The European Union 1994: Annual Review of Activities

Edited by

Neill Nugent

General Editors: Simon Bulmer and Andrew Scott

Blackwell Publishers

ISBN 0-631-19686-2

First published 1995

Blackwell Publishers Ltd
108 Cowley Road, Oxford OX4 1JF, UK

Basil Blackwell Inc.
3 Cambridge Center
Cambridge, MA 02142, USA

British Library Cataloguing in Publication Data
applied for

Library of Congress
Cataloging in Publication Data applied for

This journal is printed on acid free paper
Printed in Great Britain by Whitstable Litho, Kent

CONTENTS

Journal of Common Market Studies Volume 33, Annual Review
August 1995

List of Abbreviations

ACP	African, Caribbean, and Pacific Countries
ASEAN	Association of South East Asian Nations
CAP	Common Agricultural Policy
CCEE	Countries of Central and Eastern Europe
CCP	Common Commercial Policy
CDA	Christian Democratic Appeal (of the Netherlands)
CDU	Christian Democratic Union (of Germany)
CFI	Court of First Instance
CFP	Common Fisheries Policy
CFSP	Common Foreign and Security Policy
CIs	Community Initiatives
COM/COM DOC	Commission Document
COR	Committee of the Regions
COREPER	Committee of Permanent Representatives
CSCE	Conference on Security and Co-operation in Europe
DG	Directorate General
EAGGF	European Agricultural Guidance and Guarantee Fund
EC	European Community
ECJ	European Court of Justice
ECOSOC	Economic and Social Committee
ECSC	European Coal and Steel Community
ECOFIN	Council of Economic and Finance Ministers
ECU	European Currency Unit
EEA	European Economic Area, also European Environmental Agency
EEC	European Economic Community
EFTA	European Free Trade Association
EIB	European Investment Bank
EIF	European Investment Fund
EMI	European Monetary Institute

EMS	European Monetary System
EMU	Economic and Monetary Union
EP	European Parliament
EPC	European Political Co-operation
ERDF	European Regional Development Fund
ERM	Exchange Rate Mechanism
ESF	European Social Fund
EURATOM	European Atomic Energy Community
FDP	Free Democratic Party (of Germany)
FYROM	Former Yugoslav Republic of Macedonia
GATS	General Agreement on Trade in Services
GATT	General Agreement on Tariffs and Trade
GDP	Gross Domestic Product
GNP	Gross National Product
GSP	Generalized System of Preferences
IGC	Intergovernmental Conference
JHA	Justice and Home Affairs
MCR	Merger Control Regulation
MEP	Member of the European Parliament
NATO	North Atlantic Treaty Organization
OECD	Organization for Economic Co-operation and Development
OJ	Official Journal of the European Communities
OSCE	Organization on Security and Co-operation in Europe
PDS	Party of Democratic Socialism (of Germany)
PE DOC	Committee Report of the European Parliament
PRC	People's Republic of China
SADC	South African Development Community
SEA	Single European Act
SEC	Internal Commission General Secretariat Document
SEM	Single European Market
SIS	Schengen Information System
SMEs	Small and Medium-Sized Enterprises
SPD	Social Democratic Party (of Germany)
TACs	Total Allowable Catches
TAD	Transatlantic Declaration
TEU	Treaty on European Union
TRIPs	Trade Related Aspects of Intellectual Property Rights
UK	United Kingdom
UN	United Nations
VAT	Value Added Tax
VERs	Voluntary Export Restraints
VVD	People's Party for Freedom and Democracy (of the Netherlands)
WEU	Western European Union
WTO	World Trade Organization

Journal of Common Market Studies
Volume 33, Annual Review
August 1995

Editorial: Redefining Europe

NEILL NUGENT
Manchester Metropolitan University

I. The Changing Shape(s) of Europe

The political and economic shape of the European Union (EU), of the wider Europe, and of the relations between the EU and the wider Europe, continued to evolve in 1994.

The European Union

The most important aspect of the evolution as regards the EU was the successful completion of preparations to enable three countries – Austria, Finland, and Sweden – to become full members of the Union on 1 January 1995. Accession terms were also agreed with the Norwegian Government but, as in 1972, the Norwegian people chose not to accept their Government's advice and in a national referendum held in October rejected EU membership.

Amongst the consequences for the EU of this latest enlargement are: an increase in the size of its population by 21 million, to a total of around 370 million; an increase in the number of official languages from 9 to 11 (Finnish and Swedish being added); an increase in the Gross Domestic Product (GDP) by 7 per cent to a total of 5,900 billion ECU; and an increase in the size of the land mass by about one third, with the land area now stretching from the Mediterranean to the Arctic and including, for the first time, a common border – 700 miles in length – with Russia.

The whole enlargement issue is examined at some length by Fraser Cameron in the keynote article.

The Wider Europe

The most significant aspects of the reshaping of Europe from the viewpoint of the wider – non-EU – Europe were the continued, though in many respects rather faltering, consolidation of economic liberalization and political democratization in the countries of central and eastern Europe (CCEE) and the continued pursuit by these countries of means which enable them to locate themselves firmly within western, and more particularly within western European, spheres of orbit.

Some of these means are focused on the complex and changing security architecture of the post-Cold War era. 1994 saw both setbacks and progress for the CCEE in this respect. A significant setback was that it became increasingly likely during the year that those CCEE which have expressed interest in North Atlantic Treaty Organization (NATO) membership – Hungary, Poland, the Czech Republic, and Slovakia – may have to wait some time before their hopes are fulfilled. An important reason for this is that during 1994 President Yeltsin made his opposition to CCEE membership of NATO quite clear. He talked, indeed, of any such NATO expansion resulting in a 'cold peace'. As for progress on the security front, there was a significant advance in May when nine east European and Baltic States were admitted as 'associate' partners of the Western European Union (WEU) – Hungary, Poland, the Czech Republic, Slovakia, Romania, Bulgaria, Lithuania, Latvia, and Estonia.

Other means used by the CCEE to become part of the western world are focused on the EU. Development in this context in 1994 ranged from the lodging of EU membership applications by Hungary (on 31 March) and Poland (on 4 April) to the continued negotiation, and in some cases conclusion, of co-operation and trade agreements of various kinds with the EU (see below).

European Union – Wider Europe Relations

There were several specific developments and agreements in 1994 designed to consolidate and/or enhance relations between the EU and its neighbours. These developments and agreements included: (1) on 1 February, Europe Agreements between the EU and Hungary and the EU and Poland entered into force; (2) in July, Partnership and Co-operation Agreements between the EU and the Ukraine and the EU and Russia were signed; (3) also in July, free trade agreements between the EU and the Baltic States were concluded; (4) in December, it was decided, at the second meeting of the European Economic Area (EEA) Council, that although, with the enlargement of the EU, only Iceland and Norway now remained as non-EU EEA members, the EEA would continue to function along the established lines, and that Liechtenstein would participate in the EEA from 1 May 1995 provided that amendments to the Liechtenstein–Switzerland Customs Treaty had entered into force by that date.

Beyond such specific developments and agreements, a significant aspect of the evolution of EU–wider Europe relations in 1995 was a more concerted attempt than had been seen previously on the part of the EU to develop a strategy for conducting its relations with non-Member States. A very general set of goals and operating principles was already in existence, based on establishing closer relations and – following decisions taken at the Copenhagen summit in June 1993 – recognizing that for the CCEE and for Malta and Cyprus eventual accession was a realistic goal once certain conditions had been satisfied. These goals and operating principles were taken further in 1994, with the June European Council meeting at Corfu calling on: (1) the Council 'to evaluate, together with the Commission, the global policy of the European Union in the Mediterranean and possible initiatives to strengthen this policy in the short and medium term' (European Council, 1994a, p. 14); (2) the Commission 'to make specific proposals as soon as possible for the further implementation of the Europe Agreements [with the CCEE] and the decisions taken by the European Council in Copenhagen' (*ibid.*, p. 16); and (3) the Presidency and the Commission to report to the European Council at its next meeting on the progress made 'on the process of alignment [of the CCEE] since the Copenhagen European Council, and on the strategy to be followed with a view to preparing for accession' (*ibid.*, p. 16).

The reports which had been requested at Corfu were duly delivered to the Essen summit, after being channelled through meetings of the General Affairs Council. They enabled the summit to clarify the EU's thinking about the countries to its south and east.

With the Mediterranean countries, it was affirmed that the Mediterranean 'represents a priority area of strategic importance for the European Union'. Building on the already existing close relations and structures of the EU's Mediterranean policy, the establishment of a Euro–Mediterranean partnership was envisaged which would provide for an all-round strengthening of existing arrangements. Amongst specific measures which were referred to in the summit's Presidency Conclusions, were a request for progress with individual country partnership negotiations, the conclusion of negotiations with Turkey on the projected customs union and other matters, and confirmation 'that the next phase of enlargement of the Union will involve Cyprus and Malta' (European Council, 1994b, p. 15).

With the CCEE, the Essen Council confirmed and sought to further extend the strategy which the EU had been pursuing since the Copenhagen summit, namely, encouraging and assisting the associated states to prepare for membership through a framework of EU–CCEE dialogue and consultations. This framework, it was decided, would now be placed in the context of a 'structured relationship' which would see a formal timetabling of meetings at political and administrative levels between the EU and associated CCEE: so, Heads of Government will meet at least once a year 'on the margins of a European Council meeting', Foreign Ministers and Justice/Home Affairs Ministers will meet at least twice a year, and the likes of Agriculture, Finance, Transport, Environment and Education Ministers will meet at least once a year. These meetings are intended to promote and monitor adaptation progress in the associated states, to facilitate associated state co-operation with, or participation in, EU programmes, and – along with comparable meetings at parliamentary level – generally to help to make co-operation 'a normal part of the life of governments and parliaments' and thus 'be an important preparation for accession' (European Council, 1994b, p. 9). Symbolically, the first of these meetings at Heads of Government level was held at Essen itself, with the leaders of the four Visegrad States (Hungary, Poland, the Czech Republic and Slovakia), plus Bulgaria and Romania, attending for part of the last day of the summit.

On a general matter concerning the next enlargement round, the European Council, at both Corfu and Essen, confirmed an assumption which most interested parties had long been making, namely that there could be no question of opening accession negotiations before the 1996 Intergovernmental Conference (IGC) has taken place. The question was left aside of whether, with the ratification of the outcome of the 1996 IGC likely to be very difficult (not least because of the probable increased number of national referendums), the accession negotiations will open shortly after the IGC or only when the ratification picture is clear.

But whenever the accessions negotiations begin, it is clear that the history of the late 1980s/early 1990s is being, and will continue to be, at least partially repeated:

- The prospect of widening is an important factor in stimulating debate on, and producing pressures in favour of, institutional and policy deepening.
- Deepening is seen as needing to be tackled before final decisions are to be taken on widening. Indeed, progress on deepening is seen by many as a precondition of widening.
- States which are judged to have credible and acceptable membership claims are being granted interim arrangements and are being encouraged and assisted to adjust themselves to the requirements of EU membership.

II. Multi-Speed Europe?

The ongoing debate about the future character of the EU rumbled on in 1994. Indeed, it was given some momentum with the Treaty on European Union (TEU) – which had come into effect in November 1993 – beginning to make its full impact, with enlargement imminent and thoughts beginning to turn to the next enlargement round, and with the 1996 IGC coming ever closer.

The usual positions were advanced from the usual quarters: Delors emphasized how the EU must be much more than just a glorified free trade area; the French and German Governments stressed the need to make the EU more dynamic and more democratic; and the British Government emphasized the virtues of consolidation. To such traditional positions and postures a new – or almost new – dimension was, however, added to the debate, with the possibility of a multi-speed/multi-layered EU being increasingly openly considered and even advocated.

The notion of a multi-speed/multi-layered EU is, of course, not new. After all, not all EC Member States participated in the operation of the Exchange Rate Mechanism (ERM) of the European Monetary System (EMS) from the late 1970s. At Maastricht a multi-layered system was virtually constitutionalized, with provision for the single currency to come into effect with only some Member States participating, with the opt-out given to the UK from the Social Chapter, and with the WEU being identified as 'an integral part of the development of the Union' even though only nine EU states (subsequently ten) were WEU members. Such multi-layering was taken further in 1994 with an agreement in December by seven EU Member States (France, Germany, Spain, Portugal and the three Benelux countries) that they would start applying the much-delayed Schengen Agreement – which removes internal border checks on people – from 26 March 1995.

The prospect of differentiated integration is thus well established, with roots going back to the 1970s. Prior to 1994, however, it was usually portrayed by people in authoritative positions as something to be regretted, and where it existed as something to be rectified as soon as possible. (Even UK politicians subscribed to this view, though they mostly foresaw the rectification as being effected by a repatriation of policy and decision-making responsibilities.) There were, however, signs in 1994 of such attitudes changing and of it coming to be recognized that a multi-speed/multi-layered Europe would be increasingly inevitable as membership grew and, significantly, that it might also be, in some respect at least, increasingly desirable.

The most powerful and most publicized expression of view along these lines appeared in a policy paper entitled *Reflections on European Policy* which was issued at the beginning of September by the CDU/CSU grouping in the Bundestag. The starting point of the paper was that circumstances – most notably the end of the Cold War, enlargement, structural economic change, and different perceptions by Member States of internal and external priorities – had brought the EU to a critical stage in its development. In this context, it was in the interests of both Germany and the EU that the integration process should proceed. If it did not proceed, Europe might begin to fracture and drift apart. To head off and prevent fracturing and drifting apart, a key element of the integration strategy must be to permit, even to encourage, the notion of a multi-speed – though not an *à la carte* – Europe focused around a strengthened hard core of probably five countries (Germany, France, Belgium, Luxembourg and the Netherlands).

To demonstrate how starkly this argument was presented, it is worth quoting a few key passages from the document:

> To achieve this [flexible but strong EU institutions] the 'variable geometry' or 'multi-speed' approach should as far as possible be sanctioned and institutionalised in the Union Treaty or the new quasi-constitutional document [after the next IGC]. … It is essential that no country should be allowed to use its right of veto to block the efforts of other countries more able and willing to intensify their co-operation and deepen integration …
>
> In addition to ensuring that the decision-making process within the European Union becomes more efficient and democratic, the existing 'hard core' of countries oriented to greater integration and closer co-operation must be further strengthened. At present, the core comprises five or six countries. This core must not be closed to other Member States; rather, it must be open to every Member State willing and able to meet its requirements …
>
> The formation of a core group of countries is not an end in itself but a means of reconciling the two ostensibly conflicting goals of widening and deepening the European Union. (CDU/CSU, 1994, pp.12–13)

The CDU/CSU paper was not the first occasion in 1994 that the notion of a multi-speed Europe, or even of an inner EU core, had been raised by an authoritative source. Indeed, publication of the paper had been preceded in late August by a call from the French Prime Minister, Edouard Balladur, for a Europe of three circles (Balladur, 1994). Why then did the CDU/CSU paper create so much fuss? For four principal reasons: (1) it was perceived as advocating not so much a multi-speed Europe as a two-speed Europe within the EU; (2) it identified which Member States would be likely to be in the fast stream and which in the slow stream; (3) it was based on a carefully and thoroughly thought out case; and (4) it emanated from a very important political source in the EU's largest and most powerful Member State.

Not surprisingly, therefore, there was widespread critical reaction to the paper, most particularly in the capitals of projected slow-stream countries. For example, the Spanish Prime Minister, Felipe Gonzales, attacked the ideas as being 'politically inopportune', while the Italian Prime Minister, Silvio Berlusconi telephoned Chancellor Kohl to enquire why one of the EC's Founding Members was being relegated to the second division. In the UK, the Prime Minister, John Major, used a speech he was due to deliver at Leiden as an opportunity to make it clear that the vision of a multi-speed Europe which he had spoken of in the past was quite different from this new vision of a two-speed Europe:

> It seems to me perfectly healthy for all Member States to agree that some should integrate more closely or more quickly in certain areas. There is nothing novel in this. It is the principle we agreed on economic and monetary union at Maastricht. It may also happen on defence.
>
> But the corollary is that no Member State should be excluded from an area of policy in which it wants and is qualified to participate ...
>
> So I see a real danger in talks of a 'hard core', inner and outer circles, a two-tier Europe. I recoil from ideas for a Union in which some would be more equal than others. There is not, and never should be, an exclusive 'hard core' either of countries or of policies. The European Union involves a wide range of common policies and areas of close co-operation. No Member States should lay claim to a privileged status on the basis of their participation in some of them. (Major, 1994, p. 8)

What was concerning Major was that his vision of Europe – based on a common core of SEM-related policies and laws around which could be clustered various *à la carte*, primarily intergovernmental, arrangements – was being threatened by a fast and slow stream Europe, with Britain clearly in the latter stream. The prospect of a streamed Europe is, however, arguably enhanced by the UK's Social Chapter opt-out and EMU opt-in, for they have made it more difficult for those who do not wish, or are not able, to be in a fast stream, to slow down the integration process to their own pace. The fact is that at Maastricht the UK Government was instrumental in giving constitutional validity to the notion that integrationist advance need not necessarily involve all Member States.

Doubtless, as the 1996 IGC approaches, much more will be heard of the need and desirability of a unified Europe, of a two-speed Europe, of a multi-speed Europe, and of a Europe *à la carte*. In this debate the voice of the EP is likely to be more significant than it was in the 1985 and 1990–91 deepening rounds. Indeed, in 1994 the European Council prepared the way for an EP IGC-related role, by agreeing that two EP representatives would sit alongside representatives of the Ministers of Foreign Affairs and the President of the Commission in the Reflection Group which, from June 1995, is to prepare the work of the IGC.

In the IGC debates and negotiations, the EP's general stance on the question of the pace and nature of integration will doubtless continue to be along the lines of 'maximum advance with all Member States participating'. However, if called to make a choice, it will not sacrifice too much integration to get everyone on board. Indeed, an early signal of the Parliament's view on what should happen in the 1996 IGC was sent out via a debate it held in mid-September in the wake of the CDU/CSU paper and Major's speech. The EP voted by 342 votes to 37, with 32 abstentions, in favour of a resolution which rejected 'an *à la carte* Europe in which each Member State is entitled to disassociate itself from any Community policy', but which asserted that, 'if a small minority of states attempted to block all progress during the 1996 Intergovernmental Conference, ways would have to be found of allowing states which want to pursue their efforts to achieve European integration to still do so' (European Parliament, 1994, p. 20).

III. Institutional Developments

There were several significant institutional developments in 1994:

Enlargement and Voting in the Council

The European Council had decided at its December 1993 Brussels meeting on the allocation of seats and representations to EU institutions of the four states which were negotiating to join the Union. However, no agreement was reached at the Brussels summit on the threshold for a qualified majority, and therefore also for a blocking majority, in the Council of Ministers. With the accession negotiations completed in March, the General Affairs Council had to try to resolve the issue, and in so doing ran into considerable difficulties.

The problem was that there was a fundamental disagreement over whether, with the total number of Council votes being increased from 76 to 90 to accommodate the four applicant states, there should be a correspondingly proportionate increase in the number of votes required for a qualified majority/ blocking minority. The governments of most Member States took the view that the increases should indeed be proportionate, so that the minimum required for a qualified majority would remain at around 70 per cent of the total number of votes and the minimum for a blocking minority would remain at around 30 per cent. The UK Government, however, with some support from Spain, objected to proportionate increases, maintaining that this would not be the *status quo* since it would mean an increase in the number of states which would be required to constitute a blocking minority: two large states and one small state would, for example, no longer be enough.

After several meetings of the General Affairs Council, a classic compromise solution was reached at a specially convened meeting at Ioannina in late March.

The qualified majority was raised to 64 votes and the blocking minority to 27 votes (the 70 per cent/30 per cent solution), but it was conceded that 'if members of the Council representing a total of 23 to 26 votes indicate their intention to oppose the adoption by the Council of a decision by a qualified majority' then 'a reasonable time' would be allowed to elapse to see if an agreement could be found before the new blocking minority figure of 27 was used (Council, 1994, p. 2). Both 'sides' were thus able to save face, even if the solution was clearly only temporary and the issue would have to be readdressed no later than the 1996 IGC.

As things turned out, in one key respect the issue had to be readdressed in 1994 itself, for the vote by the Norwegian people not to ratify EU accession necessitated a recalculation of the figures. With the number of votes in the Council now reduced to a total of 87 (Norway had been allocated 3 votes), the General Affairs Council at its meeting on 19–20 December made proportionate adjustments: the normal qualified majority was reset at 62 votes (and the blocking minority was therefore reset at 26 votes), whilst the 23 to 26 votes of the 'Ioannina compromise' were reset at 23 to 25 votes.

Elections to the European Parliament

The fourth set of direct elections to the EP was held on 9 and 12 June 1994. Once again, they failed to fulfil the hopes of those who look to them for evidence of growing 'Europeanization':

- Turnout was down again, with only 56.5 per cent of those who were eligible to vote doing so. This compared with 62 per cent in 1979, 61 per cent in 1984, and 58 per cent in 1989.
- Campaigns – and they were, in practice, national campaigns rather than a single European campaign – were, as before, mostly conducted on domestic issues rather than European issues.
- Voters displayed their customary habit of using the elections primarily for national purposes. Evidence of this was no more clearly seen than in the fact that there was an electoral shift (to the left or right as appropriate) away from the parties of national government in all but two of the 12 Member States – Germany, where the CDU/CSU retained popularity, and Italy, where the Berlusconi-led Government was newly installed.
- In several countries – most notably France and Denmark – there was a clearly detectable 'anti-EU' vote, either via the emergence of new parties or via support for established 'Eurosceptic' parties.
- There was little to suggest that genuine European political parties were much nearer to emerging. It is true that more time and effort were put in than previously by the major EP political groups – through their respective European confederations – in developing agreed manifestos, but the documents

they produced were mostly vague and, in any event, were described as being non-binding when their contents created difficulties. (The UK Labour Party, for example, when attacked for the allegedly anti-competitive implications of the 35-hour week goal contained in the Socialist manifesto, simply denied that it was obligated to support such a goal.)

As for the outcome of the elections, only a few of the more important features will be noted here, since full results are given in Richard Corbett's article:

- The EP continued to be very much a multi-party Parliament, with an increase in the number of small national parties gaining representation, and a slight increase – from eight to nine, plus Independents – in the number of political groups in the Parliament.
- The two dominant groups in the 1989–94 Parliament maintained their positions of strength: the Socialist Group (PES) was virtually the same, with 198 MEPs as compared with 197 (losses in France and Italy were offset by an increase in the UK representation); the Christian Democrat/Conservative Group (EPP) fell slightly from 162 to 157 (losses in Italy and the UK were largely compensated for by increases in Germany and Spain).
- The overall balance of forces in the EP was little affected, with neither the left nor the right having a clear majority. However, the right was clearly more fractured than it had been in the previous Parliament, mainly because the Italian Christian Democrats, who had been a cornerstone of the EPP, were largely replaced by Berlusconi's Forza Italia – whose 27 MEPs constituted a single country Forza Europa political group in the new Parliament. The effective functioning of the EP would clearly continue to be heavily dependent on co-operation between the major political groups of the centre left and centre right.

EP elections have long featured in the ongoing debate about the EU's 'democratic deficit'. The 1994 elections did little to alter the terms of that debate. On the contrary, indeed, the familiar contrasting conclusions between 'intergovernmentalists' and 'integrationists' were soon being drawn about the implications of the elections. John Major, for example, argued in his Leiden speech:

> The European Parliament sees itself as the future democratic focus for the Union. But this is a flawed ambition, because the European Union is an association of states, deriving its basic democratic legitimacy through national parliaments. That should remain the case. People will continue to see national parliaments as their democratic focus ...
>
> The European Parliament is not the answer to the democratic deficit, as the pitiable low turnout in this year's European elections so vividly demonstrated. The upshot, sadly, has been an unrepresentative and rather incoherent range of

> parties in the new European parliament, in which fringe, protest and opposition groups are over-represented. (Major, 1994, p. 8)

The main counterview to the sort of argument advanced by Major has always rested on the assertion that the EP must be, as the only directly elected EU institution, the main channel for dealing with the democratic deficit, and that the problem of low turnout should be dealt with by giving the Parliament significant powers and so making it worth voting for. As David Martin, a Vice President of the EP and the author of the Martin Reports which pressed the 1990–91 IGC to give much stronger powers to the EP, wrote in early 1995 in respect of the 1994 elections:

> A great deal of unease was caused by the fact that turnout at the European parliamentary elections fell for the fourth time in succession. ... This fall is not surprising. The European electorate is not stupid, it knows that the real power in Europe lies with the secretive Council and the appointed Commission. (Martin, 1995, p.17)

Both sides of this argument clearly contain suppositions which are questionable. In no small part because of that very fact, it can be assumed that much more will be heard of the arguments in the context of the 1996 IGC discussions.

A Successor to Jacques Delors

With the TEU entering into force on 1 November 1993, 1994 saw many of the procedures it established used for the first time. This first usage of TEU procedures is dealt with by Richard Corbett in his article, but one of the usages – that relating to the nomination of the person to replace Jacques Delors as President of the Commission – was so dramatic as to merit additional attention here.

Article 158 (EC), which was newly created by the TEU, states: 'The governments of the Member States shall nominate by common accord, after consulting the European Parliament, the person they intend to appoint as President of the Commission'. The European Council, which had long assumed the responsibility for nominating the President, interpreted Article 158 as meaning little change, and engaged in only the most peremptory consultation with the EP before the Corfu summit in June – when the nomination was supposed to be made. Understandably this led to considerable dissatisfaction on the part of MEPs. It was not, however, MEPs' dissatisfaction that created problems at Corfu, but John Major, who vetoed the candidature of the Belgian Prime Minister, Jean-Luc Dehaene, despite Dehaene being acceptable to the other 11 Heads of Government. The public reason for the veto was that Dehaene was too integrationist by nature, but two other factors were clearly also important for Major: he was displeased that he had not been fully consulted by Kohl or

Mitterrand before they started promoting Dehaene, and he wanted to show his restless backbenchers that he could be 'tough in Europe'. The failure to agree on a nominee at Corfu resulted in the incoming German Presidency taking the lead in finding another candidate and, after extensive consultations – though, again, barely at all with the EP – agreement was reached on the Luxembourg Prime Minister, Jacques Santer. He was formally nominated at a special half-day summit in Brussels in mid-July.

The Brussels summit was not, however, the end of the nomination process, for the EP was resolved to take maximum advantage of the ill-defined consultative role it had been given in Article 158. The groundwork had been well prepared, with a rewrite of the EP's Rules of Procedure in 1993. A new Rule 32 stipulated that:

- the President of the EP 'shall request the candidate proposed to make a statement to Parliament';
- following the statement, 'Parliament shall approve or reject the proposed nomination by a majority of the votes cast';
- if the vote should be negative 'the President [of the EP] shall request the governments of the Member States to withdraw their proposal and present a new proposal to Parliament' (European Parliament, 1993, p. 35).

The EP was thus ready to act as if it had the power of confirmation and, by implication, the power of veto, over the European Council's nominee. That, in practice, it did have such a power was confirmed after the Corfu summit when Chancellor Kohl, the incoming President in Office of the European Council, stated that if the EP rejected whoever was eventually nominated, he would not renominate that person.

In the event, it looked for a while as though Santer would not be confirmed, for many MEPs made it plain they could not support him – either for ideological reasons (Santer is a Christian Democrat) or, more commonly, because of dissatisfaction with the inadequate consultation with the EP before his name (and, before him, Dehaene's name) was announced. Only extensive politicking – involving Spanish and Greek Socialist MEPs being 'reminded' that their Socialist Prime Ministers had supported Santer, and involving also Santer addressing the main political groups as well as the EP in plenary session – produced a confirmatory vote, albeit by a narrow majority: there were 260 votes in favour, 238 against, and 23 abstentions.

IV. Policy Developments

On the policy front, 1994 was primarily a year of continuation and consolidation, with few new initiatives of major significance. Since detailed accounts of all policy developments are given in the articles by John Redmond and by David Allen and Michael Smith, attention here will be confined to observations and comments on matters of particular interest.

Internal Policies

Considerable attention was given in 1994 to following up the Commission's 1993 White Paper on growth, competitiveness and employment. It featured as an important agenda item at the Corfu and Essen summits, and figured prominently at several meetings of the Council of Ministers. In the view of many observers, what materialized from the summits and Council meetings was too much exhortation and insufficient practical action. This reflected, in part at least, the fact that whilst the Member States were agreed on the need for policies to promote economic recovery, and especially employment (the US and Japan are much better at linking economic growth to employment growth), there was no consensus on what the nature of the policies should be. So, the UK Government took its customary lead in emphasizing the need for flexible and low-cost labour markets, whilst several governments made much of the need for EU spending programmes. In the event, there was something of both approaches, with proposals for the regulation of labour markets making only limited progress and with some EU spending proposals being approved –notably for trans-European networks.

The second stage of EMU began in January 1994. This meant that the European Monetary Institute (the forerunner of the European Central Bank) began its work, the national convergence programmes of the Member States increased in importance, and speculation and discussion intensified as to whether a sufficient number of countries would meet the convergence conditions so as to allow the third stage of EMU to begin at its earliest possible date of 1997. By the year's end, a consensus appeared to be emerging that whilst a sufficient number of countries might just about qualify for the third stage if the convergence conditions were not applied too rigorously, continuing structural problems in the national economies allied with technical difficulties in moving to the single currency made 1999 a more realistic target date.

The social dimension of EU policies commanded considerable attention in 1994. It did so in two particular respects. First, in July the Commission published its long-awaited White Paper on social policy. It concentrated on overall objectives rather than specific legislative proposals and listed the priorities as combatting unemployment, improving job skills, encouraging high labour standards, developing the European labour market, enhancing equality of opportunity between men and women, maintaining and updating the European model of the Welfare State, and extending the social dialogue. Somewhat controversially, it reiterated the call which Social Affairs Commissioner, Padraig Flynn, made several times during 1994 for social policy to be again based on one legal framework; that is to say, for the UK opt-out to be removed at the 1996 IGC. Second, the TEU Protocol and Agreement on Social Policy were used for the first time so as to allow the Eleven (all Member States other than the UK) to make legislation. The first usage, in September, enabled the European Works Council Directive to be passed.

External Policies

Four issues had been especially prominent in the EU's external relations in 1993: enlargement, the Uruguay Round negotiations, the situation in the former Yugoslavia, and relations with the CCEE and the successor states of the former Soviet Union (see the 1993 *Annual Review*). In 1994 the character of each of these issues changed in significant ways:

- The enlargement negotiations were, as was noted earlier, completed by March, with the consequence that attention switched to the implications of the impending enlargement for the existing EU (the row over qualified majority voting in the Council) and to the four national ratification referendums. The conduct of the referendums was, of course, primarily a matter for the national politicians of the states concerned, but EU representatives did what they could to offer assistance. For example, Commissioners made 'helpful' speeches, many MEPs actively participated in the referendum campaigns, and – astutely, but ultimately without the hoped-for effect – Jacques Santer allocated the fisheries portfolio in the incoming Commission to the Norwegian Commissioner-designate, Thorvald Stoltenberg.
- All outstanding major issues in the GATT Uruguay Round negotiations had been resolved in December 1993, so negotiations in 1994 were largely concerned with tying up loose ends. After this had been done, the new GATT world trade agreement was signed in April in Marrakesh by 118 countries and the EC. Attention was then turned to ratification and within the EU it was decided, after some legal argument, that both national parliaments and the EP (using the Article 228 assent procedure) would need to give their approval. Such approval was duly given.
- The hostilities in the former Yugoslavia, and more especially in Bosnia, continued in 1994, but they did not figure so prominently on EU agendas. Existing policies and commitments were maintained (see the 1993 *Annual Review*), but there was generally a greater acceptance than there had been in previous stages of the hostilities that if the parties to the conflict were not willing to stop fighting then there was relatively little that the EU and its Member States could, or would, do beyond continue contributing to

humanitarian aid and peace-monitoring efforts, keeping up (limited) pressure on the Serbs, and playing a leading part in peace-brokering activities – be these championed by the EU itself or channelled through the UN, NATO, the five-member Contact Group (UK, France, Germany, Russia and the US), or the Conference on Security and Co-operation in Europe. (There was some hope that the CSCE Heads of Government meeting in Budapest on 5–6 December would produce a breakthrough of some kind, but it did not. In fact, it produced very little of anything other than a change of name to Organization on Security and Co-operation in Europe). The reluctance of the EU to try a radically different approach to the former Yugoslavia was demonstrated in the closing months of the year when, amidst some mutual recriminations, it distanced itself from attempts by the United States both to adopt a tougher stance towards the Serbs and to lift the arms embargo, which applied to the whole of the former Yugoslavia, in the case of the Bosnians. (In November the US, in what was largely a symbolic gesture, announced that it would no longer assist in enforcing the arms embargo against the Bosnian Government. It did not, however, lift the embargo itself.)

- Relations with the CCEE were discussed earlier on in this Editorial. In essence, they were deepened in various ways, most notably by the creation of the 'structured relationship' which was formally agreed and launched at the Essen summit. As for the successor states of the former Soviet Union, relations continued to be consolidated via, for example, the signing in June of the Partnership and Co-operation Agreements with the Ukraine and with Russia, and with the Essen Council expressing its wish that Europe Agreements be concluded quickly with the Baltic States (and Slovenia) 'so that these States can be included in the accession preparation strategy' (European Council, 1994b, p. 12).

There were no major new external policy matters which concerned the EU in 1994.

V. Into a New Era

1994 was the last year of Jacques Delors' ten years as President of the Commission. This is not the place to offer an evaluation of those ten years, but it is worth making the point that the attention and the hullabaloo which surrounded the nomination of his successor, Jacques Santer, in mid-1994 are testimony to the impact that Delors made during his time as President. During the ten years, the EC/EU, the Commission, and the Presidency of the Commission, all increased enormously in significance and assumed a position and an importance in public affairs that was barely imaginable when the Delors I College assumed office in January 1985.

One era thus came towards its end in 1994 and a new era beckoned. What that new era will produce remains to be seen, though it has to be said that the portents for the incoming Santer Commission are not as favourable as, in retrospect, they were for Delors in 1985. Santer himself, for example, does not have the driving force of his predecessor – which is partly why he was chosen. The ramifications of the 1992 Danish and French referendums are still being felt, with subsidiarity and decentralization still very much in the air. The debate about the future of Europe contains, as has been shown, the seeds of serious divisions. And many national governments, especially in the large Member States, command less authority than they did a decade ago: as the Santer Commission assumed office in January 1995, Kohl had only a narrow parliamentary majority following the 1994 German legislative elections, Gonzáles was preoccupied by political crisis and corruption in Spain, Mitterrand was preparing to leave office, Major was worrying about Eurosceptic opposition in his own party, and Berlusconi had resigned and Italy was seemingly back to having another interim government.

On the other hand, the integration process seems almost to have had its own inherent force since the mid-1980s (that 'spillover effect' again?) and there is no shortage of influential political actors who wish to see it continue. Moreover, as was argued earlier, the time has probably passed when the many must always wait for the few.

References

Balladur, E. (1994) *Le Figaro,* 30 August. Balladur expressed his ideas at greater length in an article in *Le Monde*, 30 November.

CDU/CSU Grouping in the German Bundestag (1994) *Reflections on European Policy*. The full text of the paper, and the one used here, are reproduced in *European Access* No. 5, October pp. 11–15.

Council of the European Union (1994) *Press Release* 6004/94 (Presse 57).

European Council (1994a) *Presidency Conclusions*. Corfu, 24–25 June (Brussels: General Secretariat of the Council).

European Council (1994b) *Presidency Conclusions.* Essen 9–10 December (Brussels: General Secretariat of the Council).

European Parliament (1993) *Rules of Procedure* (Brussels: European Parliament).

European Parliament (1994) *The Week* 26–30 September (Luxembourg: Directorate-General for Information and Public Relations, European Parliament).

Major, J. (1994) 'Europe: A Future That Works'. Lecture delivered at the University of Leiden, 7 September. The full lecture is printed in *European Access,* No. 5, October pp. 6–10.

Journal of Common Market Studies Volume 33, Annual Review
August 1995

Keynote Article: The European Union and the Fourth Enlargement

FRASER CAMERON*
European Commission

I. Introduction

The enlargement of the European Union (EU) in January 1995 to include Austria, Sweden and Finland signified a further enhancement of the EU's position as the largest political and economic bloc in the world. The accession of these three states was the fourth enlargement to the European Communities. The original six members were joined by the UK, Denmark and Ireland in 1973, Greece in 1981, and Spain and Portugal in 1986. One of the main current debates in Europe is how to proceed with the fifth enlargement – to include the countries of central and eastern Europe (CCEE) which have signed association agreements with the EU and the Mediterranean states (Malta and Cyprus). The next Intergovernmental Conference (IGC) in 1996 will be have the task *inter alia* of agreeing the necessary institutional reforms for an enlarged Union with perhaps 20-plus members.

This article examines the background to the most recent enlargement, discusses the motives for the European Free Trade Association (EFTA) countries' (or EFTANs') application for membership and EU reactions, reviews the course and outcome of the negotiations, considers the implications of an enlarged Union, and looks forward to the next enlargement.

* I am grateful to a number of colleagues, G. Avery, E. Grillo-Pasquerelli and D. Spence, for their comments on earlier drafts of this article which is written in a personal capacity. Any errors remain my own.

II. From Maastricht to Edinburgh

Austria was the first of the 'fourth wave' countries to apply to join the EU in July 1989, followed by Sweden in June 1991, Finland in March 1992, and Norway in November 1992. Switzerland also applied to join in May 1992 but its application was put into cold storage following the negative outcome of the referendum on the European Economic Area (EEA) on 6 December 1992.

One of the least publicized decisions at the Maastricht European Council in December 1991 was an invitation to the European Commission to produce a report on enlargement for the Lisbon European Council six months later. The Commission planned to produce a radical report for this summit but the Danish 'No' on 2 May, just a few weeks prior to the European Council, resulted in a watered down version.[1] The Lisbon summit accepted the Commission's distinction between three different groups of candidates, with the EFTA countries being given priority over the CCEE and the Mediterranean countries (Turkey, Cyprus and Malta) because of the extent to which they had accepted the EC *acquis* in the European Economic Area (EEA) agreement. (The EEA had been agreed in October 1991, but formal signing and implementation were delayed when the European Court ruled In December 1991 that the joint EU–EEA arbitration mechanisms were incompatible with the Treaties of Rome and Maastricht. It was signed in May 1992 and eventually came into force in January 1994.)

Largely as a result of the shock following the Danish 'No', the European Council also agreed that the next enlargement could take place within the existing institutional framework. However, although the EFTANs were thus placed on a fast track, there was a dispute between Member States as to when negotiations should open. The UK, Germany and Denmark argued for an early start, whilst Spain and the other cohesion countries insisted that there could be no opening of negotiations until the Maastricht Treaty on European Union (TEU) was ratified and agreement had been reached on the Delors II package covering own resources. These conditions were relaxed as a result of the successful budgetary agreement at the Edinburgh European Council in December 1992 and the compromise on the Danish opt-outs, which paved the way for a second referendum and subsequent entry into force of the TEU. The European Council agreed that negotiations with the candidate countries could be opened in early 1993, but could not be concluded before the ratification of the Maastricht Treaty was completed.

[1] The report had intended to link enlargement to institutional reform. See Commission of the European Communities (1992), 'Europe and the Challenge of Enlargement', *Bulletin of the European Communities*, Supplement 3/92.

III. Why the EFTANs Applied

There were two main reasons why the EFTANs applied to join the EC. The first was the obvious success of the EC's Single European Market (SEM) programme. As the pace of integration gathered momentum in the late 1980s, after a period of Eurosclerosis, the EFTANs made clear their desire to be part of the SEM even though they still shied away from full membership of the EC. President Delors reacted to this pressure by proposing a more structured partnership with common decision-making and administrative decisions. The EFTA countries welcomed this alternative and negotiations began in 1990 to create the EEA. The EEA, which was eventually signed in 1992, and involved the EFTANs accepting over 14,000 pages of Community legislation, was not a customs union but rather an improved free trade area allowing the EFTANs to participate in the SEM. Further, it specifically excluded agricultural policy, fisheries, structural policy, taxation and foreign policy, although it did commit the EFTANs to contribute to the Cohesion Fund. However, even before the EEA entered into force, the EFTANs realized the shortcomings of the EEA, notably that it offered no real influence on EC decision-making. Only full EC membership allowed participation in decisions.

The second, and perhaps more important reason, was political. With the fall of the Berlin Wall and the collapse of communism in the eastern half of the continent, a previous hindrance to EC membership on the part of the neutrals (Austria, Sweden and Finland) was swept away. All three states emphasized the important role which the EC was playing in terms of promoting peace and stability in Europe. There had been general acceptance in the neutral states that their foreign policy status was incompatible with membership of the EC. Following the geo-political earthquake which hit eastern Europe in 1989–90 and the subsequent end of the East–West conflict, the neutrals swiftly accepted that their neutrality would no longer be a bar to full membership, even though the EC was busy planning further moves towards integration of foreign policy and holding out the prospect of an eventual common defence policy which, in the words of the TEU, 'might in time lead to a common defence'. Only Austria, which applied in July 1989, before the fall of the Berlin Wall, had specifically entered a reservation on its neutrality.

In stating their reasons for applying to join the EC, the EFTAN governments, parliaments and elite opinion showed a remarkable consensus. Each statement by government ministers to national parliaments mentioned the importance of the EC for the stability of Europe, recognized the limitations of the EEA, and accepted that pooling sovereignty would actually increase their influence to achieve policy aims. Typical was the statement of Prime Minister Bildt to the

Swedish Parliament on 12 July 1992: 'Sweden can only preserve its influence in all key policy areas by full membership of the Union'.

Similarly, Prime Minister Brundtland told the Norwegian Parliament on 16 December 1992 :

> It is no longer possible to tell Norwegian voters that we can carry out all our tasks by means of decisions in Norway alone. If we cut ourselves off from the fora [EC] where decisions are made, we are in reality restricting our freedom of action.

IV. The Negotiations

Organization

Article O of the TEU states that :

> Any European state may apply to become a Member of the Union. It shall address its application to the Council, which shall act unanimously after consulting the Commission and after receiving the assent of the European Parliament, which shall act by an absolute majority of its component members.
>
> The conditions of admission and adjustment to the Treaties on which the Union is founded shall be the subject of an agreement between the Member States and the applicant state. This agreement shall be submitted for ratification by all the contracting states in accordance with their respective constitutional requirements.

Having received favourable opinions from the Commission, which were confirmed by the Council, the accession negotiations took place, following EC custom, in an Accession Conference chaired by the Presidency of the Council.[2] Although the Council has overall responsibility for accession negotiations, in practice the Commission is given considerable powers to seek compromises with the acceding states. It is the first port of call for the applicants, it identifies and examines the problems, and it proposes and presents solutions. The Commission also has to examine secondary legislation and the *acquis communautaire* for compatibility with the applicants. A specially convened Commission Task Force for Enlargement (TFE), headed by a Dane, Steffen Smidt, and comprising representatives from most of the Commission services, bore the brunt of the work covering enlargement from the EU side.

Given that in this instance the EEA countries were acceding to the European Union, the Political Committee (comprising senior Foreign Ministry officials from the Member States and Commission), and the Co-ordinators Group

[2] The Commission's opinion on Austria, SEC (91) 1590, was published on 1.8.91, that on Sweden, SEC (92) 1582, on 7.8.92, that on Finland, SEC (92) 2048, on 4.11.92 and that on Norway, SEC (93) 142, on 24.3.93.

(comprising senior Interior Ministry officials and the Commission), were also involved for the chapters on the Common Foreign and Security Policy (CFSP) and Justice and Home Affairs respectively.

One of the Commission's main roles is to make proposals to the Council for 'common positions' of the Union. It does so following an assessment of the position papers of the applicants, what they might be likely to accept, tempered with a judgement of how far the Member States would be prepared to go. It is not an exaggeration to say that the most lengthy and arduous part of the negotiations was not between the Union and the applicants but between the Member States themselves. For example, during the final marathon of the 15–16 March Council/ Conference session, it took the Member States nearly 12 hours to reach a common EU position *vis-à-vis* Norway's remaining demands on a few crucial points in the fisheries sector. The difficulty of reaching agreement on the Union side was compounded by the fact that all decisions on 'common positions' had to be reached by unanimity, not qualified majority.

The negotiations were opened (officially) with Austria, Sweden and Finland on 1 February 1993 and with Norway, which applied later, on 5 April. They were conducted in parallel, at various levels, in the framework of separate conferences meeting at Ministerial or Deputies (Ambassadorial) level. When the TEU entered into force on 1 November 1993, they were formally transformed into negotiations for accession to the European Union. The negotiations on an important number of chapters were facilitated by the existence of free trade agreements between the Community and the candidates, and the entry into force on 1 January 1994 of the EEA whereby the candidates were already well acquainted with and committed to accepting in their national legislation most of the *acquis* concerning the Single Market, as well as a number of 'flanking policies'.

The Content

As with previous enlargement negotiations the most difficult chapters were those concerning the Common Agricultural Policy (CAP), regional policy, and budgetary arrangements. In addition, there were problems over fisheries and energy (Norway), road transit (Austria), and alcohol monopolies (the Nordics). One of the most contentious chapters was that on institutions which was not a dispute between the EU and the candidates but rather an internal EU wrangle (see below).

Agriculture was one of the most difficult chapters (although less so for Sweden) because it was the economic sector requiring the biggest adjustments as a result of membership. The four candidates each had a distinctive national system of support for agriculture, which – unlike the industrial sector – never figured in their mutual free trade under EFTA. The candidates argued that these support systems were essential in view of the difficult natural conditions, including in Austria a high proportion of Alpine regions, and in the three Nordic countries remote northern territories with low temperatures, limited daylight and low population. In fact all the acceding countries traditionally maintained agricultural price and support levels higher than those of the Union, although in recent years Sweden had undertaken reforms which brought its prices in many areas even below those of the Union. The two main problems to be resolved were the transitional period for agricultural prices and the adaptation of the CAP to take account of the particular problems of the new members.

The Union insisted that, in view of the SEM and the need to avoid border controls for trade between Member States, the acceding countries should adopt common agricultural prices immediately on accession. The acceptance of this principle was a key element in the final round of negotiations. It was accompanied by agreement on the payment of national aid over a five-year period to farmers in Austria, Finland and Norway, to compensate for the reduction in prices. The cost to national budgets would be partially offset by a special 'agro-budgetary' contribution from the Community over four years. The 'mountain and less-favoured areas' designated in the acceding countries would allow their agriculture to benefit from important income support for farms with handicaps of climate and terrain. In addition, it was agreed that national aid for 'northern agriculture' (essentially farms north of 62°N) would be authorized.

Another contentious area, linked to agriculture, was regional policy. Although the newcomers are relatively prosperous in relation to other members of the Union, they do have areas of low income and high unemployment; and in the Nordic countries large areas with very low population densities. One part of Austria (Burgenland) was designated eligible for 'Objective 1' status under the EU Structural Funds. In the case of the Nordic countries, it was decided to create a new 'Objective 6' permitting the designation of regions with very low population density.

One of the major concerns of the applicant countries during the negotiations was to maintain a high level of health, safety and environmental standards after accession. Despite much trumpeting of higher environmental standards it became clear during the negotiations that the number of problem areas were not very substantial. For a few, exceptional, well-justified cases, it was agreed that each acceding country could maintain its national rules for a transitional period of four years. The derogations relate to the classification, packaging and labelling of pesticides and certain other dangerous substances, the marketing and use of some chemical products, and the composition of fertilizers and batteries. During this transitional period the EU is to review the relevant provisions according to normal procedures and at the end of the period the *acquis* will apply to the new Member States in the same way as the present Member States.

An important issue in competition policy was the future existence of the Nordic State alcohol monopolies. The Nordic countries agreed, as they already had under the EEA, to accept the competition rules and case law of the EC which establishes that import and wholesale monopolies run counter to the EC Treaty; there is no case law on retail monopolies and these can be continued as long as they do not discriminate against products from other Member States.

A particular and highly sensitive problem for Austria was the problem of transit of heavy goods vehicles. In view of the environmental threat to the Alpine passes, and the narrow roads leading to them, the EC had concluded in 1992 a bilateral agreement with Austria to control the number of vehicles by means of an 'ecopoint' system of transit licences. Austria's case for a further derogation of the normal unrestricted rights of passage for heavy goods vehicles through Member States was considerably strengthened by the Swiss vote against new transit routes in a referendum on 20 February 1994. The final agreement with Austria allowed for a further nine years of the 'ecopoint' system during which time the objective will be to reduce lorry pollution by 60 per cent.

In the energy field there were two main problems. The first, mainly for Sweden, concerned some of the implications of membership of Euratom, e.g. the competence of the Euratom Supply Agency in the field of trade in nuclear materials and the role of the Commission as regards safeguard measures. In the end, Sweden and the other applicants bowed to EU competence. A joint declaration which recognized the acceding countries right to decide for themselves whether or not to produce nuclear energy resolved the popular fear that Euratom would somehow force the new members to go nuclear. The other problem concerned Norway's demand for sovereignty over oil resources. This demand was met by a protocol recognizing this sovereignty within the limits of Community law. In parallel, agreement was reached by the Member States on an oil licensing directive in a form acceptable to Norway (which in practice negotiated it as a 13th Member State!).

The fisheries issue, particularly with respect to Norway, was one of the more difficult and complex subjects of the negotiations. This was the result of the need, on the one hand, to incorporate into the Common Fisheries Policy (CFP) a large fishing nation that had developed its own comprehensive approach to fisheries policy and, on the other hand, to find solutions to a number of internal concerns of the Union in this sector. The agreed solution was that in return for Norway accepting the present CFP *acquis* it was granted transitional periods regarding management of resources and control of fishing activities.

There were no problems on external trade. The Union agreed to negotiate free trade agreements with the Baltic States in order to align itself with the Nordic countries. This was an interesting example of the Nordics influencing EC decision-making and indirectly propelling the EC to opening association agreements with the Baltic States.

In other policy areas, temporary derogations were granted with regard to the ownership of secondary residences (a particular Austrian request), the import of tax-free alcoholic beverages and tobacco products and, for Sweden and Norway, the continuing use of snuff. Special provisions were made for the Sami people living in the Arctic region, for the Åland islands, and for the Svalbard archipelago (which would have remained outside the EU in the case of Norwegian accession).

As regards the chapters relating to the new policies of the Union introduced by the Maastricht Treaty (Economic and Monetary Union, Common Foreign and Security Policy and Justice and Home Affairs), the candidates accepted without difficulty the underlying principles and political objectives on which these policies were based, as well as the associated *acquis*.

The CFSP Chapter

Given the considerable debate on the compatibility of the neutral stance of Austria, Finland and Sweden with the CFSP, it is worth examining this part of the negotiations in more detail. The dialogue between the Union and the applicants revealed a wide consensus on foreign and security policy issues. The applicants had been 'shadowing' European Political Co-operation (EPC) for some time, and there were no surprises on either side. Indeed there was general agreement that the four applicants would strengthen the CFSP. All were active members in the international arena, had accomplished diplomatic services, and would be able to assume the Council Presidency without any serious problems. Furthermore, with the increasing emphasis on financial and economic diplomacy, the applicants could be expected to provide increased resources to strengthen the CFSP. The Nordics were keen for the Union to pay more attention to the Arctic and Baltic regions, whilst Austria, given its geographical position, was more concerned with problems in central and eastern Europe and the Balkans.

Whilst the candidates had been pursuing an active dialogue with the EU on CFSP matters, the actual negotiations on this chapter could not begin until the entry into force of the TEU on 1 November 1993. The Presidency stated its intention to close the TEU chapters before the end of the year, which meant that there was little time for formal consultations and negotiation. Exploratory talks at the level of deputies were conducted by the Chairman of COREPER and the Deputy Secretary General of the Commission. The talks were designed to verify that the applicants accepted the CFSP *acquis* including Article J4 (common defence), to determine the necessity of modifying domestic legislation, and to establish whether any candidate wished to make a unilateral declaration. Predictably there were no problems encountered by the Nordics as their neutrality was not enshrined in any constitutional act. The Austrians assured the Presidency that the Government intended to make the necessary adaptations to domestic legislation (particularly sanctions legislation) to ensure compatibility with the TEU. On the basis of these talks, the Presidency then proposed a formula which noted that the Nordics had no problems in accepting the Treaty objectives and *acquis* and that Austria intended making the necessary adaptations. Some Member States, and the Austrians, preferred a formula covering all the candidates and hence the final wording was as follows :

> The Union notes the confirmation by Austria, Sweden, Finland and Norway of their full acceptance of the rights and obligations attaching to the Union and its institutional framework, known as the '*acquis communautaire*' as it applies to present member states. This includes the content, principles and political objectives of the Treaties, including those of the TEU.
>
> The Union and Austria, Sweden, Finland and Norway agree that :
>
> - accession to the Union should strengthen the internal coherence of the Union and its capacity to act effectively in foreign and security policy;
> - the acceding states will from the time of their accession be ready and able to participate fully and actively in the CFSP as defined in the TEU;
> - the acceding states will, on accession, take on in their entirety and without reservation the objectives of the Treaty, the provisions of its Title V, and the relevant declarations attached to it;
> - the acceding states will be ready and able to support the specific policies of the Union in force at the time of their accession.
>
> With regard to member states' obligations deriving from the TEU concerning the implementation of the CFSP, it is understood that on the day of accession the legal framework of the acceding countries will be compatible with the *acquis.*

The final agreement was thus a compromise between those who wished to see the neutral applicants enter into 'specific and binding commitments' and those who were prepared to accept the assurances of the applicants at face value.

Institutional Changes

The appropriate adjustments to the institutions of the Union were made on the basis of the existing institutional provisions in the TEU – a decision which followed on from the Conclusions of the Lisbon European Council in June 1992. This did not, however, prevent the UK attempting to increase the weight of larger

Member States in Council voting by seeking to lower the threshold for the blocking minority. The British won no consistent support from other Member States apart from Spain, and after holding out for a number of weeks after the close of negotiations were forced to back down at the Council meeting in Ioannina on 29 March. Sweden and Austria were each granted four votes and Finland and Norway three votes. The qualified majority was fixed at 64 (62 after the Norwegian 'No') which maintained the present balance, i.e. 71 per cent of the total votes. The Commission was to be increased to 21 members (later reduced to 20 when Norway dropped out) whilst the number of Euro-parliamentarians was fixed at Sweden (22), Austria (21), Finland (16) and Norway (15). Other EU institutions would have their membership adjusted mechanically to take account of the relative weight of each new member country.

Assessment

The negotiations were conducted during three Presidencies – those of Denmark, Belgium and Greece. There may have been some difference in political priorities, but all three Presidencies pushed the negotiations along at a brisk speed. The Danes were to some extent handicapped by their second referendum and were content to let the Commission undertake the necessary groundwork. The Belgians were keen to close as many chapters as possible during their Presidency and this determination resulted in agreement on the Maastricht chapters, as well as standards and the single market at the ministerial session on 21 December 1993. The crucial breakthrough came at the marathon meeting in Brussels, 25 February–1 March 1994 at which the Greek chairman of the Council, Theodoros Pangalos, and the German Foreign Minister, Klaus Kinkel, played important roles in brokering the final compromise formulae.

The negotiations were concluded with Austria, Sweden and Finland on 1 March 1994, but later with Norway, on 15 March, owing to the need to settle the fisheries issue in particular. Following the Ioaninna agreement amongst the Member States, the Accession Conference then formally agreed on all the negotiating chapters on 30 March. Parallel to the negotiations, drafting had been taking place on an Accession Treaty and Accession Act together with annexes, protocols and declarations. These were agreed at the final session of the Conference on 12 April, which allowed their transmission to the European Parliament before its historic vote, as per Article O of the TEU, approving enlargement by substantial majorities on 4 May. There had been some concern that the EP might use the enlargement assent procedure as a tool to demand extra powers, but in the event there were large majorities for all the applicants. The votes were as follows: Sweden (381 in favour, 21 against and 60 abstentions), Austria (378 in favour, 24 against and 60 abstentions), Finland (377 in favour,

21 against and 61 abstentions), Norway (376 in favour, 24 against and 57 abstentions). The Treaty on Accession was formally signed by Heads of Government at the European Council in Corfu on 24 June. Signature of the Treaty signalled the start of the interim period which enabled representatives of the accession countries to attend meetings of the Council and various other Union bodies as observers.

V. The Referendums

Ratification procedures then followed in all the Member States. They were remarkably similar, involving both consultative referendums and an affirmative vote in the national parliaments. Although the referendums were consultative, each government undertook to accept the results.

Austria

The 'Yes' campaign was solidly supported by the two major parties, SPO and OVP, in the governing coalition as well as by most of the media, business and trades union leaders. They pointed to the economic benefits of membership and warned of Austria's isolation in the event of a 'No' vote. The 'No' campaign was led by Jorg Haider, the colourful leader of the right-wing liberal FPO, whose outright opposition led to a split in his party. The Greens were also opposed on environmental grounds. The campaign was rather lacklustre, coming to life only in the final fortnight with a plethora of scare stories about Austrians being forced to build nuclear power stations and to eat unsafe yoghourts from Spain. It was also alleged that the Germans would 'buy up' Austria which would lose its independence. Strangely, there was hardly a reference to the neutrality issue in the campaign.

On 12 June, the Austrians voted by 67 per cent to 33 per cent, on an 81 per cent turnout, in favour of EU membership. All Länder voted in favour, even in Tyrol where opposition to the transit agreement had been strongest.

Finland

The 'Yes' campaign was supported officially by all the major political parties, the media, business leaders (especially the forestry lobby) and the trades unions. But some room for dissent was allowed, particularly in the Centre Party of Prime Minister Aho which was heavily dependent on farmers' votes. The farming issue tended to dominate the campaign, with the 'Yes' camp arguing that Finland could not live in total isolation from Europe and that the deal on the CAP allowed the Government to continue to assist farmers in remote areas. The 'No' camp, a loose coalition of disgruntled farmers' organizations, Communists and Greens, attacked the remote Brussels bureaucracy and warned of the dangers for Finnish independence should Finland join the EU.

On 16 October, the Finns voted by 57 per cent to 43 per cent, on a 74 per cent turnout, in favour of membership. There was, however, a marked difference between the more urban south (strongly pro-EU) and the more rural north (stronger anti-EU).

Sweden

For many observers, Sweden, as the economically strongest and most populous of the potential new members, was the key country. If Sweden voted 'No' then there would have been no prospect of securing a 'Yes' vote in Norway, and even a danger that the Finnish Parliament would have failed to pass the enabling legislation.

A change of government in September 1994 brought back to power Ingvar Carlsson, the Social Democrat Prime Minister who had made Sweden's application in 1991. His predecessor, the Conservative Carl Bildt, had been a highly enthusiastic advocate of membership but his cuts in public spending had alienated public opinion, parts of which saw the strict economic policy as being dictated by Brussels. The political, economic and media elites were strongly in favour of membership, but there was considerable scepticism from women's organizations and the various strands of the environmental movement, including the vociferous animal welfare lobby. The Social Democrats were also split, with some members of Carlsson's cabinet being allowed to campaign on the 'No' side. This meant that the Government was unable to launch a united 'Yes' campaign and allowed itself to be diverted by a number of scare stories. Shortly before the referendum, Jacques Santer, the President-designate of the new Commission, announced the division of portfolios for the new Commission in which he gave Anita Gradin, the Swedish nominee, responsibility for equal opportunities, judicial affairs and the fight against fraud. This may have had some impact on the campaign, but the decisive factor was the major effort by the Prime Minister in the final week warning Swedes of the dire economic consequences of a 'No'.

In the referendum on 13 November, the Swedes voted 52 per cent in favour and 47 per cent against, on a turnout of 82 per cent. As was the case in Finland, there was a marked contrast between the negative trend in the rural north and the positive vote in the more urban south. Women were more sceptical than men.

Norway

It had always been hoped that the domino effect would influence Norwegians to vote in favour of membership. Norway had by far the strongest 'No' camp, with two major political parties (Centre and Left Socialist) as well as an array of farming, fishing and green organizations opposed to membership. Brundtland's ruling Labour Party was itself split on membership and did not really begin campaigning until after the Swedish referendum when Brundtland and other political and economic leaders began to hammer home the danger of Norway being left isolated in Europe. Jacques Santer also tried to influence the debate by offering the fisheries portfolio to the Norwegian Commissioner-designate, Thorvald Stoltenberg. In the final fortnight the 'Yes' camp made up a lot of ground, particularly in the cities, but in the end this could not compensate for the overwhelming 'No' from the rest of the country. A majority of Norwegians felt confident about their ability to go it alone, with their economy bolstered by considerable energy resources and their security covered by NATO.

In the referendum held over two days on 27–28 November, the Norwegians rejected membership by 52 per cent to 48 per cent on a 89 per cent turnout, an almost identical result to 1972. It is interesting to note that a swing of just 38,000 votes would have led to a 'Yes' victory.

The referendums in all four countries revealed stronger support for the EU amongst well-educated, male, city-dwellers; women, especially those employed in public service jobs, and rural inhabitants tended to vote against membership. Party splits were evident in all countries, the most serious being Aho's Centre Party in Finland, Carlsson's Social Democrats in Sweden, and Brundtland's Labour Party in Norway.

VI. Implications of the Norwegian 'No'

Within 24 hours of the referendum result being known, Norway's active observers in COREPER and the multitude of Council working groups had made their farewells. The diplomatic service, united in support of EU membership, were shocked even though they had been mentally prepared for the result. Brundtland stated that Norway would continue to seek active co-operation with the EU whilst breathing life into the EEA.

On the EU side, there were many expressions of regret, and External Political Relations Commissioner, Hans van den Broek, promised 'to keep the door open' for Norway. The fact that Norway remains a prospective net contributor to the budget probably guarantees it a favourable response in the future. But, in reality, the door is likely to remain closed for some time, and Norway will now fall back a long way in the EU's priority list.

The Council and Commission immediately set about revising the Treaty of Accession, deleting all provisions concerning or referring to Norway, and adjusting the votes in the Council, etc. The Council adjustments were purely mathematical – instead of 90 votes there would be a total of 87 and the blocking minority would fall from 27 to 26.

VII. Impact of the New Members

Internal

The accession of the three new Member States will increase the Union's territory by a third, which will still make it less than half the surface area of the US and only a fifth as large as Russia. Its population will rise by 6.2 per cent to just over 370 million and its GDP by 7 per cent. The enlarged EU will have a GDP nearly 30 per cent higher than the US and twice that of Japan. It will also have a 1200 kilometer border with Russia. Although comprising only 7 per cent of the world's population, the enlarged EU provides 53 per cent of all development aid, holds 37 per cent of global financial reserves, produces 27 per cent of the world's automobiles, and is responsible for 19 per cent of world trade (excluding intra-EU trade).

An analysis of political attitudes in the new members and their negotiating strategy would suggest that their accession will have a significant impact on a number of important policy areas. There is, first, the question of whether the Nordics will form a bloc in the EU. There will certainly be many occasions when they will vote together but their historic rivalries and very different economic structures should not be forgotten. The prospect of a coherent Nordic bloc has also diminished with Norway's rejection of membership. The example of Norway making its way outside the EU could also provide a rallying point for the anti-EU camp in Denmark, Sweden and, to a lesser extent, in Finland.

There can be no doubt that the newcomers will press for higher standards in environment and social policy. They are also determined to press for more openness and transparency in EU decision-making, and to support demands that Member States should enforce directives to which they have agreed. They will be supporters of a strong regional policy and keen to put subsidiarity into practice. They may find it more difficult to maintain the vagaries of their tax system and their companies could be more exposed to takeovers. With the exception of Sweden, their farmers will lobby to maintain direct income subsidies, thus making CAP reform more difficult. In terms of meeting the criteria for EMU, the EFTANs would be amongst those likely to be in the first wave.

Initially, the changes are likely to be more of tone and style, but as the newcomers find their feet they will begin to make an impact. They will do so against a background of a considerable band of 'Eurosceptics' at home, which may inhibit the new members from supporting proposals to deepen the EU.

External

In external affairs, the EFTANs are likely to push for more EU attention to Russia, central and eastern Europe and the developing world. Sweden and Finland both meet the UN aid targets of 0.7 per cent of GDP for development assistance and have an impressive record in dealing with the Third World. The newcomers share the goal of early membership for the CCEE and will push for the Baltic States to catch up with the CCEE. The EFTANs have long contributed to UN peace-keeping, and will seek to support enhanced EU/WEU capabilities in this field. Although Norway, as a NATO member, will continue to play a full role in European defence, there will now be a further gap between present and potential memberships of EU/WEU and NATO. This is a worrying development for those who would like to see a single identity of EU/WEU/NATO membership, but one with which the various institutions will have to live for the immediate future. The three newcomers have taken up observer status in the WEU, which marks a further step away from neutrality.

Enlargement will affect the EU's trade policies, with the newcomers in general likely to support a more open trade policy albeit with reservations on the agricultural front.

VIII. The Next Enlargement

The magnetism of the European Union and the swiftness of the EFTAN enlargement has already fuelled speculation about the next wave of enlargement. The European Council in Copenhagen in June 1993 made the historic statement that:

> the associated countries of central and eastern Europe that so desire shall become members of the European Union. Accession will take place as soon as an associated country is able to assume the obligations of membership by satisfying the economic and political conditions required.

These requirements include stability of political institutions, a functioning market economy, capacity to cope with competitive pressures, and acceptance of the Union's objectives as regards political, economic and monetary union. The Council also drew attention to the Union's capacity to absorb new members. This institutional aspect was deemed 'an important consideration' affecting the interests of both the Union and the candidate countries.

The Corfu European Council invited the Commission to make specific proposals to speed up the implementation of the Copenhagen Conclusions, and at the Essen European Council in December 1994, the Heads of Government approved the Commission's plan for a White Paper setting out the requirements for the candidate countries to integrate themselves in the internal market. They also approved plans for an enhanced dialogue with the CCEE on a wide range of policy areas from CFSP to environment and transport. At Essen there was, however, no mention of how to meet the cost of integrating the CCEE, nor of the necessity of reforming the CAP and the Structural Funds.

But Corfu had also singled out Malta and Cyprus as being involved in the next phase of enlargement, and made a linkage between enlargement and the 1996 IGC when it stated that 'the institutional conditions of ensuring the proper functioning of the Union must be created at the 1996 Intergovernmental Conference, which for that reason must take place before accession negotiations begin' with countries of central and eastern Europe. This meant that the institutional question should not be fudged again and the same European Council agreed to establish a Reflection Group under Spanish chairmanship to produce reform proposals by the December 1995 European Council. Specifically, the conclusions of the Corfu European Council invited the Reflection Group 'to elaborate options in the perspective of the future enlargement of the Union set out in the conclusions of the European Council in Brussels and in the Ioannina agreement [weighting of votes, the threshold for qualified majority decisions, number of members of the Commission, and any other measure deemed necessary to facilitate the work of the institutions and guarantee their effective operation in the perspective of enlargement]'.

Essentially the question for the 1996 IGC is how to organize a Union of perhaps over 20 members on the basis of democracy, transparency and efficiency. Two types of questions will need to be addressed: constitutional and institutional. As regards the constitution of the Union, each new accession increases the burden of work and the diversity of issues to be handled. This suggests that the IGC will have to pay greater attention to the application of the subsidiarity principle. What should be the balance between decisions taken and tasks attributed at the Union, national and regional level? How can greater involvement in, and acceptance of, the Union's activities by its citizens be achieved? On the institutional side, attention will need to focus on how to improve the preparation, taking, and implementation of decisions in an enlarged Union which will inevitably involve more complex and diverse considerations.

The opening shots in this debate were fired on 1 September 1994 by Karl Lamers, the German CDU Foreign Affairs spokesman, when he published proposals for a hard-core Europe involving Germany, France and the Benelux countries. The central point of the Lamers paper was that those Member States ready, willing and able to take further steps towards integration should not be prevented from doing so. John Major responded in his Leiden speech on 7 September 1994 with calls for a more flexible, *à la carte* Europe, in which Member States could essentially pick and choose in which policies they wished to participate. In France, Prime Minister, Edouard Balladur, spoke in favour of '*géometrie variable*' – a concept which implies that all Member States accept shared goals but may take different times to reach them.

Whatever the future shape of Europe, there is common agreement on the need for substantial reforms, not least of an institutional nature. Perhaps the most sensitive of the institutional issues is the question of changes to the voting system in the Council. The larger states will certainly press strongly for greater attention to size of population. Other contentious issues include the nature and composition of the six-monthly rotating Presidency/troika system; the manner in which the Council transacts business; and the linguistic regimes and costs of interpretation/translation.

As regards the Commission, there is wide consensus on the need to reduce the number of Commissioners – but that is the end of the consensus. If rotating Commissioners cannot be agreed, then it may be worthwhile exploring the option of denationalizing the Commission and drawing the Parliament into the nomination process. The difficulties surrounding the appointment of Jacques Santer have certainly fuelled calls for a more open and democratic system of choosing the Commission President.

As for the Parliament, although it has gained important new powers under the TEU, it remains far from satisfied with its position *vis-à-vis* the other institutions, and will certainly seek to use its potential to block further enlargements unless it gains additional powers, particularly in co-decision.

The agenda for the 1996 IGC is thus lengthy and complex, and it must be very doubtful whether the deliberations can be concluded within a year. The outcome will very much depend on the political environment at the time and in particular the willingness of the Heads of Government in the larger Member States to make compromises.

IX. Conclusion

Although the 1993–94 enlargement negotiations involved more countries than any previous round of enlargement, they were the least problematic in that the EFTANs were prosperous, were stable democracies, and were closely linked to the EC through the EEA. The negotiations took place more rapidly than any earlier enlargement negotiations and the agreed transition periods were shorter than any previously agreed. The final deal was reached only 13 months after the opening of the Accession Conference and only 16 months after the last of the four applications (by Norway).

The speed of the negotiations demonstrated both the willingness of the Union to accept the EEA applicants at a time of some internal confusion and disarray, and the high degree of preparedness on the part of the applicant states. The negotiations were also facilitated by the considerable degree of harmonization that had occurred within the EEA framework. Nevertheless, there were major problems to overcome in the agricultural and regional sectors, as well as a host of topics of lesser importance. The Commission Task Force under Commissioner van den Broek was generally acknowledged to have played a significant role in seeking compromises, whilst Theodoros Pangalos and Klaus Kinkel made a decisive impact at the final negotiating marathon at the end of February.

The impact of the new members is likely, overall, to be more positive than negative, but they will not have much time to adjust to Union membership before they are confronted with the challenge of the 1996 IGC. No further enlargement of the EU, to the east or south, will be possible until there is an agreement on institutional reform at the IGC. The 1996 rendezvous will thus have major implications for the future of Europe.

Journal of Common Market Studies Volume 33, Annual Review
August 1995

Governance and Institutional Developments

RICHARD CORBETT*
*Deputy Secretary General, Parliamentary Group of the PES**

I. Introduction

Developments in the governance and institutions of the European Union in 1994 were dominated by the first experiences in applying the Treaty on European Union (TEU), commonly known as the Maastricht Treaty, and by preparations for enlargement to the applicant states from the European Free Trade Association (EFTA). There were also some ongoing institutional developments of a less spectacular nature.

II. Application of the Maastricht Procedures

Development of the 'Pillars'

The two 'pillars' of a largely intergovernmental character set up by the TEU went through their first full year of operation in 1994. In neither case were developments spectacular.

Against the background of the ongoing war in former Yugoslavia, and worrying events in other parts of eastern Europe, the Common and Foreign Security Policy (CFSP) failed to chalk up any spectacular successes. Only seven joint actions had been approved pursuant to Article J.3 of the TEU by the end

* The views expressed are those of the author and do not necessarily reflect those of his employer.

of 1994 (four in 1993 and three in 1994) and six common positions (five in 1994). A hundred and ten CFSP declarations were adopted.

The joint actions were mostly small scale. Two related to international conferences (the stability pact and the non-proliferation treaty), two related to observing elections (in Russia and South Africa, carried out with considerable assistance from the European Parliament), and one to support the Palestinian police, with help from the Western European Union (WEU). The issue of how to finance CSFP actions (Community budget or national contributions) had still not been definitively resolved by the end of the year.

The WEU continued to develop its role, adopting the Kirchberg Declaration on 9 May, reaffirming WEU's commitments to develop 'separable but not separate' military capabilities with NATO, and envisaging the possible development of a WEU maritime force and an independent European satellite system. The WEU Council Presidency was reduced from one year to six months in length in order to coincide with that of the EU Council, with Spain due to be the first country holding a simultaneous Presidency in 1995. A new category of WEU 'associate partners' was created whereby the Visegrad countries, the Baltic States, Romania and Bulgaria became associated with the WEU with the right to participate in Council meetings.

Foreign policy objectives continued to be pursued through the Community pillar as well, notably through the various financial mechanisms providing assistance for central and eastern European countries, including macroeconomic financial assistance.

As to the Justice and Home Affairs pillar, not a single convention was adopted during 1994, and only one joint action (concerning travel facilities for school pupils from third countries residing in the Member States). Council failed to agree on the terms for establishing Europol. Two 'resolutions' were adopted on the admission of third country nationals for employment and for study.

Economic and Monetary Union

The first set of recommendations for economic policy guidelines of the Member States and of the Community were drawn up in conformity with Article 3(2) of the EC Treaty. This rather cumbersome procedure involves the Commission preparing a recommendation for the Council which reports to the European Council, following which the Council adopts recommendations for the Member States. Recommendations remained rather general. More concrete was the first use of the 'excessive deficit procedure' whereby Council adopted recommendations to ten Member States pursuant to Article 104 C of the EC Treaty. These recommendations were eventually adopted by Council after the lifting of a scrutiny reserve by the French delegation pending the consultation of the French Parliament by the French Government on the terms of the recommendation that Council would be making to France! The recommendations to the ten Member States were made public, despite provision in the Treaty for such recommendations to remain initially confidential.

Interinstitutional Agreement on Committees of Inquiry

Article 138 C of the Treaty as amended by the TEU required the European Parliament (EP), the Council and the Commission to determine 'by common accord' the detailed provisions governing the rights of EP committees of inquiry. Negotiations had begun in 1994, and concluded on 20 December 1994. The position of the Parliament and the Council had diverged in particular on the issues of Parliament's right to oblige national officials to appear before committees of inquiry, access of the committees to confidential documents and the term of office of such committees. In the text agreed, the right to determine the time limit for a committee was left to the EP, provided it did not exceed 12 months, twice renewable by three months. Member States and Community institutions are required to designate officials to appear before a committee of inquiry upon the request of the committee, unless grounds of secrecy or public or national security dictate otherwise by virtue of national or Community legislation. Member States and Community institutions must similarly provide the committee with 'the documents necessary for the performance of its duties'. Where national or Community legislation provides for secrecy, this must be 'notified to the European Parliament by a representative authorized to commit the Governments of the Member States [or Institution] concerned'. Hearings and testimony at the committee of inquiry will take place in public except when requested by a quarter of the members of the committee, by Community or national authorities, or by witnesses and experts.

Social Protocol

The first use of the protocol on social policy annexed to the TEU, which contains an agreement to which the UK is not a party, took place on 22 September when the Council adopted a directive on European Works Councils, providing for information and consultation of employees in Community-scale undertakings (directive 94/45/EC). Recourse to the protocol was necessary following the failure to overcome UK objections in the normal EC procedure in an area requiring unanimity.

First Use of the Co-decision Procedure

1994 saw the first 'acts of the European Parliament and the Council' with 30 co-decision procedures completed. In 18 cases, agreement was reached between the two institutions without needing to convene the conciliation committee. In 11 cases, the conciliation committee agreed a text which was then approved by Council and Parliament. In one case, the conciliation committee failed to reach agreement, Council reconfirmed its common position but this was rejected by the EP by an absolute majority, and consequently failed (voice telephony directive, see below).

In these 30 cases, there was relatively little difficulty in negotiating compromises on the substance of the legislation in question, important though some of it was. Nor were there insurmountable difficulties as regards the application of the procedure. The six-week deadlines proved to be flexible with Council and Parliament agreeing that the conciliation committee's deadline would run as of the first meeting of the committee and that the deadlines for the institutions to vote would run only after discounting a time lag for translations. It was also established that the conciliation committee is not limited to negotiating on amendments adopted by the Parliament by an absolute majority, but can introduce any new text capable of facilitating a compromise. This included points on which the majority – but not an absolute majority – of Parliament had approved amendments.

Where major difficulties did arise between the two institutions was on two 'horizontal' issues: provisions for Commission implementing measures or secondary legislation arising from co-decision acts, and the fixing in legislative acts of volumes of expenditure estimated to be necessary.

On implementing measures, Parliament had objected for many years to the so-called 'comitology' system, whereby Commission decisions were subject to scrutiny by committees of national civil servants empowered, in certain cases, to block the Commission decision and refer the matter to Council. Comitology was criticized by Parliament for being bureaucratic, for giving only Council-appointed committees the right to scrutinize the Commission, and for the fact that an implementing measure referred back to the legislature by such committees is referred to Council alone and not to Parliament and Council.

With the co-decision procedure, Parliament was in a stronger position to oppose unacceptable comitology provisions in legislative texts, and also argued that there was a new legal situation in that the traditional comitology provisions were based on Article 145 of the EC Treaty which allowed Council to lay down conditions for the exercise of implementing measures for legislation adopted *by Council* – but co-decision legislation was not adopted by Council but *by*

Parliament and Council, a distinction clearly made in Article 189 of the EC Treaty.

This interpretation was not accepted by the Council and the issue was fought out on each individual item of legislation containing comitology provisions. Although some compromises fudged the issue, Parliament refused to back down and went so far as to reject the voice telephony directive on these grounds. Council was eventually persuaded to negotiate with Parliament leading to the adoption of a *modus vivendi* on 20 December. This *modus vivendi* provides for all draft general implementing acts to be sent to the Parliament at the same time and under the same conditions as to the comitology-type committee. The Commission must take account of any comments by the EP and 'keep it informed at every stage of the procedure of the action which it intends to take on them'. Where a matter is referred to the Council, the latter may not adopt an implementing act without first carrying out a consultation procedure with the Parliament and, in the event of an unfavourable opinion from Parliament, 'taking due account of the European Parliament's point of view' and trying to 'seek a solution in the appropriate framework'. Whilst not fully satisfying the Parliament, the *modus vivendi* goes well beyond all previous provisions for giving Parliament a role in scrutinizing implementing measures. It was also agreed that the 1996 Intergovernmental Conference (IGC) should re-examine the issue.

The question of the 'amounts deemed necessary' (fixing in legislative acts amounts which, in the view of the Parliament, should be determined in the annual budgetary procedure), also gave rise to conflict. When this threatened to prevent the adoption of the Socrates and Youth for Europe exchange programmes, Council eventually agreed to negotiate a joint declaration whereby Council accepted that 'amounts deemed necessary' would only be incorporated into legislation (pursuant to the co-decision procedure or otherwise) when jointly agreed by Parliament and Council. Even then they should serve only as a reference from which the budgetary authority could depart if it could justify doing so by objectively valid reasons. In all other cases, legislation would no longer refer to such amounts.

The resolution of these two 'horizontal' problems illustrated the knock-on effect of co-decision into areas where Council was initially reluctant to concede ground, but where it was ultimately obliged to negotiate a compromise solution. The fact that such compromises were found augurs well for the future of the co-decision procedure.

Appointment of the Commission

The TEU brought in a new procedure for appointing the Commission whereby the Member States first agree on a candidate for President, on whom they must consult the EP, and then the Commission as a whole is subject to a vote of confidence by the Parliament. Both phases gave rise to important innovations.

The choice of a President was clouded by the UK's veto on the candidacy of the Belgian Prime Minister, Jean-Luc Dehaene, at the Corfu European Council. Although all other Member States agreed to Dehaene's candidacy, the requirement for unanimous agreement among the Member States allowed the UK to prevent his name going forward. An extraordinary European Council convened in Brussels a month later agreed on the compromise candidacy of Jacques Santer, the Luxembourg Prime Minister.

Given the circumstances, the debate and the vote in the EP on Jacques Santer was no formality. A combination of those opposing Jacques Santer, and those who had major reservations about the procedure and the UK veto, threatened his approval by the Parliament. This opposition was not overcome by his meetings with the main political groups in the Parliament prior to the vote. In the event, Parliament approved his appointment by 260 votes to 238, with the majority composed mainly of Christian Democrats, Gaullists, Forza Italia and a minority of the Socialist group (largely from governing parties whose representative in the European Council had approved the nomination). The process at least confirmed that the 'consultative' vote in the Parliament amounts to a vote of confirmation with both the President of the European Council (Chancellor Kohl) and Jacques Santer himself confirming that a negative vote in the Parliament would require the European Council to find another candidate. (The appointment of Santer is also considered in the editorial by Neill Nugent.)

The second phase of the procedure required a vote of confidence from the EP once the Commission as a whole had been put together by the national governments in consultation with the President-designate. Parliament sought to build on this Treaty provision by providing in its revised Rules of Procedure (see the 1993 *Annual Review*) that the individual members of the Commission-designate must appear before the relevant parliamentary committee corresponding to their prospective portfolio for a public confirmation hearing. This provision was not universally popular within the Commission and, indeed, the outgoing Commission expressed grave reservations. Nonetheless, it became clear that the EP would simply not schedule a vote at all on the new Commission until it had complied with this requirement. Jacques Santer and his colleagues therefore accepted to go through the procedure, which in turn required a prior agreement on the distribution of portfolios – something that no previous Commission had managed to do before taking office. The Commission-designate reached agreement on the distribution of portfolios in early November, thereby leaving adequate time for Parliament to conduct the hearings.

Parliament nonetheless postponed the hearings and the vote of confidence until January 1995 – thereby prolonging the life of the Delors III Commission –

in order to allow MEPs from the new Member States (who only became members on 1 January) to take part in the vote. Parliament felt that a Commission governing 15 Member States and including representatives from each of them should be voted in by MEPs from all 15.

The hearings, when they took place in January 1995, focused considerable media attention on the aptitude of the candidates. There was strong criticism of the performance of some candidates, but short of rejecting the Commission as a whole, MEPs could only press for a re-allocation of responsibilities. This took place in the case of Commissioner Flynn whose chairmanship of a Commission committee on equal opportunities was reallocated to President Santer. Following this, and an undertaking by the incoming Commission to renegotiate the 'Code of Conduct' that governs EP–Commission relations, the EP gave a vote of confidence to the new Commission by 417 votes to 104.

The allocation of portfolios among the new Commissioners is as follows:

Jacques Santer:	– General co-ordination – EMU (with Yves-Thibault de Silguy) – CFSP (with Hans van den Broek) – IGC (with Marcelino Oreja) – Staff matters
Manuel Marin:	– External relations with the Mediterranean, Middle and Near East, Latin America and Asia (except Japan, China, South Korea, Hong Kong, Macao and Taiwan)
Martin Bangemann:	– Industrial affairs – Information technology and telecommunications
Sir Leon Brittan:	– External relations with North America, Australia, New Zealand, Japan, China, South Korea, Hong Kong, Macao, and Taiwan – Common commercial policy – Relations with the OECD and WTO
Karel van Miert	– Competition
Hans van den Broek	– External relations with central and eastern Europe, the former Soviet Union, Turkey, Cyprus, Malta and other European Countries – CFSP
Joao de Deus Pinheiro	– External relations with the ACP countries

Padraig Flynn	– Employment and social affairs
Marcelino Oreja	– Relations with the European Parliament – Culture and audiovisual – IGC (in agreement with the President)
Edith Cresson	– Science, research and development: training and youth education
Ritt Bjerregaard	– Environment – Nuclear security
Monika Wulf-Mathies	– Regional policies – Cohesion Fund
Neil Kinnock	– Transport (including trans-European networks)
Mario Monti	– Internal market – Financial services
Emma Bonino	– Consumer policy – Fisheries
Yves-Thibault de Silguy	– Economic and financial affairs – Monetary matters (in agreement with the President)
Christos Papoutsis	– Energy – Euratom – Small and medium-sized enterprises – Tourism
Anita Gradin	– Home and judicial affairs – Anti-fraud measures
Franz Fischler	– Agriculture and rural development
Erkki Liikanen	– Budget – Personnel and administration

Building on the precedents set by Jacques Delors, President Santer was instrumental in allocating the portfolios.This involved a clash with Sir Leon Brittan who sought the CFSP portfolio, which went to Hans van den Broek. One new feature is the grouping of Commissioners sharing a field under the chairmanship of the President (e.g. in external relations).

Ombudsman

The EP began the procedure for appointing the first ombudsman. Six candidates were considered by the Parliament's committee on petitions with a view to submitting a name to the plenary of the Parliament. However, the committee repeatedly held a tied vote between the two most successful candidates. This caused a delay in the appointment such that the final vote could only be held in 1995. As this would be after the accession of the new Member States, it was agreed to start the procedure again from scratch in order to allow candidates from the new Member States to apply as well.

III. Preparations for Enlargement

As Fraser Cameron shows in his keynote article, the accession negotiations with Austria, Sweden, Finland and Norway were completed by the end of March. Parliament gave its necessary assent on 4 May by overwhelming majorities. The results of the negotiations had also to be approved by the national parliaments of the Member States, a process completed just in time for the end of the year deadline to be respected. Meanwhile, the acceding states held referendums on their accession, with a majority of 66.6 per cent giving their support in Austria (12 June), 56.9 per cent in Finland (16 October) and 52.3 per cent in Sweden (13 November). Norway, however, decided not to join with 52.8 per cent voting against (28 November).

Institutional Aspects of Enlargement

Although agreement was reached without difficulty on the number of votes to be attributed to each applicant state in the Council (Sweden and Austria 4; Finland and Norway 3), the issue of what should constitute the new threshold for obtaining a qualified majority (previously 44 out of 76 votes) had to be defined for a new Council with a total (it was thought before Norway decided not to join) of 90 votes. Most Member States wanted the new threshold to be 64, which represented the same proportion (71 per cent) as the previous level, as with each previous enlargement. The UK wanted the threshold to be 68, representing the same blocking minority of 23 votes. This, however, would have made decision-taking more difficult and was vigourously opposed by a majority of Member States and by the European Parliament, where MEPs made it clear that Parliament would not give its assent to enlargement if the Accession Treaty contained such a weakening of the Union. The issue deadlocked the enlargement negotiations just at the moment when agreement had been reached on all the outstanding policy questions. Eventually, a special meeting of the Council in Ioannina on

27–29 March approved a compromise whereby a threshold was indeed adapted to 64 votes in the Treaty, but an accompanying political declaration stated that, where a measure was opposed by 23–26 votes, then discussions would continue to try to reach a larger majority of at least 68 votes 'within a reasonable time'. It was specified that this 'reasonable time' was without prejudice to time limits laid down by the Treaties and by secondary legislation, notably the time limits in the co-operation and the co-decision procedures, and that the Council rules of procedure (which provide for a vote to be taken at the request of the Commission or a single Member State provided a simple majority agrees) remained in force. It was agreed that the whole system of qualified majority voting would have to be re-examined in the 1996 IGC.

As regards the number of seats in the EP, the EU forwarded in the negotiations the figures proposed by Parliament itself, namely 15 for Norway, 16 for Finland, 20 for Austria and 21 for Sweden. However, Sweden made a strong case for having a greater number on the basis of recent population trends, but its argument that it should have 25 seats (like Belgium, Portugal and Greece) was not accepted. The EP accepted that Sweden should have 22 members and this figure was eventually accepted in the enlargement negotiations. Austria, however, argued that if Sweden was increasing to 22, then it should increase to 21 and this too was accepted. As a result Austria is now the only Member State of the EU not to have the number of MEPs that the EP has itself proposed (the pre-enlargement Member States have the number agreed at the Edinburgh European Council – which accepted without amendment Parliament's own proposal).

It was agreed that for the other institutions (the Commission and the Courts), each new Member State would obtain one member.

The Accession Treaty also made provision for a change in the rotation of the Council Presidency, as had been suggested by the EP. The new order of rotation seeks to obtain more balanced troikas which nearly always include one of the larger Member States. Furthermore, Council can now agree unanimously to change the order of rotation.

Budgetary Consequences of Enlargement

The financial perspective laying down ceilings for each category of expenditure until 1999 needed revision to take account of enlargement. The Commission, Parliament and Council agreed on a new financial perspective on 29 November, which was approved by the Council on 5 December and voted by Parliament on 13 December and signed the same day. Essentially, it provides for an increase of about 5 per cent in Community expenditure, with an above average increase for internal policies and external action and a below average increase for the structural funds and administrative expenditure. The ceiling on agriculture expenditure was increased by 74 per cent of the increased GNP provided by enlargement (about 5 per cent of expenditure). At the same time, the institutions took advantage of this adjustment to make other changes to the financial perspectives not arising from enlargement, notably to increase the ceilings on structural operations to cater for Community finance for the peace programme in Northern Ireland and for a programme to modernize the Portuguese textile industry following the GATT agreement. The new figures allow for the 'safety margin' for future adaptations to be increased from 0.01 per cent of GDP to 0.03 per cent.

IV. Other Institutional Developments

Besides questions relating to the new Maastricht procedures and the prospective enlargement of the Union, normal institutional life continued in the context of the existing Treaties.

The Commission

1994 was the final year of the third Commission headed by Jacques Delors and the last of his ten-year incumbency as President.

The work of the Commission focused on measures to implement the White Paper on growth, competitiveness and employment adopted by the Brussels European Council in 1993, as well as on the enlargement negotiations, the adoption of the fourth framework programme for research and technological development, the proposals for trans-European networks, and the application of the enlarged Structural Funds.

The annual legislative programme for 1994 was approved through a joint declaration by the EP and the Commission on 9 February and published in the *Official Journal*.

During the year, the Commission adopted 7,034 instruments (regulations, decisions, directives, recommendations and opinions) and sent to Council 558 proposals and 272 memoranda or reports. There were 14, 070 permanent posts and 848 temporary posts on its establishment plan, supplemented by 3,316 (and 181 temporary posts) in its research bodies, 465 in the Office of Publications, 76 at the Centre for Development of Vocational Training (Berlin) and 71 at the Foundation for the Improvement of Working and Living Conditions (Dublin).

The Council

The Council was chaired by Greece during the first six months and by Germany for the second half of the year. The priorities and performances of the two Presidencies are considered in the article by Brigid Laffan.

The Council held 92 meetings in 1994 in the following formations:

– General Affairs	16	
– Economic and Finance (Ecofin)	11	
– Agriculture	11	
– Fishing	5	
– Justice and Home Affairs	4	
– Environment	4	
– Industry	4	
– Research	4	
– Social Affairs	4	
– Transport	4	
– Internal Market	3	
– Health	3	
– Telecommunications	2	
– Energy	2	
– Budget	2	
– Education	2	
– Youth	2	
– Culture	2	
– Consumer Protection	2	
– Development	2	
– Civil Protection	1	
– Joint meetings	2	(Environment/Transport; Industry/Telecommunications)

Council adopted 46 directives, 274 regulations and 148 decisions. It had 2,289 permanent posts on its establishment plan.

The European Council

The European Council met three times in 1994. Besides its regular meetings in June (Corfu) and December (Essen), it had an additional short meeting in July in Brussels in order to agree on a candidate for the President of the Commission, following the UK's veto of Jean-Luc Dehaene in Corfu. Participants from the applicant states took part in the meetings (including Norway except for the Essen meeting). The European Council had a short meeting with the Heads of State or Government of the six associated countries from central and eastern Europe at the Essen meeting.

European Parliament

The fourth set of direct elections to the EP – and the first in which Union citizens residing in a Member State of which they were not nationals had the right to vote at their place of residence – were held from 9 to 12 June. As reported in previous *Annual Reviews,* the size of the Parliament was increased from 518 to 567. Turnout dropped by 2 per cent compared to the previous direct elections, remaining low when compared to national elections but high when compared to, for instance, US congressional elections. The most spectacular drop in turnout was in the Netherlands, which had held nation-wide local elections followed by national elections in the preceding months.

In most Member States, the election campaign was dominated, like local election campaigns, by national issues. Nonetheless, European issues did feature and the main party political federations made greater use than previously of the common election manifestos.

The results of the elections produced little change on the left of the political spectrum, but fragmentation on the centre-right. On the left, the Party of European Socialists retained the same number of seats as before the elections (albeit in a larger Parliament) and remained flanked by the Greens, former Communists and a 'Radical' group that replaced the former Rainbow group. On the centre-right, the Christian Democratic EPP lost seats and two new groups appeared: Forza Europa as the European emanation of Berlusconi's Forza Italia (the only group in the history of Parliament to have consisted entirely of MEPs from a single nationality) and the 'Europe of the Nations' group consisting of opponents of the TEU, based largely on the list of Philippe de Villiers and Jimmy Goldsmith which obtained support on an anti-EU and anti-GATT platform in France. The Liberals and the (largely Gaullist and Fianna Fáil) 'European Democratic Alliance' were returned with only small changes, whereas the former European Right group was unable to attract sufficient members to maintain its status as a political group after the elections.

The sizes of political groups after the elections were as follows:

– Party of European Socialist (PES)	198
– European People's Party (EPP)	157
– European Liberal, Democratic and Reformist Party (ELDR)	43
– Confederal Group of the European United Left (EUL)	28
– Forza Europa (FE)	27
– European Democratic Alliance (EDA)	26
– Greens	23
– European Radical Alliance (ERA)	19
– Europe of the Nations (EN)	19
– Non–affiliated	27

An important feature of the EP after the elections, as before, is the need for negotiation and compromise among the political groups. The centre-right has a small theoretical majority but it cannot deliver on most issues, because of the anti-European and extreme right elements. Consequently (and also because of the need to assemble an absolute majority to amend or reject Council's position in many of the legislative and budgetary procedures), negotiation and compromise between the PES and EPP groups remain essential.

At its inaugural session after the elections, Parliament elected Klaus Hänsch (PES/Germany) as its new President for two and a half years. It created a new Standing Committee on Fishing (previously a subcommittee of the Agriculture Committee) bringing the total number of standing committees to 20. A temporary committee was created (for a year) on employment to follow through the implementation of the Delors White Paper on growth, competitiveness, and employment, and to develop other proposals to fight unemployment.

Parliament's involvement in the enlargement issue, in the appointment of the new Commission, in the application of the new legislative procedures, in the appointment of the ombudsman and in the preparation of the IGC are described elsewhere in this article. Parliament adopted 168 opinions under the simple consultation procedure, 33 first readings and 21 second readings under the co-operation procedure, 18 first readings, 34 second readings and 8 third readings under the co-decision procedure and 11 assents. It also adopted a number of own-initiative reports and resolutions. Members of the Parliament addressed 2,505 written questions to the Commission and 401 to the Council, 100 oral questions (with debate) to the Commission and 66 to the Council, and posed 565 questions at question time to the Commission and 248 to the Council. There were 3,249 permanent and 541 temporary posts on the establishment plan.

Court of Justice and Court of First Instance

(See the separate article on legal developments by Jo Shaw in this *Annual Review.*)

Court of Auditors

Besides its annual report and six specific reports on various Community organs, the Court adopted four special reports (on exports refunds and the dairy sector, European Development Fund (EDF) import programmes, beef market intervention and on the open environment). There were 360 permanent and 67 temporary post on its establishment plan.

Committee of the Regions (CoR)

The Committee, established under the TEU, held its inaugural session on 9–10 March. Jacques Blanc, President of Languedoc-Roussillon, was elected President for a two-year term. Rules of Procedure were drawn up and approved by the Council on 25 May. The Committee delivered its first opinion on draft legislation at its second session in April, adopting some 27 opinions (including 3 own initiative reports) by the end of the year. The CoR has set up nine commissions (regional development, transport and communications, urban policies, land use, agriculture, citizens Europe, research and culture, education and training, cohesion, social policy and public health, institutional affairs) and four subcommissions.

The CoR sought to hold its meetings in the plenary of the EP building in Brussels rather than in the Economic and Social Committee. Parliament has, however, been reluctant to allow it to use the parliamentary chamber itself, offering temporary use of other meeting rooms instead.

CoR Members belonging to political parties affiliated to the PES and the EPP have established political groups. They have not, however, been given any facilities by the CoR and this development has been opposed by the CoR's President.

Economic and Social Committee

The Committee adopted 121 opinions on Commission proposals or memoranda and 23 own initiative opinions in the ten plenary sessions held in 1994. In October, it elected a new President, Carlos Ferrer. There were 510 posts on the Committee's establishment plan.

European Monetary Institute (EMI)

The EMI was established on 1 January 1994 with the start of stage II of Economic and Monetary Union. The main task of its President, Alexandre Lamfalussy, and the EMI Council in 1994 was to get the EMI off the ground. It moved into its own premises in Frankfurt after operating provisionally from the Bank for International Settlements in Basle for the first months of the year.

National Parliaments

For the reasons mentioned in last year's *Annual Review*, no meeting of the Conference of Parliaments envisaged under the TEU took place. Instead, the Conference of European Affairs Committees continued with its bi-annual meetings in Athens and in Bonn. The presidents of the national parliaments and of the European Parliament also met. At these meetings, the French Parliament continued to press for a greater interinstitutionalized involvement of national parliaments in the EU's legislative procedures and in the preparations for the 1996 IGC without ,however, obtaining support from other national parliaments.

Preparation of the 1996 Intergovernmental Conference

The Corfu European Council, confirming the agreement reached by the Council at Ioannina, agreed to establish a 'Reflection Group' to prepare the 1996 IGC. This Reflection Group would begin work in June 1995 under the Spanish Presidency. It would consist of personal representatives of the Foreign Ministers and two members of the EP. Parliament appointed Elisabeth Guigou (PES/France and former Minister of European Affairs during the Maastricht negotiations) and Elmar Brok (EPP/Germany) as its representatives. The national representatives had not yet all been nominated by the end of 1994.

The European Council also invited each of the Institutions to prepare a report for the Reflection Group. Parliament's report is being prepared by its Committee on Institutional Affairs (rapporteurs: David Martin (PES/UK, and Vice-President of the European Parliament, formerly Parliament's rapporteur during the Maastricht negotiations) and Jean-Louis Bourlanges (EPP/France).

Budgetary Matters

Despite the new interinstitutional agreements on the budget signed in October 1993, the 1994 budgetary procedure (on the 1995 budget) ended in conflict. This initially centred on the issue of whether the budget should assume that Member States would (at last) ratify the Edinburgh Agreement raising the ceiling of the Community's own resources (Parliament eventually won this battle by entering the corresponding amounts with a footnote freezing certain appropriations until ratification took place). The second contentious issue concerned how far the budget should already make provision for enlargement (with amounts eventually being entered into a reserve on the understanding that a supplementary and the amending budget would be presented early in 1995 to allocate this reserve to different items). By the end of the procedure, however, the conflict centred on the classification of certain (agricultural) items as compulsory expenditure or non-compulsory expenditure. On the former, Council has the final say in that it can overrule by a qualified majority any Parliament amendment cutting expenditure. On the latter, Parliament can, by a three-fifths majority, overrule Council (within the jointly agreed expenditure ceilings). In this dispute, Parliament was seeking to reduce certain items of agricultural expenditure and its ability to do so depended on the classification of the items in questions. As the final vote on the budget is in the Parliament, it pressed ahead with its own interpretation which Council has now challenged in the Court.

Journal of Common Market Studies
Volume 33, Annual Review
August 1995

Internal Policy Developments

JOHN REDMOND
University of Birmingham

I. Introduction

1994 lacked the drama of 1993, as much of what took place involved finishing off earlier initiatives or engaging in the rather routine activities that are the stuff of European integration. This was certainly the case with most of the economic (and related) internal policy activities. Similarly, agriculture was dominated by the negotiations over the annual price package, and there was a continuation of the efforts to resolve the problems in the fish market which began in 1993. However, there were major developments in social and environmental policy which, significantly, involved initiatives from which the UK was excluded and, perhaps most importantly, the debate on Economic and Monetary Union (EMU) began to address the really important issues relating to Stage III and the single currency. On the other hand, despite sterling efforts by the Commission and the German Presidency, the Justice and Home Affairs (JHA) pillar made little progress.

Ultimately, 1994 was therefore a quiet, but certainly not an uninteresting, year.

II. Economic and Related Policies

Internal Market Developments

The excitement that had been attached to the '1992' programme had completely dissipated by the beginning of 1994 as the completion of the Single European Market (SEM) became increasingly concerned with detail. Consequently, the focus was on filling the gaps and pursuing those recalcitrant Member States which were still being slow in transposing SEM regulations into national law. The Commission sought to maintain the momentum by instituting a series of 'internal market weeks' in Member States during which the general public and business interests could obtain more information and point to problems but, in general, the mood was very much 'so far so good but could do better'.

In October, the progress of the SEM was criticized from two sources:

- The Economic and Social Committee (Ecosoc) published a report which identified 62 'substantive obstacles' to the functioning of the internal market, which were apportioned between the four freedoms as follows: goods (32), services (15), capital (2) and people (13).
- A Eurochambers (Association of European Chambers of Commerce and Industry) study found a degree of concern amongst companies, particularly small and medium-sized enterprises (SMEs), about the extent to which the SEM programme had been implemented.

Nevertheless, in its report to the Essen Summit in December, the Commission was basically optimistic, noting that, in general terms, the SEM was functioning well. Indeed, earlier in the year evidence that goods were moving more freely and much more quickly had been cited, derived from a study using nine Euro-Info Centres in seven countries. (A much broader study is due to be completed in 1996.) However, the Commission also observed that several significant problems remained, notably:

- In some sectors the measures adopted in the Council had not been transposed into national law in all Member States and, moreover, their practical implementation left much to be desired.
- The Council had still not reached agreement on a number of outstanding measures, most notably the abolition of border controls on persons.
- Other significant gaps concerned the continuation of double taxation of companies with business in more than one Member State, the insufficient liberalization of certain sectors – energy and telecommunications in particular – and the need to establish a final value added tax (VAT) regime.

The Commission also reported on transposition rates in detail. Superficially, the average rate of transposition – 89 per cent – appeared high, but this concealed significant differences between sectors. Delays were particularly widespread in the areas of intellectual property, public procurement, insurance and, to a lesser extent, company law.

The most visible failure continued to be the inability to implement free movement of people at EU level. Indeed, attempts to implement the (more limited) Schengen Agreement also failed in 1994 mainly because of technical difficulties with the Schengen Information System (SIS). Moreover, it became clear that two of the intended participants – Italy and Greece – could not join in initially because of technical difficulties with connection to the SIS. This left the remaining seven countries – Belgium, the Netherlands, Luxembourg, France, Germany, Spain and Portugal – with a receding target starting date; eventually it was agreed to begin in March 1995. Meanwhile, the British and the Irish remained aloof and the Danes asked for observer status (which was also given to Austria in anticipation of its accession). From an EU perspective, a functioning SIS would be valuable as it may be made available to the non-Schengen EU Member States and could serve as the basis for the intended EIS (European Information System) which could allow agreement on the free movement of people throughout the whole Union.

Finally, there were three other SEM areas where progress was limited or non-existent. First, the Commission expressed concern early in the year about the liberalization of public procurement markets; although the legislative framework was in place the involvement of foreign companies, and particularly SMEs, in these markets remained disappointing. Second, the 1989 agreement on a Community patent remained blocked since less than half the Member States had ratified it, despite efforts to make progress in the December Council meeting. Third, no progress was made towards the adoption of the European company statute.

Economic and Monetary Union

Unlike in the past two years, there was no exchange rate drama in the Exchange Rate Mechanism (ERM). Indeed, Stage II of EMU began very much with a whimper rather than a bang, with the European Monetary Institute (EMI) being created against a sombre and pessimistic backdrop. However, Stage II did bring significant changes in the procedures for the analysis and management of economic policy. The essential element is no longer the annual economic report but two more binding exercises: the 'Broad Guidelines for the Economic Policies of the Member States and the Union'[1] was approved in June and stressed the co-ordination of national policies; and the 'Multilateral Surveillance' of develop-

[1] The document is reproduced by Agence Europe, *Europe Documents* No. 1892, 14 July 1994.

ments in the economic policies of the Member States was undertaken in December and took a guardedly optimistic view of the EU economy.

Much of the second half of the year was spent on the 'excessive deficits procedure'. Under the Treaty of European Union (TEU) the Commission is charged with monitoring the public deficits of Member States, identifying situations in which they are 'excessive', and addressing recommendations (which have to be approved by the Council) to remedy the position to the Member States concerned. The criteria for 'excess' are the two convergence criteria that relate to public debt:

- annual budget deficits should not exceed 3 per cent of GDP;
- accumulated (total) public debt must not exceed 60 per cent of GDP).

The Commission decided that ten of the Member States had 'excessive' deficits, with Belgium, Greece and Italy having the most severe problems and only Germany looking likely to fulfil both criteria in 1995. Luxembourg, alone, already fulfilled both criteria and was therefore automatically excluded from the procedure. However, Ireland was also excluded on the grounds not of fulfilling the criteria, but of exhibiting a strong trend in the right direction: specifically the ratio of its total debt had fallen from 116 per cent of GDP in 1987 to 93 per cent in 1994 with the anticipation of further falls to come. This raised an issue of principle which made the Germans, in particular, very uncomfortable: it could be interpreted as implying that it is sufficient for a country to be showing a sufficiently strong downward trend in its public debt ratio – even if it is still well above 60 per cent of GDP – to fulfil the TEU criteria. This may open the door for participation in Stage III of EMU for countries like Italy and Belgium which had ratios of 116 and 134 per cent respectively in 1994.

More generally, the position with regard to a number of substantive issues was clarified during the course of the year:

- The prospects for Stage III beginning in 1997 were increasingly seen as being 'unlikely', but for 1999 they were judged as being 'good'. This much was admitted by the head of the EMI himself.
- There was increasing acknowledgement that Stage III would involve two phases. Exchange rates would be fixed in the first stage, but a common currency would be delayed until the second stage because of practical considerations relating to its introduction.
- It became clear that the current 15 per cent band of fluctuation was generally considered to be the 'normal band of fluctuation' as referred to in the TEU and the band within which a country had to maintain its currency for the two years preceding Stage III in order to qualify for participation in the final stage of EMU.

- The Irish case implied that trends, not levels, might be used to evaluate the budget deficits of prospective participants in Stage III.

The last two points suggested a margin of flexibility with the TEU convergence criteria although resolute German opposition is likely to preclude any further tendencies in that direction.

Finally, as Neill Nugent shows in his Editorial, the possibility of a multi-speed Europe was thrust into the limelight and widely discussed towards the end of the year. This followed the publication of a paper by the parliamentary group of the main German party (CDU/CSU) – 'Reflections on European Policy' (The Schäuble–Lamers Paper)[2] – which advocated that a 'hard core' of EU Member States should press ahead with monetary union (and other policies) regardless of formal decisions taken in 1997 and 1999.

Growth, Competitiveness and Employment

The Commission devoted much of its energy in 1994 to progressing the 1993 White Paper,[3] the contents of which served primarily as an agenda and which needed to be converted into practical actions to have the desired effects on employment. With this objective in mind, two committees, each named after their (Commissioner) chairman, were set up in January. The 'Bangemann Group' was concerned with exploring how Europe might adapt to the development of new information and communications technologies; its work falls within the chapter of the White Paper dealing with trans-European networks (TENs) in telecommunications. Its report was primarily concerned with liberalization of the information and telecommunications markets and the need for a single (minimal) regulatory framework. In addition it favoured the creation of a digital broadband TEN for applications in fields such as distance learning, health care, teleworking and SMEs.

The Christophersen Group was charged with preparing the ground for the creation of TENs in transport and energy. Its report proposed 14 transport TENs and 10 energy (gas or electricity) TENs.[4] It identified funding problems for the transport projects, particularly those in 'rich' regions which were not eligible for Structural or Cohesion Funds. Only half the transport TENs appeared to be fully funded and the agreement that the European Investment Bank (EIB) will open a 'special window' may well be insufficient to fill the gap. The Commission, though not the European Parliament (EP), has shied away from the idea of additional EU lending through some kind of 'Eurobond' in the face of opposition

[2] This is reproduced, together with a subsequent speech by Lamers, in Lamers, K. (1994) *A German Agenda for European Union* (London: Federal Trust).

[3] Commission of the European Communities (1993) *Growth, Competitiveness, Employment – the Challenges and Ways Forward into the 21st Century* COM(93) 700 final, December.

[4] A full list is provided in European Council, *Presidency Conclusions* Essen 9–10 December 1994, Annex I.

from some Member States, but the issue will have to be resolved eventually. The group has now been asked to make proposals for environmental TENs in 1995.

Finally, the Commission also made proposals at the Essen summit to reduce unemployment directly by increasing the flexibility of labour markets. It is generally disappointed with the response to the White Paper in this respect and the minimal achievements so far.

Structural Funds and Regional Policy

In 1994, regional policy was very much dominated by unfinished business from previous years, notably the definition of Community initiatives, the establishment of the Committee of the Regions (COR), and the formulation of a permanent regulation for the Cohesion Fund to replace the temporary regime that had been in force since 1 April 1993. The Cohesion Fund regulation was held up by the delay in creating the COR, since it required an opinion from the COR, but eventually a definitive and final instrument for the Cohesion Fund was adopted by the Council in May.

Community initiatives (CIs) are designed by the Commission to address EU-wide problems, and account for 9 per cent of structural fund expenditure (13.45bn ECU) over the 1994–99 period. It was decided in 1994 that there would be 13 initiatives: PESCA (fisheries: 0.25bn ECU), URBAN (urban areas: 0.6bn ECU), SMEs (small and medium-sized enterprises: 1bn ECU), the Portuguese textile and clothing industry (0.4bn ECU), RETEX (textile regions: 0.5bn ECU), KONVER (areas dependent on the defence sector: 0.5bn ECU), RESIDER II (steel regions: 0.5bn ECU), RECHAR II (coal mining areas: 0.4bn ECU), ADAPT (adaptation of the workforce to industrial change: 1.4bn ECU), human resources (NOW, HORIZON and YOUTHSTART: 1.4bn ECU), REGIS II (for the most remote regions: 0.6bn ECU), LEADER II (rural development: 1.4bn ECU) and INTERREG II (cross-border co-operation and energy networks: 2.9bn ECU). There is also a reserve of 1.6bn ECU to be distributed later. Some 60 per cent of the total funding is reserved for Objective 1 regions.

The Committee of the Regions eventually met for the first time in March. Having elected its officers, its first major business was to give an opinion on the Cohesion Fund regulation. It went on to hold four further plenary sessions in 1994 – in Brussels since it had not established a permanent home even after nearly a year – and dealt with a whole range of issues. Perhaps least surprisingly it adopted a rather forceful position in favour of the clear application of subsidiarity with regard to the division of responsibilities between the Member States, the Union, and regional and local authorities. The COR is a consultative body that is intended to be 'closer to the citizens' representing, as it does, the full range of regions and localities. However, it sits rather uneasily with the Ecosoc which has a similar role (and is the same size) and, to some extent, with the

European Parliament also. How the three institutions will relate to each other remains to be seen. Towards the end of the year, the COR began to organize itself into political groupings, beginning with the Socialists, the European People's Party, and a 'Mediterranean Europe' Group. A 'Radical Group' is also likely to be formed.

Industrial and Competition Policies

The principal focus of industrial policy continued to be the steel industry, and specifically the private steel sector. The Commission needed to extract from the private sector over half of the required minimum 19 million tonnes of cuts in capacity necessary to make its restructuring programme viable. If the necessary commitments were not forthcoming the Commission threatened to withdraw its 'accompanying measures' and, in effect, abandon the restructuring programme. These accompanying measures included 240 million ECU made available between 1993 and 1995 to finance social measures to mitigate the effects of steel closures on workers, and external measures to restrict steel imports. By the summer, the issue hinged on a flexible interpretation of the aid code in order to allow Italian national aid to independent producers in the Brescia region, who would then be prepared to close down part of their production facilities and reduce capacity by 5–6 million tonnes. This package deal was eventually agreed. Unfortunately, by this point, part of the arrangements for the public sector had begun to unravel. The restructuring of the (East) German firm, Eko-Stahl, was dependent on it being taken over by the Riva group, but this fell through in May and an alternative buyer had to be found – Cockerill-Sambre – to put the restructuring package back on track. However, in late October the Commission's patience with the private sector finally ran out when it became clear that the required cuts would not be in place by the 8 November deadline. The steel restructuring plan was therefore abandoned and with it most of the accompanying measures. No formal plan now exists, although the overcapacity problem remains.

More generally, in September, the Commission put forward an industrial competitiveness policy for the EU.[5] This had four main elements: the promotion of intangible or immaterial investment; the development of industrial co-operation; the implementation and enforcement of fair competition; and the modernization of the role of public authorities. The Commission also proposed an integrated programme for SMEs.

Turning to competition policy, the Commission stated its intention to continue to impose severe financial penalties on enterprises violating the competition rules. Transgressors who produced steel beams (17 producers with fines totalling

[5] Commission of the European Communities (1994) *An Industrial Competitiveness Policy for the European Union* COM(94) 319.

104m ECU), cardboard (19 producers: 132m ECU), and cement (33 producers: 248m ECU) had good reason to believe this. However, towards the end of the year, the Commission was forced to defend its policy on state aid against charges of laxity – for example, the authorization of aid for Air France – from the Confederation of British Industry (CBI), not to mention rival companies.

Other Developments

The two *transport* 'Committees of Wise Men', set up in 1993, both reported. The first, on civil aviation, reported in February. It highlighted the need for deregulation and liberalization, improvements in infrastructure (notably for air traffic control), and a common EU approach to relations with third countries. In June the Commission adopted an action programme which reflected these priorities. The second committee, on road (freight) transport, reported in July, and made three basic recommendations: a competitive framework must be created by ensuring free access to both the market and the profession and by comprehensive enforcement of EU regulations; effective road transport infrastructure must be assured through appropriate investment and management; and there must be harmonization of the social framework across Member States. Concern over maritime safety continued and, in November, the Council took positive steps with regard to the control and inspection of ships in EU ports, the notification of ships in EU waters, the safety of roll on/roll off ferries, and the minimum level of training for those at sea.

In the *energy* field the EU's main focus in 1994 was on negotiating the implementation of the 'European Charter on Energy'. This is concerned with the efficient and co-operative development of the energy resources of eastern Europe and, in particular, the creation of a stable framework within which operators in the energy sector can invest. A two-stage approach was pursued, with the first involving the adoption of the main elements in the form of a 'Treaty of the Charter' (known formerly as the 'Basic Agreement'); the second is to follow within three years and will include all remaining parts of the charter. The Treaty was eventually signed in Lisbon in December. However, on the negative side, the Commission's modified draft of its proposal for achieving a single market in gas and electricity made no more progress than the original version. The most intractable problem remained how to accommodate third party access.

Another energy problem in 1994 was that the funding for the THERMIE II programme (1995–98), which seeks to continue EU support for the promotion of technological innovation in the energy sector, was blocked by France, Germany and the UK.

Turning to *research and development* the efforts to finalize the Fourth Framework Programme (1994–98) continued. The Council had agreed a budget of 12bn ECU (with a 1bn ECU reserve) but, early in the year, the Parliament sought to increase this by 400m ECU. It was feared that any further delay might disrupt research activity. Nevertheless, compromise through the conciliation procedure proved difficult. Eventually, however, it was agreed (in effect) to commit 300m ECU of the reserve immediately, thus increasing the budget to 12.3bn ECU (with a reserve of 700m ECU). Various minor issues relating to the EU's Joint Research Centre were also settled. During the course of the year it proved possible to approve all 20 of the individual programmes making up the Framework Programme and thereby avoid a break in funding. Meanwhile, in March, the Court of Auditors reported on the major item of expenditure in the Framework Programme – ESPRIT – and criticized it for its slowness and shortcomings in the exploitation of findings.

The Commission proposed its new Socrates programme for *education* to replace ERASMUS and LINGUA and extend EU actions to primary and secondary schools (in line with its 1993 Green Paper). However, efforts by the Council to reduce the budget from 1bn ECU to 760m ECU led to a dispute which had not been resolved by the end of the year. The Commission's parallel proposal for its Leonardo programme for vocational training (to replace COMETT and others) was agreed, but only after its budget had been reduced from 800m ECU to 620m ECU. The Jean Monnet Project supported 236 new initiatives in 1994, of which 53 were 'chairs'.

In 1994 the Commission proposed action programmes on *health* promotion, on measures to combat AIDS and other communicable diseases, and its third action plan against cancer (1995–99). More negatively, it continued to prove impossible to agree the draft directive banning tobacco advertising.

In April, the Commission approved its first report on *tourism* and the first Tourism Council since mid-1992 was held, although with little significant result.

III. EU Finances

Perhaps the most important issue in 1994 was the need to give effect (in operational legal texts) to the decision taken at Edinburgh to implement the 1993–99 financial perspective. This became critical because the own resource ceiling was to begin rising in 1995, initially to 1.21 per cent of EU GDP. (There had been no problem in 1993–94 because the ceiling had not changed.) What made this difficult was the Italian decision to make its approval conditional on an increase in its milk quota and the retrospective application of that increase back to 1991, thereby reducing fines for overproduction in the past. This was opposed by other Member States; indeed, the Commission decision to apply the higher quota in 1989 and 1990 had prompted the UK and the Netherlands to take legal proceedings in the Court of Justice. The argument dragged on, thus threatening the 1995 budget and, in particular, limiting the Parliament's margin of manoeuvre to modify expenditure (upwards). The issue was eventually resolved in October: the retrospective milk quota increases would apply to Italy (and also to Spain which had similarly transgressed) from 1992, but not for 1989–91, and the Court case was dropped.

The perennial issue of fraud was addressed with a package of proposals in March. The major recommendations were:

- better co-operation between Member States;
- strengthening the Commission's anti-fraud services, inspections, and presence on the ground generally;
- improvements in the legal framework for combatting fraud.

Subsequently, as part of this 'new strategy', the Commission proposed two new instruments to fight fraud: a regulation to define the concept and the penalties to be imposed; and a convention to create a specific offence of 'fraud against the EU'. The Commission also proposed paying informers, and in the autumn set up an experimental 'hotline' on which citizens could report any suspicions of fraud.

Past budgets continued to attract criticism: the Court of Auditors was unhappy with some aspects of the 1993 budget, and the Parliament put off giving the Commission a discharge of the 1992 budget until after it had fully digested the milk quota decision. A possible looming budgetary problem was signalled with the German Government indicating that Germany was reaching the limit of what it was prepared to contribute to EU funds and that other Member States of comparable per capita income ought to be prepared to shoulder their share of the burden.

The Commission's preliminary draft budget for 1995 reflected the constraints of the downturn in the growth of GNP, and envisaged only a modest 3.9 per cent increase in expenditure. The Council, at its first reading, subsequently inserted modest cuts in spending on internal policies, but the EP, in its customary manner, generally to sought to increase expenditure. Most importantly, the EP at its first meeting voted in favour of:

- an addition of 6.21bn ECU to take account of enlargement;
- the creation of a small credit line for the Common Foreign and Security Policy (CSFP);
- the reclassification of some of the 'compulsory' Common Agricultural Policy (CAP) expenditure on which the Council has the last word.

The first issue was resolved in early December when the adjustment to the financial perspective to accommodate the 1995 enlargement was agreed. Approximately 4bn ECU extra will be available to spend each year (to 1999). The second point was conceded, and the third point remained unresolved even when the Parliament finally approved the 1995 budget for an EU of 15 in mid-December. The matter may be referred to the Court of Justice.

Table 1 : European Community Budget, 1994 and 1995, Appropriations for Commitments

	1994 Budget (ECU m)	*1995 Budget (ECU m)*	*1995 Budget (% of total)*	*% Change 1995 over 1994*
1. COMMON AGRICULTURAL POLICY				
Guarantee (price support)	34,520.0	35,559.0	44.0	+3.0
Accompanying measures	267.0	1,416.5	1.7	+430.5
Enlargement reserve	–	950.0	1.2	–
Total 1	34,787.0	37,925.5	46.9	+9.0
2. STRUCTURAL OPERATIONS				
EAGGF guidance	3,343.0	3,316.0	4.1	–0.8
FIFG (fisheries guidance)	419.0	439.0	0.5	+4.8
ERDF	9,030.0	10,593.0	13.1	+17.3
ESF	6,457.0	6,444.0	8.0	–0.2
Community initiatives	1,706.0	2,144.0	2.7	+25.7
Transnational/innovation measures	368.0	242.0	0.3	–34.2
Cohesion Fund	1,853.0	2,152.0	2.7	+16.1
EEA financial mechanism	–	108.0	0.1	–
Enlargement reserve	–	891.0	1.1	–
Total 2	23,176.0	26,329.0	32.5	+13.6
3. INTERNAL POLICIES				
Research	2,622.4	2,968.7	3.7	+13.2
Other agricultural operations	208.8	207.7	0.3	–0.5
Other regional operations	31.0	51.3	0.1	+65.5
Transport	16.0	24.0	–	+50.0
Fisheries and the sea	25.6	26.1	–	+2.0
Education, vocational training, youth	287.5	361.5	0.4	+25.7
Culture and audiovisual media	151.9	137.7	0.2	–9.3
Information and communication	47.5	57.0	0.1	+20.0
Other social operations	156.6	174.6	0.2	+11.5
Energy	83.0	62.0	0.1	–25.3
Euratom nuclear safeguards	19.5	18.8	–	–3.6
Environment	133.5	137.0	0.2	+2.0
Consumer protection	16.0	20.8	–	+30.0
Aid for reconstruction	9.3	6.3	–	–32.3
Internal market	173.8	152.5	0.2	–12.3
Industry	40.5	117.7	0.1	+190.6
Information market	12.0	13.0	–	+8.3
Statistical information	30.0	33.0	–	+10.0
Trans-European networks	289.8	381.0	0.5	+31.5
Co-operation in the field of justice	2.0	5.0	–	+150.0
Enlargement reserve	–	100.0	0.1	–
Total 3	4,353.6	5,055.7	6.2	+16.1
4. EXTERNAL ACTION				
Food and humanitarian aid	855.1	847.9	1.0	–0.8
Co-operation with Latin America and Asia	648.7	670.5	0.8	+3.4
Co-operation with Mediterranean countries	399.9	487.4	0.6	+21.8
Co-operation with central/eastern Europe	1,463.0	1,582.6	1.9	+8.2
Other co-operation	637.0	699.8	0.9	+9.9
External aspects of certain EU policies	284.2	294.2	0.4	+3.5
Common foreign and security policy	20.0	110.0	0.1	+450.0
Enlargement reserve	-	190.0	0.2	–
Total 4	4,307.8	4,881.4	6.0	+13.3

Table 1: *(Contd)*

	1994 Budget (ECU m)	*1995 Budget (ECU m)*	*1995 Budget (% of total)*	*% Change 1995 over 1994*
5. ADMINISTRATION				
Commission	2,428.7	2,504.3	3.1	+3.1
Other institutions	1,205.9	1,337.7	1.7	+10.7
Enlargement reserve	–	166.3	0.2	–
Total 5	3,634.6	4,008.3	5.0	+10.3
6. RESERVES				
Monetary reserve	1,000.0	500.0	0.6	–50.0
Guarantee	318.0	323.0	0.4	+1.6
Emergency and reserve	212.0	323.0	0.4	+52.4
Total 6	1,530.0	1,146.0	1.4	–25.1
7. COMPENSATION				
Compensation	–	1,547.0	1.9	–
Total 7	–	1,547.0	1.9	–
TOTAL APPROPRIATIONS FOR COMMITMENTS	71,789.1	80,892.9	100.0	+12.7
of which:				
Compulsory	37,222.1	41,420.5	51.2	+11.3
Non-compulsory	34,567.0	39,472.4	48.8	+14.2
TOTAL APPROPRIATIONS FOR PAYMENTS	68,354.6	76,527.1	100.0	+12.0
of which:				
Compulsory	37,203.5	41,402.3	54.1	+11.3
Non-compulsory	31,151.1	35,124.8	45.9	+12.8

Source: Commission of the European Communities (1995) Twenty-Eighth General Report, Table 26, pp. 391–2 (adapted).

Table 2 : Budget Revenue (% of total)

	1994 (Out-turns)	*1995 (Estimates)*
VAT	51.1	50.4
Customs duties	17.5	18.4
GNP-based own resources	25.9	27.7
Agricultural levies	1.3	1.2
Sugar and isoglucose levies	1.9	1.6
Other	2.3	0.7
Actually assigned own resources (% GDP)	1.119	1.176
Maximum assigned own resources (% GDP)	1.20	1.20

Source: Commission of the European Communities (1995) Twenty-Eighth General Report, Table 27, p. 393 (adapted).

The volume of loans granted by the EIB amounted to 19.9bn ECU in 1994 (compared to 19.6bn in 1993), of which 17.7bn ECU were loaned within the EU and 2.2bn ECU were advanced to third countries under the EU's co-operation policy. The loans (within the EU) were provided for regional development (12bn ECU), communications infrastructure (5.7bn ECU), industrial objectives and SMEs (1.8bn ECU), environmental projects (4.9bn ECU) and energy projects (3.5bn ECU). (The total exceeds 19.9bn ECU because some projects fall into two categories.) Italy (19 per cent) regained its position from Spain (18 per cent) as the leading recipient of loans but these two, along with the France (14 per cent), Germany (14 per cent) and the UK (14 per cent), continued to account for nearly four-fifths of all internal loans.

IV. Agriculture and Fisheries

Agriculture

The Commission's proposed price package for the 1994–95 marketing year had three main elements:

- price cuts (or equivalent measures) for cereals, beef and veal, pigmeat, butter, potato starch, and dried fodder;
- price freezes for other products;
- strict observance of budgetary constraints.

The Council gave the package a muted welcome although, with typical inconsistency, virtually every individual item was criticized by those Member States who felt their own producers were threatened by it. Farmers' groups (predictably) opposed the package, and Ecosoc and the EP were not entirely happy on the grounds that it offered little encouragement to farmers and was solely dictated by budgetary considerations. The Council was unable to make progress at meetings in April, May and June (at which the Greek Presidency submitted four compromise packages). The Commission blamed unreasonable and unrelated (to prices) demands by Member States. Finally, agreement was reached in July – by qualified majority – on a package which offered a wide range of concessions to Member States. The Commission noted that this could be accommodated within the guidelines for agricultural expenditure and so reluctantly accepted the increase in spending.

The Court of Auditors was critical about fraud in export refunds, particularly in the milk sector. It also attacked the tobacco sector, not only on the grounds of fraud, but also mediocre management by the Commission and lax application of EU rules by Member States, all of which combined to make the sector excessively expensive. The Commission proposed the establishment of a 'blacklist' of past offenders to help identify fraudsters.

The EU's new regime for bananas was also under fire on both external and internal fronts. Early in the year, a General Agreement on Tariffs and Trade (GATT) panel found against it for discriminating against Latin American ('dollar') bananas in favour of those produced by African, Pacific and Caribbean (ACP) countries, whilst internally the German case against the banana regime ran its course until it was rejected by the Court of Justice in October.

In March, the Commission rejected a call from Germany to ban exports of live cattle and beef from the UK (because of BSE or 'mad cow disease'), holding that current EU measures were sufficient. This eventually prompted the Germans to threaten to introduce national measures. However, the issue was resolved when the Commission introduced a number of supplementary measures in July, but the Anglo-German dispute was then reactivated when an argument emerged in September over how strictly these new measures should be implemented.

Problems were created by enormous surpluses in the wine sector. In May, the Commission proposed a draft reform package which sought to adapt production to demand, improve wine quality, and reduce costs. The centrepiece of the plan was an EU production quota system which would cut production by 35.6m hectolitres. The plan met with a predictable (negative) response from wine producers in general, and Italy and Spain in particular. A North–South divide quickly emerged in the Council whenever the plan was discussed.

Towards the end of the year, the Union begin to address two difficult issues which were resolved in December:

- The implementation of the agricultural chapter of the Uruguay Round agreement. This requires adaption of the appropriate EU regulation and some Member States feared that the flexible and pragmatic approach to decision-making advocated by the Commission might be used to expand its powers. However, it proved possible to resolve this and other contentious issues.
- The reform of the agri-monetary system which had been postponed at the end of 1993 by an agreement which effectively extended the current regime until the end of 1994. The main change proposed by the Commission was the abolition of the switch-over mechanism; this inevitably met with German resistance. It did go ahead, but a compensation system in case of currency re-evaluations was introduced which the Danes and the British considered to be a 'mini switch over' and so they actually voted against the package.

As was shown in the previous section, the problems relating to Italian (and Spanish and Greek) milk quotas were resolved in October. Finally, during the course of the year, the Commission initiated proposals to adjust the regimes for sugar, and fruit and vegetables.

Fisheries

The fisheries crisis continued. The system of minimum import prices for key species was not renewed at the beginning of 1994 but was reinstated, after French pressure, in February and continued until mid-May. In July, a Commission communication considered the fisheries crisis and attributed it to structural factors; in particular there was a lack of competitiveness due to fleet overcapacity, overfishing, low productivity and inappropriate commercial structures. The suggested solution was improved resource management and the control of catches, the elimination of overcapacity, and better market management (but not import restrictions).

A political agreement was reached (in the context of Norway's accession negotiations) that the end of the transition period at which point Spain and Portugal are to be integrated into the Common Fisheries Policy (CFP) be brought forward from 2003 to 1996. The principles and timetable for this integration were quickly settled in June, but specific access and monitoring arrangements for particular zones and fish resources proved much more difficult to agree. Continued failure raised the spectre of a Spanish veto of the 1995 enlargement. Ultimately agreement was reached only at the eleventh hour and then by qualified majority (as the UK abstained).

There were three other important developments during the year. First, new Canadian legislation authorizing its inspectors to seize vessels fishing outside its 200-mile limit which failed to comply with international conservation regulations caused some disquiet in the EU. Second, the Council, for the first time, agreed a significant package of conservation measures in the Mediterranean. Third, in December, the Commission proposed reduced total allowable catches (TACs) (and quotas) for 1995, but the cuts were moderated by the Council and the final levels agreed for most species were similar to those for 1994.

V. Social Policy

Debate on the Commission's 1993 Green Paper continued in the first half of the year and this was followed, in July, by a White Paper on European social policy[6] looking forward to the years 1995–99 which emphasized the following, in particular:

- the need for a new mix between economic and social policies;
- jobs are the top priority;
- the European legislative base must be completed and rigorously applied;
- there must be a strengthening of co-operation and action.

[6] Commission of the European Communities (1994) White Paper: *European Social Policy: A Way Forward for the Union* COM(94) 333.

The White Paper set out a strategy with jobs at the top of the agenda, but it also sought to emphasize that social policy goes beyond employment.

In April, the Commission proposed its directive concerning worker information and consultation in large companies and the creation of European Works Councils; this was based on the Social Protocol of the TEU and therefore excluded the UK (which had opted out). The directive was generally welcomed by employees but not employers who considered it, in the form it was put forward, to be unduly centralized and bureaucratic. However, it was eventually adopted in September and became the first decision to be taken without the UK. This success prompted the Eleven, in the face of a British blockage to the directive on parental leave, to decide to try and progress that through the Social Protocol of the TEU. In December, in response to continued British intransigence, it was also decided to take the directive on atypical (for example, part-time) work through the same route. The end of the year provided two further examples of the UK's opt-out possibly being counterproductive: in November United Biscuits became the first British company to set up a Works Council voluntarily; whilst in early December, there was some evidence that the other Member States were losing patience with the UK after the 'failure' of the (first) December Council meeting, which was widely attributed to British inflexibility.

In June, the Council adopted the directive on the protection of young people at work and also agreed to create a 'European Agency for Health and Safety at Work'; this will be located in Bilbao and will exchange technical, economic and scientific information in this area between Member States. In November, the Commission launched Eures (European Employment Services), a computerized database which offers workers and employers information, advice and assistance with placement and recruitment through 350 'Euro-advisers' across the EU.

Finally, one particularly contentious issue continued to cause difficulties: the UK Government, having abstained in the vote on the directive on working time (which the other 11 passed) in 1993, carried out its threat to take the matter to the Court of Justice on the grounds that the legal base was incorrect. The UK Government remained implacably opposed to the contention that an individual might be prevented from working the number of hours which he or she wants to.

VI. Environmental Policy

In 1994 the Commission sought to revise and strengthen a number of existing directives, notably:

- the 1982 'Seveso directive' on protection against risks of major accidents involving dangerous substances;
- the 1975 directive on standards of bathing water;
- the 1979 directive on the conservation of wild birds;

- the 1985 directive on the evaluation of the environmental impact of major projects (especially infrastructures).

In May, the Council set out the broad lines for a joint approach to the environment and tourism aimed at promoting lasting development of tourism in the EU by giving priority to the protection of the most vulnerable areas. The troubled directive on packaging and packaging waste was finally agreed in November, but only after a highly contentious passage through the conciliation procedure. In December, the Commission published its interim report on environmental measures and the sustainable development strategy launched in 1992. It conceded that, although a start had been made, the results were disappointing.

Early in the year, in an attempt to move forward on the CO_2/energy tax, a high level group was convened to clarify the various issues. It reported its conclusions in June:

- the Member States accepted the principle of the tax (with the exception of the UK), although the cohesion states (Spain, Greece, Ireland and Portugal) were concerned about sharing costs and Luxembourg was concerned about effects on competitiveness;
- the view that the CO_2 tax might be incorporated into a harmonized system of minimum rates of excise duty was supported by a number of Member States;
- a majority of Member States favoured a gradual introduction of the tax;
- renewable energy resources should be exempt;
- there would have to be burden sharing possibly in the shape of giving certain Member States more time to introduce the tax.

The German Presidency then tried to make progress by proposing a system making it possible to use existing excise duties in a targeted fashion, in stages, in order to achieve the required reductions in CO_2 emissions (instead of creating a special tax). However, this was opposed by the UK.

In October, it emerged that Belgium and the Netherlands were considering introducing an energy tax unilaterally if nothing was decided at EU level. This developed into a proposal for an optional taxation scheme that would be applied in an EU framework by those Member States which wished to do so. This allowed a two-pronged strategy to be developed in the December Council:

- the Commission would continue to move towards a directive to introduce a CO_2 tax via targeted excise duties;
- at the same time, the Commission would prepare guidelines to enable Member States to adopt a CO_2 tax unilaterally but on the basis of common parameters.

It is not quite clear whether the UK has opted out or been thrown out but, for some, this was a worrying development.

VII. Justice and Home Affairs Policy

Implementation of the third pillar of the TEU continued to be held back by slow procedures – for example, the need for unanimity in the Council – and limitations in the powers of the Commission. In December, the EP expressed the view that co-operation in this area had been insufficient, blaming inadequate treaty provision and the insistence of some Member States on the rigorous application of intergovernmental procedures.

In February the Commission adopted a communication on *immigration* and the right of *asylum* which was intended to generate debate and ultimately action. It was concerned with:

- action on the causes of migratory pressure through co-operation with the main countries from which immigrants come;
- measures to control migration flows;
- strengthening integration policies for legal immigrants to help with their assimilation.

However, when the Council examined the communication it quickly became clear that this marked only the beginning of a very long process. Nevertheless, the Council did take a decision in June to introduce a restrictive policy for immigration 'for employment purposes', which it now considers to be purely exceptional.

In June, the Commission presented a communication to the Council and the EP which proposed an action plan to combat *drugs* based on three key points: preventing addiction, reducing drug trafficking, and strengthening measures taken at the international level. The Commission also proposed an action programme to help prevent drug dependence with a budget of 30m ECU over five years. In March the Parliament called for better co-ordination of policies to combat *terrorism*.

Police co-operation made little progress. Despite the best efforts of the German Presidency, it proved impossible to agree the Europol Convention. There were specific problems relating to the inclusion of terrorism, institutional problems (concerning Europol's relationship with the EU institutions), and access to sensitive data. However, more ominously, there was a fundamental difference of philosophy between those who wished to interpret the third pillar in a European Union sense and those who wanted a strictly intergovernmental approach and, indeed, sometimes seemed intent on clawing back what they had conceded at Maastricht. Negotiations will continue in 1995.

Journal of Common Market Studies Volume 33, Annual Review
August 1995

External Policy Developments

DAVID ALLEN and MICHAEL SMITH
Loughborough University

I. General Themes

The 1993 *Annual Review* pointed to the continuity of many EU concerns in the external policy field, and to a large extent this was the tone of developments in 1994. Despite the very mixed record of Union policy in the affairs of the 'new Europe', and particularly in the former Yugoslavia, there could be no escape from continuing entanglement and responsibility. The same was true of the former Soviet Union, with the need to respond to an at times bewildering variety of developments with relatively limited policy tools. In the global political economy, the move from agreement in the General Agreement on Tariffs and Trade (GATT) Uruguay Round to implementation of both its institutional and its substantive provisions was a central concern, which also had significant internal repercussions for EU policy-making. The final stages of the accession negotiations with the four European Free Trade Association (EFTA) applicants equally pointed up the intimate link between the internal functioning of the Union and the management of the external environment, as demonstrated by Fraser Cameron in his article.

Alongside this set of continuities, however, went a number of new directions. Some of these might have been predicted: the need to put real flesh on the bones of the Common Foreign and Security Policy (CFSP), the need to review the Lomé agreements with African, Caribbean and Pacific (ACP) countries, the parallel need to revise the Community's Generalized Scheme of Preferences, the demand for follow-through on the Transatlantic Declaration and other agreements with major political and trading partners. No less significant were two areas of considerable dynamism which had previously been in abeyance or unsuspected. The first was the development of a more comprehensive strategy towards key areas of the world such as Asia and Latin America, which generated a good deal of 'diplomacy' during the year. The second was the emergence of a varied 'new agenda' for EU external policies, covering areas such as transportation and competition policy, and leading to new patterns of diplomatic activity as well as to new policy initiatives.

The Common Foreign and Security Policy

The Treaty on European Union (TEU) came into effect in November 1993, so 1994 was therefore the first full year of the Common Foreign and Security Policy (CFSP). It was not an auspicious start with the Union divided over Macedonia, ineffectual with regard to the war in Bosnia, and upstaged by unilateral French action in Rwanda. On the institutional front the year began with French-inspired concern about the lack of a central decision-making authority for the CFSP. However, this concern was matched by a Franco-British determination that neither the Commission nor the newly enlarged Council Secretariat should be encouraged to fill that particular void. The year ended with the promise of further institutional change as Jacques Santer, the incoming Commission President, appointed four Commissioners with external and CFSP-related responsibilities, but announced that he would retain for himself the ultimate responsibility for co-ordinating their activities.

In Bosnia, the joint action of the European Union was expanded to take on the task of administering the town of Mostar. In July, Hans Koschnik, a former mayor of Bremen, was sworn in as the administrator of Mostar for a two-year term. Koschnik is assisted by a 200-strong European police force, EU funding to the tune of 80 million ECU for 1995, plus a grant of 35 million ECU for the reconstruction of Mostar, including the ancient Ottoman bridge destroyed so spectacularly by Croat artillery.

EU involvement in attempts to resolve the wider conflict in Bosnia reflected the impatience of some Member States with the Union's impotence and division. Britain, France and Germany (occasionally accompanied by the troika partners) joined forces with the US and Russia in the so-called 'Contact Group', and various peace plans, which were mainly variations on the original Vance-Own proposals of January 1993 involving the complex division of Bosnia, were proposed to little avail. In support of these plans the EU sought to exert influence by tightening its sanctions against the Bosnian Serbs and relaxing those that were aimed at Belgrade. In December, when the US announced its withdrawal from the joint US-WEU arms embargo patrol of the Adriatic, the EU members of the WEU decided to carry on alone.

In February, Greece marked its tenure of the Council Presidency by unilaterally embargoing the Former Yugoslav Republic of Macedonia (FYROM) by denying it access to the vital port of Salonika. This act, which was seen in EU circles as an attempt to draw attention to Greek unhappiness with the threat to use air power against the Bosnian Serbs, resulted in considerable pressure on Greece by the other Member States. This eventually led to the European Commission going to the European Court of Justice to seek an interim ban on the embargo and a longer-term judgment on the legality of the Greek action. At the end of July the Court ruled against the Commission with regard to the interim ban, but the definitive Court judgment was not expected to be produced for 18 months or so.

There were four other joint actions that should be mentioned: the EU successfully 'observed' the holding of South Africa's first post-apartheid elections; it put its weight behind the continuing peace process in the Middle East by participating in the preparation for elections in the Palestinian homelands and by providing some funds for the establishment of a Palestinian police force; in May it hosted the inaugural conference in Paris that launched the Stability Pact which is designed to enhance security relations between and with the states of eastern and central Europe; finally, the EU chose to make support for the principle of nuclear non-proliferation the subject of a joint action. and to this end it sought to encourage as many states as possible to adhere to the Non-Proliferation Treaty and thus to participate positively in the approaching Signatories Conference in 1995.

As well as the joint actions, the CFSP followed the familiar pattern established by the European Political Co-operation (EPC) process over the years and issued a number of statements outlining the EU's position on various issues. In the main these statements concentrated on two specific areas – Africa and the territory of the former Soviet Union. The EU had cause to note and worry about deviations from the democratic process in a number of African states, most obviously Rwanda, Burundi, Nigeria, Mozambique, Lesotho, the Congo, Somalia and the Gambia, whilst it was pleased to congratulate Togo, Uganda, Malawi and Ethiopia on their successful holding of elections and Niger on its search for peace with its neighbours. Action in the form of an arms embargo was taken against Sudan and a troika of Development Ministers was sent to Malawi to investigate the fate of refugees from Rwanda. The EU has sent 200 million ECU for the relief of Rwandans since October 1993, and in July it met with the ACP states to seek the release of further European Development Fund money for Rwanda.

Statements concerning the states of the former Soviet Union focused on three main areas. First, in the case of conflicts in Georgia and Azerbaijan, the EU was broadly supportive of Russian 'peace' efforts. Secondly, those states which have announced a willingness to sign up to the Non-Proliferation Treaty (Kazakhstan, Georgia, Kyrgysztan) also received EU support. Finally, there was enthusiastic EU endorsement of Russian decisions finally to withdraw from the Baltic States, linked with concern about the treatment of non-citizens (mainly Russians) by the Baltic States themselves. As their accession drew ever nearer, the applicant states of Sweden, Finland, Austria and Norway began to associate themselves with these CFSP statements.

The TEU named the Western European Union (WEU) as the potential defence arm of the Union and some progress was made during the year towards the definition of its role and tasks. At the January North Atlantic Treaty Organization (NATO) summit, the US made clear that it now supported the idea of a European defence identity and that it was prepared to consider, via the concept of Combined Joint Task Forces, allowing the WEU to use NATO facilities when engaged on military missions limited to European participation (an offer that was mischievously matched by Russia later in the year). France (already linked with Germany, Belgium and Spain via the Eurocorps) was the main advocate for developing the WEU's role, but British interest during the year was stimulated by a recognition of the evolving US position. At Chartres in the autumn, Britain and France laid the groundwork for future military co-operation and Britain announced that many of its units committed to NATO would also be made available to the WEU.

Finally, some institutional developments concerning the CFSP should be recorded. In Brussels, an expanded unit of the Council Secretariat (incorporating the old EPC Secretariat) under Brian Crowe, a senior British diplomat, took on the task of preparing for the expanded business of the Council of the Union where EC and CFSP business is collectively handled. Some, but not all, CFSP and Council working groups have been merged, but the relationship between the Political Committee and COREPER in preparing for Council business remains unclear. It would appear that the Political Committee reports to the Council of Foreign Ministers through COREPER, but with COREPER mainly taking note of rather than interfering with Political Committee positions. Whilst the Commission continued to develop the role of DG 1A, it became clear towards the end of the year that the new President of the Commission intended to shake up the external relations and CFSP portfolios and that this would mean a considerable reorganization of DG 1 and DG 1A in 1995.

External Trade and the Common Commercial Policy

As already noted, the major preoccupation of external trade policy during 1994 was the need to move from agreement to ratification and implementation of the Uruguay Round trade negotiations. The tangled tale of ratification and its impact on EC competence is told by Jo Shaw in her article on legal developments: here the concern is with the policy directions which emerged during the year. Perhaps the most significant area of development was in the 'new agenda' linked to the agreements: calls were made by the European Parliament and others for the inclusion of a 'social clause' dealing with labour standards and human rights in the foundation of the World Trade Organization (WTO), and the related issue of environmental standards in trade was also the object of attention. Since the Uruguay Round agreements were finally ratified by the EU and other major states only towards the very end of 1994, the impact of the 'new agenda' concerns was not fully felt during the year, but would be a key issue for the future.

At the same time, there was the question of the leadership of the WTO itself. The EU's support of the candidature of Renato Ruggiero for the post of Secretary-General was paralleled by candidates from both the Americas and Asia, and this led to a good deal of friction, particularly with the USA. Some of this friction could be seen in the continued meetings of the so-called 'quad group' (the EU, the USA, Japan and Canada), which focused on the specific terms of the Uruguay Round final agreement and on the continuing negotiations relating to financial services, intellectual property and other areas.

The EU was thus deeply implicated in the 'end-game' of the Uruguay Round and the beginning of the new trade agenda, but at the same time it was attempting to streamline its own commercial policy instruments and their application through the mechanism of the European Community (EC), which remains the central channel for trade policy. Part of the deal by which the EU accepted the Uruguay Round agreements had been the promise to review trade instruments internally. For some, such as the French, this meant strengthening trade defences; for others, it meant cutting down the apparatus of quotas and other provisions in line with the principles of deregulation and the development of the single market. During the middle of the year, debate came to centre on two issues: first, the development of a new 'illicit practices regulation', which some saw as a threatening and protectionist instrument and which allowed commercial concerns to petition for EC trade actions against unfair traders; second, the problems of quotas particularly in relation to the growing trade with the People's Republic of China (see below), which generated a good deal of heat.

Two other 'internal' debates should be mentioned here, since they show the ways in which trade policy and internal economic development are inextricably linked. The first was the unexpected *contretemps* over the competence of the

Commission to negotiate and agree antitrust collaboration with the USA, which meant that during the autumn of 1994 there had to be a rapid internal 'renegotiation' of the agreement entailing Council adoption (the Commission had assumed that this was effectively an 'administrative' measure and thus fully within EC competence). The second was the attempt within the framework of the EC to reach a new dispensation about export credits, which revealed important fault-lines between members.

A number of more specific, often acrimonious, disputes arose during 1994 in the 'traditional' trade policy field, and they are covered where appropriate below. The final general theme to be highlighted here is far from 'traditional', and potentially of immense long-term significance. During the year, there was growing, not to say compelling, evidence of the ways in which 'internal' EU policies feed through into the external policy domain, involving not only new subject matter but also new patterns of Commission and other policy-making. Only the general flavour can be given here, but the key examples included the following: the international follow-up on the White Paper on growth, competitiveness and employment, which involved Commissioners Bangemann and Christopherson in intensive diplomacy; major developments in aviation and transport policies, centring on the notion of 'open skies' and entailing complex dealings with the USA; competition policy issues particularly in shipping and shipbuilding; and the conclusion of the European Energy Charter which moved into its final phase during the second half of the year. Subsequent *Reviews* will no doubt return to this area, since it is potentially crucial to both the substance and the process of Union external policies.

Development Co-operation Policy

The most important event of the year was the mid-term review of the Fourth Lomé Convention, held in Mbabane in Swaziland in May. Whilst the Commission placed great weight on the need for enhanced conditionality (democracy, good governance and human rights), a developing political dialogue, and improved management procedures, the ACP states were worried that more stringent conditionality would lead to them being disadvantaged compared to other recipients of EU assistance. The ACP states were also worried about the impact of the GATT agreement on their commodity trade with the EU, and on the likely increased cost of their imports of meat, cereals and dairy products once EU export subsidies were reduced to meet GATT obligations. There seemed to be general agreement that, despite the start of negotiations for Lomé V, the Lomé system, as it has developed to date was unlikely to continue and that any new accord would be much more specific. The EU will certainly seek to differentiate between states of different development levels and possibly between various regions. The globalization of world trade, as exemplified by the Uruguay Round, probably means that ACP preferences will have to disappear in the long run, and the EU has a clear interest in moving away from special relationships based on its colonial past, towards arrangements that are based on 'real needs' and which are compatible with the GATT.

The Commission has also begun a long-term review of its Generalized System of Preferences with a view to introducing reforms for the 1995-2004 period. In September the EU played an important role in the World Conference on Population and Development held in Cairo. The EU was particularly proud of its ability to remain cohesive on all the central issues and to initiate compromise positions on divisive issues such as abortion (despite the potential for intra-EU conflict between states like Ireland and Denmark).

II. Regional Themes

EFTA, the EEA and Northern Europe

The key issue in this area during 1994 was the accession negotiations, followed by the ratification process, leading to the entry into the EU of Austria, Finland and Sweden. Since these are covered in the keynote article by Fraser Cameron, readers are referred there. In the context of this article, it is important to note that the accession negotiations did not entirely pre-empt the establishment and initial activities of the European Economic Area (EEA): during the first half of the year, the institutional arrangements of the EEA were set up, and the initial meetings of a number of bodies were held. Not only this, but the agreement was amended to apply the EU *acquis* of legislation and other provisions up to the end of 1993 – a significant extension. There was also substantial work on the amendment of EU trade legislation (for example on anti-dumping) to bring the position of the EEA members into line with that of EU members. In December, the EEA Council, at its second meeting, reaffirmed the relevance of the organization, and prepared for the entry of Liechtenstein, but the much reduced membership clearly raised some questions about the continuing vigour of the EEA as a whole.

The Swiss, of course, had rejected not only EU membership but also the EEA in their 1992 referendum. 1994 saw the continuation and the intensification of efforts to arrive at a *modus vivendi* between the Swiss and the EU through bilateral negotiations. These were complicated by the fact that on one central issue, that of Alpine transit, the Swiss promptly held another referendum which supported the abolition of all lorry transit rights by 2004. Unsurprisingly, the negotiations on this issue were rather tense, and it became linked also to the possible conclusion of an 'open skies' agreement involving Swissair in the context of EU and EU/US tensions. On other agenda items, there was progress:

the Council was able to adopt negotiating directives in October, and on such issues as immigration and agriculture there were prospects of agreement. The situation remained unresolved at the end of 1994, and also became linked in different ways to EU relations with Norway (on freedom of movement) and Austria (on transit provisions). During the year, the Swiss also reaffirmed their neutrality and indeed voted not to become involved in United Nations peace-keeping: the link to debates about neutrality within the EU – and particularly in Austria and Sweden – remains to be seen.

Central and Eastern Europe

The rise of nationalism in Russia illustrated by the electoral success of Vladimir Zhirinovsky in 1993 and the fear that Moscow might seek to re-establish its sphere of influence in eastern Europe led to a reassessment early in 1994 of EU policy towards the countries of central and eastern Europe (CCEE). By the end of the year, the German Presidency was able to make a 'pre-accession strategy' for the applicants the centrepiece of the Essen European Council – a historic meeting, because the leaders of Poland, Hungary the Czech and Slovak Republics, Romania and Bulgaria all attended the closing session. Although the EU once again resisted attempts to commit itself to a detailed timetable for further enlargement, it is clear that the process is now irreversible and that it could start soon after the completion of the 1996 Intergovernmental Conference. Indeed, the Czech Republic has already announced that it expects to enter the EU by 1999, with Poland and Hungary both giving the year 2000 for their own accession. The German Presidency was also successful in gaining Council support for its proposal (prearranged with the French) to ask the Commission to produce a White Paper (along the lines of the Cockfield White Paper for the single market) laying out in some detail the measures that would be necessary for the applicant states to adopt in order to prepare for membership. The idea was that the White Paper would be ready for discussion by the Fifteen plus the six aspiring CEE members at the Cannes European Council, in June 1995.

It had thus become clear during the year that the eastern enlargement process would need to be speeded up and that the EU and the applicant states had many changes to contemplate in order to realize what Jacques Delors referred to in January as 'Greater Europe'. Once Hungary and Poland decided to apply for membership in the spring the Commission organized a 'brainstorming' session in March at which it contemplated the end of agricultural export subsidies for goods exported to the CCEE, an overhaul of the PHARE programme to allow a greater emphasis on infrastructure projects (it was agreed in the run-up to Essen that some 7 billion ECU would be made available in the five years between 1995 and 1999), and a plan whereby the eastern states adopted EU-style competition and other legislation in order effectively to extend the single market before actual enlargement. These plans were further refined throughout the year but at Essen, despite the progress that was made, the EU was not able to deliver the package of measures designed to dismantle its own protective armoury that the German Presidency had initially hoped for.

Despite the concern of some Member States that 'back door membership' was being offered, the EU also decided in March that it would develop its political dialogue with the six CCEE states. They are to be associated with most aspects of the CFSP, including attending selected meetings at all levels (from the European Council to CFSP Working Groups) and particularly when appropriate with CFSP statements, *démarches* and joint actions. As the EU plans for a 'Stability Pact' and NATO for a Partnership for Peace, it is also clearly the EU's intention that a place will be found in the WEU structure for the CCEE.

Progress was also made in 1994 in developing relations with the Baltic States. The Commission successfully sought a mandate to begin the negotiation of Europe Agreements and thus build on the arrangement that a free trade area between the EU and the Baltic States would be established by the start of 1995. Similarly, it became clear at the Corfu European Council that Slovenia, once it had resolved its political difficulties with Italy, could anticipate a Europe Agreement and eventual full membership. Thus by the end of the year a sort of pecking order had been established, despite Romania's unsuccessful attempts to get the EU to agree that it would deal with all applicants *en bloc*. The Czech and Slovak Republics, Hungary and Poland appeared first in the queue, followed by Bulgaria and Romania, which were followed in turn by the Baltic States and Slovenia. Slovenia, of course, must also be regarded as a Mediterranean state and its claim for membership will also lead to both Cyprus and Malta, who have been told by the European Council that they will be involved in the next round of enlargement, demanding renewed attention to their own bids.

One of the incentives for the EU to clarify the next stage of enlargement towards the east arose from the clear shift in US policy in 1994. As President Clinton was forced, for a variety of reasons, to reconsider his 'Russia First' policy, so the US became more interested in binding the states of eastern and central Europe into the West via both NATO and the EU/WEU. During Clinton's visit to Berlin in the summer it was agreed that the US and the EU would set up a Working Group to co-ordinate their policies towards the east.

Despite the progress that was made in 1994 the CCEE still complained that the EU was only slowly giving them what they most wanted which was access to the EU market. Their complaints were supported by a report published by the European Bank for Reconstruction and Development (EBRD) in October. This identified the EU's own protectionist policies as the main barrier to economic development in the east. In particular, the report highlighted a number of Voluntary Export Restraints (VERs) that the EU effectively imposed on the eastern states, along with 19 anti-dumping measures and 12 other restrictive measures. The Europe Agreements were criticized for their 'investment deterring effect' because of the high local content rules that they established for goods exported from eastern Europe to the EU.

Russia and the Other Soviet Successor States

In 1994, the long-awaited Partnership and Co-operation Agreements between the EU and the Ukraine, and the EU and Russia were finally concluded. The deal with the Ukraine was initialled just before the Ukrainian elections, and progress towards it was stimulated by EU concern about the internal situation in the Ukraine (after a year of effective neglect by the EU). Progress was also assisted by the nuclear deal negotiated by President Clinton between Russia, the US and the Ukraine early in the year and by the Ukraine's promise to adhere to the Non-Proliferation Treaty – a promise that was fulfilled when the Ukrainian Parliament ratified the Treaty in November. The Ukrainian agreement, which could lead to talks on a free trade agreement with the EU in 1998 provided progress towards market reform is maintained, was slightly overshadowed by concern in the EU about the safety of the remaining nuclear installations at Chernobyl. At the Corfu European Council it was agreed to provide 500 million ECU in grants and loans to assist the Ukraine to make these and other nuclear plants safe and this money was then topped up with an additional $200 million when the G 7 met in Naples. In December the EU eventually, after a long internal row between Britain and France, agreed to provide 85 million ECU to assist the Ukrainian balance of payments situation.

In June, President Yeltsin was welcomed to the Corfu European Council on the first stage of his triangular trip to western institutions (he also went to NATO to sign up for the Partnership for Peace and to the G 7). In Corfu, Yeltsin finally signed Russia's Partnership and Co-operation Agreement with the EU. As well as the promise of talks on a free trade area in 1998, the new Agreement commits the EU to supporting Russian accession to the GATT and the WTO and to removing all quotas on Russian exports (except steel and textiles!) by 1998. The Agreement is extremely significant for Russia: in 1993, Russian exports to the EU in 1993 accounted for 50 per cent of total exports and, with a value of $17.4 billion, considerably outweighed imports from the EU valued at $13.5 billion. The fact that the Agreement contains a number of safeguard clauses means that the EU will hope to continue its 'carrot and stick' approach to Russia by attempting to link trade concessions and further offers of aid and credits to the EU's political objectives.

The EU's developing policy towards Russia and the other former Soviet states within the CFSP framework has already been mentioned. Note should also be made of some concern in EU circles that Russia was gradually reforming its links with a number of the former Soviet states. This process can be partly explained by the fact that the EU's further eastern enlargement will exclude all but the Baltic States from the old Soviet Union and therefore it is logical that those left outside the EU should seek support and comfort from each other. The Union would obviously like to see the evolution of arrangements between the former Soviet states broadly similar to the Union itself. The fear, of course, is that something more like the old Soviet Union or Russian Empire might emerge. If these are the possibilities, the need for solid action within the CFSP will be a Union priority.

The Mediterranean and the Middle East

During the German Presidency, the French and Spanish Governments sought to balance the moves to speed up enlargement to the east by extracting an agreement that the EU would also pursue a more vigorous policy towards the Mediterranean region. With French, Spanish and Italian Council Presidencies due to succeed each other in 1995-96, this proved an effective strategy and, by the time of the Essen European Council, the EU had agreed to increase its spending in the region from 2 billion ECU between 1990 and 1994 to 5.7 billion ECU in the five years to 1999. At Essen, approval was also given to an ambitious plan put forward by the Commission to create, by 2010, a European-Mediterranean Economic Area. This would function along the lines of the EEA except that the participants from the Maghreb (Morocco, Tunisia, Algeria and Libya) and the Mashreq (Egypt, Jordan, Lebanon and Syria), along with Israel, would not be in line for eventual membership of the EU. Although the plan is to create a market of some 800 million consumers, the wealth differentials between the EU (with an average per capita income of $20,000 in 1992) and the prospective partners (with an average per capita income of $993 in 1992) are likely to grow and continue to strain the relationship.

The EU itself is divided about the best way of assisting the non-member Mediterranean states, with the northern EU states favouring trade concessions and the southern states preferring direct aid (provided mainly by the northern members!). As with its dealings with eastern Europe, the EU has proved to be still very protective when it comes to the detail of negotiation over trade concessions with its Mediterranean partners.

Alongside the more ambitious plans mentioned above, the EU continued to negotiate new bilateral arrangements with Israel, Morocco and Tunisia. Dealings with Israel, in particular, were difficult: despite additional concessions by the EU on a number of products, and despite agreeing to allow Israel to participate in the EU's fourth framework research and development programme, agreement was frustrated by Israel's demands that the EU give greater recognition to Israel's role (and consequent expenses!) in the Middle East peace process. In 1994, the EU continued to assist the Palestinians by funding their police force and a number of other infrastructure projects. In November the EU announced that it would provide 100 million ECU for the Palestinians in 1995 via the European Investment Bank (EIB).

Relations between the EU and Turkey got off to an uncertain start in 1994, with the British and German Governments defying the Greek Presidency and arranging a joint visit to Turkey, designed to show solidarity and to pave the way for the customs union that was due to be established at the end of the year. Relations were soured in July by a decision of the Court of Justice that effectively blocked direct exports from the Turkish area of Cyprus to the EU, but matters significantly worsened in December when the Turkish Government imprisoned eight Kurdish members of the Turkish Parliament. After protests in the European Parliament, and aware of a threatened Greek veto, the EU Council of Foreign Ministers agreed at the end of the year to postpone implementation of the long-awaited customs union.

Africa

Apart from the many concerns about political developments in numerous African states recorded in the CFSP section, the main focus of the EU's African policy was South Africa and the South African Development Community (SADC). Once the newly-elected President Mandela had formed his government, negotiations began which culminated in a Co-operation Agreement which was signed on behalf of the EU by External Economic Relations Commissioner Sir Leon Brittan and on behalf of South Africa by the Deputy President in early October. The agreement aims to boost co-operation in trade and development, but it also deals with questions of democracy and human rights. At the same time, the EIB was given approval to start lending the 300 million ECU that it had earmarked for South Africa. The EU is already South Africa's most important trading partner, taking more than 40 per cent of its exports and providing 33 per cent of its imports in a two-way trade worth around 15 billion ECU. The Co-operation Agreement represents the essential groundwork for an eventual formal trade agreement between the EU and South Africa. By the end of 1994 it remained unclear whether such an agreement would be part of the Lomé framework or separate from it. The EU has also admitted South Africa into the Generalized System of Preferences which is estimated to be worth some 260 million ECU to South Africa per annum.

In September the EU held its first high-level ministerial meeting in Berlin with the 11 states of the SADC. The EU sees the SADC as a way of moving on from the Lomé framework and developing multilateral co-operation aimed at regional integration. The two sides have agreed to support democracy in Southern Africa, encourage arms reduction and promote economic and trade co-operation. They also agreed to set up a foreign policy dialogue aimed at promoting peace and stability in the area – the Southern African equivalent of the European Stability Pact?

Asia

The major event of the year in strategic terms on the part of the EU was the development and initial implementation of a new approach to Asia. This was particularly a feature of the German Presidency: the Commission adopted a paper entitled 'Towards a New Asia Strategy' in July, and the overall aim of giving the EU a new and higher profile in the region was broadly supported. Partly in pursuit of this strategy, the diplomacy of Sir Leon Brittan was particularly evident in the Asian sphere, although Martin Bangemann, the Industry Commissioner, was also to be seen pursuing the information technology aspects of the White Paper on growth, competitiveness and employment. Sir Leon visited Beijing twice (see below), and also paid a full visit to both Australia and New Zealand in February, during which he expressed the view that the EU should be more fully involved in the process of APEC (Asia-Pacific Economic Co-operation), even if only as an observer. During September, in Karlsruhe, there was the latest in a series of meetings between the EU and ASEAN (Association of Southeast Asian Nations): the development of ASEAN itself has given these meetings a more pronounced tilt towards political and security issues, but there is also evidence of continuing economic tension.

The chief tensions of the year, though, came in relations with the People's Republic of China (PRC). Everyone recognizes the importance of the PRC as both a market and an exporter; likewise, everyone recognizes the difficulty of accommodating the rapidly growing Chinese economy in the global trading system now focused on the WTO. The EU has a trade and co-operation agreement with the PRC dating from 1985, and it was in the context of this agreement that the first of Sir Leon Brittan's visits to Beijing took place in February. On this occasion, a number of new working groups were set up, and the Commissioner was able to support the PRC's bid to become a founder member of the WTO (in contrast to US views as they emerged during the year).

But during the rest of the year, tensions emerged and intensified. These centred partly on human rights, and the link between evidence of abuses and trade policies – a matter on which both the Commission and the Parliament expressed themselves during the year. More materially, though, they centred on the issue of trade policy and trade quotas. The EU's attempts to streamline its trade defence mechanisms, including the elimination of many quotas, created major difficulties, for example over imports of toys and footwear from the PRC, in which the conflicting interests of EU members themselves were apparent. This was further complicated by the fact that many imports of toys in particular arise from the activities of EU manufacturers in the PRC itself. Thus the sight of the UK Department of Trade and Industry going into battle for Chinese teddy-bear imports on behalf of UK manufacturers expressed an important trend and one likely to be intensified. By the time Sir Leon Brittan visited Beijing for the second time, in November, these issues had not been fully resolved, but there appeared to be progress.

Elsewhere in Asia, the EU was entangled in the usual range of disputes and anti-dumping findings, ranging from garlic imports to TV sets. But there was also substantial activity in the building of co-operation. The Trade and Co-operation Agreement with India finally came into force on 1 August, with a five-year duration, automatically renewable. A draft co-operation agreement with Sri Lanka was signed during July, and there were initial moves towards some form of wider co-operation with Vietnam, which External Political Relations Commissioner Hans van den Broek visited during July. EU concern with the Koreas was not merely of a commercial nature, given the threat of North Korean nuclear developments and the tensions between the US and North Korea that arose during the middle of the year; the EU positioned itself resolutely behind the US stance on this potential conflagration.

Latin America

As in 1993, there was a range of institutional contacts between the EU and Latin America, and there was evidence that the Commission saw these as an important counter to the assumed spread of US influence as a result of the North American Free Trade Agreement (NAFTA) adopted in late 1993. At the end of March, in Athens, the tenth 'San Jose' meeting between the EU and Central American countries was held; importantly, this defined a new phase for the relationship with a move to planning for co-operation on a multi-annual basis. Sao Paulo in April saw the fourth ministerial meeting of the EU and the so-called 'Rio Group', which produced a declaration on future co-operation. In October, the Commission produced a communication for the Council and the Parliament dealing with relations between the EU and the Mercosur Group (Argentina, Brazil, Paraguay and Uruguay); significantly, this called for the exploration of a new form of 'interregional association' which might eventually lead to a free trade agreement.

Despite this evidence of growing co-operation, the EU-Latin America relationship during the year was dominated by the severe conflict over the trade in bananas. The EU banana regime, which had entered into force during 1993, was challenged by a number of central American producers of 'dollar bananas' on the grounds that through its quota system it discriminated in favour of bananas from ex-colonies of the UK and France. Throughout 1994, the tensions persisted, with EU efforts to forge a compromise (sometimes through apparent attempts to divide and rule the Central Americans), complicated by the findings of a GATT panel which upheld the complaint against the EU. This was further complicated by an internal challenge in the Court of Justice from the Germans (who had historically allowed free entry for bananas), by tropical storms which wiped out crops in some Caribbean countries (thus preventing them from meeting their quotas), and eventually by intervention from the US, which threatened counter-measures on behalf of corporations producing 'dollar bananas'. Although there were other trade disputes in the area, for example those over threats to Ecuadorian cut flower exports, the banana issue shows every sign of continuing to be a trade policy *cause célèbre* because of the volatile mix of cultural, economic and political interests engaged.

The United States, Japan and Other Industrial Countries

The year saw probably a larger number of American expressions of support for the EU than any in recent memory; some saw this as part of a conscious strategy by Washington to play up the prospects for a new transatlantic partnership. In January, President Clinton visited Brussels for the NATO summit and for a meeting at the Commission in the context of the Transatlantic Declaration (TAD) of 1990. He was back again in June for the D-Day commemorations, and for an address to the French National Assembly, all of which furnished him with opportunities to offer strong support and encouragement to the EU, particularly in the field of foreign and security policy. A meeting in Berlin during July, under the umbrella of the TAD, established new working groups on drugs and eastern Europe. By the end of the year, there were even suggestions that rapid progress could be made towards a new form of transatlantic treaty based on a partnership of equals. This had been proposed in a European Parliament resolution in March, and by others before, but by December it had been taken on board by at least some parts of the US administration.

In the field of foreign and security policy, though, the reality of policy was somewhat different from the rhetoric of partnership. Although the EU staunchly supported the US in terms of declared policy on distant areas such as Haiti or North Korea, closer to home and where the stakes were higher there was much less in the way of warm feelings. Nowhere was this more so than in the conflict in former Yugoslavia, where the failings of the EU were paralleled by those of the USA and underlined by the domestic swing to the Republicans in the November mid-term congressional elections. The details of the CFSP are covered elsewhere in this article, but it is important here to point out the severe tensions caused by moves in the USA to withdraw from the arms embargo, which came to a head in November with the effective cessation of US participation in the Adriatic naval operation. Although there was important collaboration in a number of areas between not only the US and the EU, but also NATO and the WEU, it was far from clear after a troubled year what the future of co-operation was to be. This was underlined by further tensions about the extent to which NATO could be expanded to central and eastern Europe, and by the ways in which this affected the EU's relations both with potential future Member States (the Visegrad countries) and with the former Soviet Union (see above).

In trade and economic policy, there was no shortage of continuing bilateral disputes, of which the sharpest was over trade in audiovisual products: this was a legacy of the Uruguay Round, focused freshly by the moves to revise the 'Television Without Frontiers' Directive of the EU. US intervention in the dispute over bananas has already been noted – an intervention which reflected corporate interests in the USA as much as sympathy with Central American producing countries. A third cause of rancour was the belief in EU circles that the President and his Secretary of Commerce had 'stolen' some major orders, including one for $6 billion of commercial aircraft to be sold to Saudi Arabia, from under the noses of EU firms. US revival of their 'section 301' weapon against perceived unfair trade also caused hackles to rise in Brussels.

The picture of bilateral conflict was complicated by a number of issues in which the EU-US relationship took on a trilateral or multilateral hue. In a way, this was true of the bananas dispute, but it was even more pronounced in relations between the EU, the US and Japan. To a degree, the EU and the US had mutual interests in improving access to the Japanese market in the context of the GATT and the WTO; indeed, this was seen by some as a function of the 'quad' group talks during the year. But the increased bilateral pressure on Japan from the USA, which led to US-Japan framework agreements in a number of areas as the year wore on, aroused considerable concern in the Commission about the extent to which the EU might be 'crowded out' in the bilateral process. Another multilateral issue was that of the leadership of the WTO itself, in which the three candidatures effectively became sponsored by the Europeans, the Americans and the East Asians. US attacks on the European candidate, Renato Ruggiero, as a protectionist, were calculated to raise further tensions, especially when combined with EU-US tensions over the replacement of the Secretary-General of the Organization for Economic Co-operation and Development (OECD).

Nonetheless, there was considerable evidence of the development of new areas of effective collaboration between the EU and the US. In part, the implementation of the Uruguay Round demanded it; in part also, the further emergence of an infrastructure of collaboration based on working groups and specialist networks in specific issue areas was notable. Thus, there was in April at least an interim conclusion of negotiations on public procurement which had been a source of acrimony in earlier years; this covered an additional $28 billion of purchasing by government and public authorities, and was accompanied by commitments from the US administration that 39 states, seven cities and a number of federal agencies would be opened up to competition. There was also considerable consultation and 'policy sharing' on the implications of the White Paper on growth, competitiveness and employment. The impact of the accession of Austria, Finland and Sweden was the subject of EU-US talks well before accession actually occurred, a marked difference from the previous enlargements. On a host of other issues – drugs, eastern Europe, air transport, Russia – there were continuous official contacts, which could not eliminate disputes but which could provide a far firmer foundation for policy co-ordination.

The EU's relations with Japan have always been more distant and limited than those with the USA but, as already noted, the Commission proposed a new Asian strategy during 1994, which was to include Japan. In February, Sir Leon Brittan launched a 'gateway to Japan' programme to encourage EU exporters and investors, but in many ways the message of 1994 was one of consolidation – of the gains made from the Uruguay Round, and of earlier agreements such as that on automobile imports – rather than of new creation, although there were hints that 1995 would see a new push on the part of the EU. The auto agreement worked smoothly, with a mid-course increase in the agreed totals for imports in the autumn. Martin Bangemann visited Tokyo in April as part of his diplomacy connected with the White Paper. The general tone was one of 'quiet diplomacy', although as noted above the temperature was raised by US-Japan negotiations on market access during the autumn, an issue raised during Sir Leon Brittan's November visit and meeting in the context of the 1991 EU-Japan Declaration (a parallel to the EU-US Transatlantic Declaration, but less wide ranging).

Finally, it must not go unremarked that during July 1994 the EU and Canada held a meeting in Bonn in the context of the EU-Canada Transatlantic Declaration. Although relations were generally on an even keel, there were the beginnings of tensions later to become much more marked over the problem of North Atlantic fisheries.

III. Concluding Remarks

1994 was a year in which the sheer range of external policy concerns for the EU was perhaps more apparent than in 1993, which had been dominated by the Uruguay Round and by the former Yugoslavia. The increasing linkage between issue areas in the world economy, and the ever more apparent connection between 'internal' and 'external' policy concerns was a key feature, alongside the consolidation and development of the CFSP. It may, indeed, come to be seen as the year in which the EU really started to acquire a comprehensive foreign policy, with all the institutional and practical implications that this entails.

Journal of Common Market Studies Volume 33, Annual Review
August 1995

Legal Developments

JO SHAW
University of Leeds

I. Introduction

The legal developments reviewed in this article are those which occurred within the Court of Justice and the Court of First Instance. As this is the first occasion on which a review of precisely this type has appeared in the *Annual Review*, a word of explanation about the focus and terminology would be useful.

The exposition in the following sections is principally doctrinal: it sets out to explain to a general audience the development by the Court of the provisions of the Treaties themselves, and of the general principles and concepts which it applies to the interpretation, application and enforcement of the Treaties and secondary legislation. It does not purport to be complete, but merely to chart the main developments. As the emphasis is on the development of principles and concepts, little attention is directed to how the Court interprets the legislative intentions of the EU policy-makers as expressed in instruments such as directives or regulations (e.g. the interpretation of the provisions of the Common Customs Tariff in its application to some innovative or novel product, or the determination of the exact scope of the Acquired Rights Directive and the extent to which it restricts contracting out activities). Such questions will be covered only if they are in some way unusual or unexpected. Some of the cases discussed in this review are mentioned not because they themselves establish important principles, but because they make it possible to draw to the attention of readers developments which began in 1992 or 1993, and which were continued in 1994.

It is to be hoped that this review of doctrinal developments will be useful to readers interested in the debates surrounding the politics of legal integration within the EU. To that end, wherever possible, some attempt is made to contextualize the case law of the Court and to explain its wider significance.

Throughout this review the term 'Community' or 'EC' law is used, rather than EU law. In legal terms, this is the correct term to use in almost all circumstances, since the bulk of 'law' emanating from the EU as a whole is adopted under the central, supranational pillar of the three Communities. To encompass the broader legal framework of European integration, the general term 'legal order of the EU' is also used.

II. The Development of the Competence and the Powers of the EU and its Institutions

Relationships between the EU and its Member States

Since the introduction of more qualified majority voting through the Single European Act in 1986, one of the ways in which the Member States have, from time to time, tested out the powers of the institutions and the scope of Community competence has been through legal basis litigation. This allows the Court to determine whether the institutions have acted within the scope of Community competence when deciding which Treaty provisions to use as the legal basis for particular legislative measures. What, for example, is the breadth of the power granted to the Council in Article 100A EC to adopt harmonization measures aimed at the completion of the internal market? In the August 1994 case of *Germany* v *Council (Product Safety Directive)*[1] the Court was faced with a challenge to the novel approach to the enforcement of harmonized standards introduced in the Product Safety Directive.[2] In the context of a measure setting out a uniform standard for safe products, Article 9 of the directive set up a process whereby the Commission could, after following a specified procedure, take temporary measures to ensure the free movement of a product against which one or more Member States had taken restrictive measures. The measures would take the form of decisions addressed to Member States. The Court rejected the argument by Germany that such individual measures could not be regarded as a form of harmonization, and therefore could not validly be adopted under the authority of Article 100A. The Court also rejected an argument by Germany that the possibility of introducing such measures violated the principle of proportion-

[1] Case C-359/92 [1994] European Court Reports (ECR) I-3681.

[2] Council Directive 92/59 OJ 1992 L228/24.

ality. This judgment indicates that a potentially more flexible concept of harmonization can be mediated through the legal basis of Article 100A.

Interinstitutional Relationships

Legal basis. In 1994 the Parliament continued its fight, through legal basis litigation, to maximize its powers within the institutional system. Under Article 173 EC, as amended by the Treaty of Maastricht, it is entitled to challenge acts of the other institutions before the Court of Justice, with a view to protecting its own prerogatives. One such prerogative is the right to be consulted. However, in *Parliament* v *Council (Lomé Convention)*[3] the Parliament failed in its attempt to persuade the Court that expenditure for development aid under the Fourth ACP–EEC Convention is Community expenditure and therefore must be governed by financial regulations made pursuant to Article 209 EC which requires it to be consulted. However, significantly, the Court held that the Parliament could, at least in principle, challenge a financial regulation adopted by the Council, acting not under Treaty powers but those of an 'internal agreement' relating to the financing and administration of Community aid, adopted by the representatives of the Governments of the Member States, 'meeting within Council'. In other words, the Parliament established the important principle that it has the standing to challenge all acts of the institutions, even those adopted pursuant to intergovernmental measures outside the Treaty itself.

In June 1994, the Court further refined the position of the Parliament. In *Parliament* v *Council (Transport of Waste)*[4] the Court rejected an action for annulment of Council Regulation 259/93[5] on the supervision and control of shipments of waste within, into, and out of the European Community. The Parliament failed in an argument that Article 113 EC (creation of the common commercial policy) should compose part of the legal basis of the regulation, but on the *technical* ground that it did not have the standing to bring such a claim since, at the time the regulation was made, Article 113 did not provide for consultation of the Parliament. On the question of the relationship between Article 100A and Article 130S, the Court held, confirming its refinement of the *Titanium Dioxide* case law,[6] that Article 100A could be excluded by the Council from the legal basis as the main thrust of the measure was towards the creation of a Community environmental policy. The fact that the regulation does affect movements of waste and thus has a bearing on the functioning of the internal market is, in effect, ancillary.

[3] Case C-316/91 [1994] ECR I-625.
[4] Case C-187/93 [1994] ECR I-2857.
[5] OJ 1993 L30/1.
[6] Case C-300/89 *Commission* v *Council (Titanium Dioxide)* [1991] ECR I-2867, as refined in Case C-155/91 *Commission* v *Council (Waste Disposal)* (17.3.93: not yet reported).

Other related issues. Closely related to the Parliament's ability to challenge the legal basis of measures is its right to seek annulment of a measure where the proper legislative procedures have not been followed. In *Parliament* v *Council (Cabotage Regulation)*[7] the Court of Justice annulled a Council regulation under Article 75 EC on the grounds that the Council had failed to reconsult the Parliament, in circumstances where it had altered the entire scheme of the proposed regulation after initially consulting the Parliament.

External Powers

1994 saw the ultimate conclusion of the General Agreement on Tariffs and Trade (GATT) Uruguay Round and a major Court decision in the field of external powers. At the request of the Commission, the Court examined three important questions concerning agreements annexed to the Agreement establishing the World Trade Organization (WTO):

- whether the Community had exclusive competence to conclude the Multilateral Agreements on Trade in Goods, so far as these concerned certain specific types of products;
- what competence the Community had to conclude the General Agreement on Trade in Services (GATS); and
- what competence the Community had to conclude the agreement on Trade-Related Aspects of Intellectual Property Rights (TRIPs).

In November, the Court delivered an advisory opinion under Article 228(6) EC setting out the nature and scope of Community competence.[8] While the Commission had acted as exclusive negotiator on behalf of the Member States and the EU during the Round, this did not prejudge the question of competence to conclude the agreements – which was ultimately a matter for the Court. The litigation essentially set the Commission (arguing for wider Community competence) against the Member States (seeking to protect national reserved powers).

Multilateral agreements on trade in goods. In principle, Article 113 confers on the Community exclusive competence to conclude international agreements in respect of trade in goods. Difficulties arise only in respect of certain specific types of products. The European Coal and Steel Community (ECSC) Treaty differs from the EC Treaty in that it does not create a customs union in respect of the products which it encompasses, leaving external competence to the Member States (Article 71 ECSC). However, the power to conclude *general* agreements under Article 113 also includes agreements which incidentally also cover ECSC products. Only a *separate* agreement covering ECSC products

[7] Case C-388/92 [1994] ECR I-2067.
[8] Opinion 1/94 on the Agreement establishing the World Trade Organization (15.11.94; not yet reported).

specifically would be affected by this restriction on Community competence and would require action by the Member States.

GATS. The Court rejected the Commission's contention that Article 113 was also the appropriate legal basis for the conclusion of the GATS, and that the Community had exclusive competence in the sphere of services. Only where trade in services involved *cross-border supplies* (where the supplier, established in one state, supplies a service to a consumer, established in another state and neither party actually moves), which are analogous to cross-border supplies of goods, did Article 113 apply. It did not apply to transport services, or to other modes of supply of services covered by GATS, namely consumption abroad (consumer travels to state where services are supplied), and commercial presence abroad and presence of natural persons abroad (supplier, whether legal or natural person, travels to the state where the consumer is situated in order to supply the services). In the alternative, the Commission sought to argue that the *ERTA* doctrine[9] of parallelism between internal and external competences and the 'Opinion 1/76 doctrine'[10] on exclusive competence to secure the attainment of Community objectives gave the Community exclusive competence. The key to the Court's conclusions was whether the Community had *general* exclusive competence, or only exclusive competence in fields where it had actually exercised its internal competence in such a way as to affect the treatment of nationals of third countries (e.g. in the Banking or Insurance Directives, where the treatment of US, Japanese and other third country banks is dealt with) or to provide a complete system of common rules governing access to a self-employed activity. The Court concluded in favour of the latter interpretation, holding, therefore, that the Community and the Member States *shared* competence to conclude the GATS.

TRIPs. In relation to the agreements on intellectual property rights (IPR), the Court found that exclusive competence based on Article 113 was limited to aspects of the agreements concerned with the control of counterfeit goods at the external frontiers of the Community. This is logical, as the Community can, acting autonomously, adopt its own unilateral measures on such matters under Article 113. *A fortiori* the same principles should apply to measures adopted on the basis of *agreements*. For the rest, the Court rejected the application of Article 113, since allowing the Community to conclude international agreements *harmonizing* the protection of IPR on that basis would effectively circumvent the *internal* institutional constraints on harmonization measures in that field (e.g.the requirement of unanimity: Article 113 requires only a qualified majority vote).

[9] Case 22/70 *Commission* v *Council (ERTA)* [1971] ECR 263.

[10] Elaborated in the context of Opinion 1/76 [1977] ECR 741 on the draft agreement establishing a European laying-up fund for inland waterway vessels.

Consequently, the Court concluded that the Community and its Member States were jointly competent to conclude TRIPs.

Problems of co-operation. The Court rejected the concern that shared competence would unnecessarily complicate the work of the EU and the Member States within the WTO. The Commission feared that lengthy debates about competence might lessen the effectiveness of the EU. The Court recognized this as a legitimate fear, but rejected its relevance to questions of competence to conclude the agreements. It emphasized instead the duty to co-operate imposed on both the Community and its Member States as being the key to the effective operation of the agreements.

The overall tenor of the *WTO Opinion* is conservative, with the Court failing either to push at the limits of Community external competence or clarify uncertainties about the notion of exclusive competence.

US–EC Competition Laws Agreement. In 1994, the Court also addressed the validity, under Community law, of the US–EC agreement on the application of their competition laws. In *France* v *Commission (EC/US Competition Laws Agreement)*,[11] the Court held that Commission was not competent to conclude an Agreement with the US on co-operation in the application and enforcement of their respective competition laws. The Court emphasized that it is the Community itself which has international legal capacity, not the individual institutions. However, it is important to know which institution, in the internal sphere, has power to act for the Community. The Court held that it is the Council which has the power to conclude such agreements under Article 228 EC, and that this particular agreement did not fall within any of the exceptions to this principle giving powers to the Commission. Nobody has contested the desirability of such an agreement in policy terms and the Council has now readopted the agreement. In the meantime, it continued to be binding on the Community in international law because at the time the Commission acted as if it had authority to conclude the agreement.

III. The Development of the Principles of Primary Community Law

This section looks at the interpretation by the Court of the key provisions of the Treaty establishing free movement rights and non-discrimination rights of a constitutional nature. Most of the key principles are already well established. Consequently, not all the areas of free movement, for example, will be discussed. One area where new developments are anticipated concerns the concept of an 'internal market' defined in Article 7A EC. However, expectations that the Court would rule during 1994 on the argument that Article 7A *requires* the dismantling

[11] Case C-327/91 [1994] ECR I-3641.

of internal border controls, were disappointed. This question is likely to be decided during the course of 1995.

Article 9 (prohibition on customs duties)

The most important case of 1994 was *Lancry* v *Direction générale des douanes*,[12] in which the Court was required to consider the scope of the earlier case of *Legros*.[13] At issue in these cases were so-called 'dock dues', levied in the French overseas departments on goods brought into those territories, irrespective of their origin or provenance (i.e. other French *départements*, other Member States, or third countries). The dock dues were used to support the economic and social development of the overseas departments. In *Legros* these were held to be contrary to Article 9 EC, as customs duties, because they destroyed the unity of the market. The Court limited the retrospective effect of its judgment, so that unless a claim for reimbursement had already been lodged at the date of the judgment, only dues paid after the judgment (16 July 1992) could be recovered from the authorities. However, before the Court gave judgment in *Legros*, the Council adopted a decision[14] requiring the abolition of the dues by 31 December 1992. The question raised in the *Lancry* case was whether the relevant provisions of this Decision were valid (i.e. could the Council derogate in this way from the primary principles of the internal market?). The Court concluded that the Council could not do this. It also reiterated its conclusions in *Legros*, making it clear that the dock dues are unlawful even where they are levied on goods coming from within France, and not actually crossing a national border.

Articles 30–36 (non-tariff barriers to the free movement of goods)

Coming after the landmark year of 1993, which saw the *Keck* case[15] redrawing the boundaries of Article 30 EC in a very significant way, 1994 was a year of consolidation for the Court. For example, in *Tankstation 't Heuske and Boermans*,[16] the Court directly applied its ruling in *Keck* to Dutch rules on opening hours for petrol stations. It applied the same reasoning to Sunday trading rules in *Punto Casa SpA* v *Sindaco del Comune di Capena*.[17] Under *Keck*, national rules applying equally to domestic and imported products which restrict or prohibit certain types of selling arrangements do not fall under the prohibition in Article 30 EC on non-tariff barriers to trade. In contrast, in *Verband Sozialer Wettbewerb eV* v *Clinique Laboratories SNC*[18] the Court applied the other half

[12] Cases C-363/93 etc. [1994] ECR I-3957.
[13] Case C-163/90 [1992] ECR I-4625.
[14] Council Decision 89/688 OJ 1989 L399/46.
[15] Cases C-267 etc./91 *Criminal Proceedings against Keck and Mithouard* [1993] ECR I-6097.
[16] Cases 401-2/92 [1994] ECR 2199.
[17] Cases 69 and 258/93 [1994] ECR 2357.
[18] Case C-315/92 [1994] ECR I-317.

of *Keck*, affirming that German rules which prohibited the marketing of a cosmetic because it bore the name 'Clinique' and might confuse the consumer, were covered by Article 30 as rules which lay down requirements to be met by goods, such as requirements on designation, form, size, weight, composition, presentation, labelling or packaging. Such a measure can only be saved if it pursues, in a proportionate manner, a legitimate public interest objective (such as the protection of consumers, or of the environment). The Court concluded that the German measures in this case were not saved.

However, the Court has not ceased to cut down the scope of Article 30. Having held in *HAG II*[19] that the so-called exhaustion of rights doctrine does not apply where ownership of a trademark right in different countries is split following expropriation, it extended this ruling in June 1994 in *IHT Internationale Heiztechnik GmbH* v *Ideal-Standard GmbH*[20] to cover the voluntary assignment of trademark rights. The exhaustion of rights doctrine precludes a trademark owner from using the national segmentation of trademark rights in order to oppose the importation, under his trademark, of goods which have been marketed in another Member State by him, or with his consent (e.g. by a licensee or subsidiary). However, a voluntary horizontal assignment of the trademark in state B does not prevent the owner of the mark in state A from challenging importations from state B. This is because the object of the right of prohibition stemming from the mark is to protect the owner against contrivances of third parties seeking to take advantage of the reputation accruing to a trademark, and that ownership right is not exhausted where the mark is used by an assignee.

Article 48 (free movement of workers)

Recent cases in this field have tended to highlight instances of covert or indirect discrimination against migrant workers. Such was the case in *Scholz* v *Opera Universitaria di Cagliari*.[21] The Court confirmed that it was contrary to Article 48 for a public authority in Italy to refuse to take into account periods of service in the public service in another Member State when determining whether the candidates for a post had the requisite experience. Such a rule obviously applies irrespective of nationality, but is one which citizens of other Member States are more likely to find burdensome.

The Court also reaffirmed its slightly contentious case law on reverse discrimination, whereby it refuses to apply Community rules or allow reliance upon Community rights in situations which are purely internal to Member States. Consequently, of course, nationals may receive worse treatment than migrant

[19] Case C-10/89 *SA CNL-SUCAL* v *HAG GF* [1990] ECR I-3711.
[20] Case C-9/93 [1994] ECR I-2789.
[21] Case C-419/92 [1994] ECR I-507.

workers. Such was the case alleged in *Steen* v *Deutsche Bundespost (No. 1)*,[22] in which a German national objected to the situation in the German post office where migrant workers can be employed under private law contracts, whereas nationals must be employed as 'civil servants'*(Beamte)*, with a number of significant consequences. The German national in question had never exercised the right to free movement. As the Court confirmed when the case was referred to it for a second time for further clarification,[23] any resulting discrimination against nationals is a matter for *national* law, in this case Article 3 of the German Basic Law.

Articles 52 and 59 (free movement of services and freedom of establishment)

The issue of reverse discrimination has also arisen in the context of free movement of services. In *Peralta*[24] the Court held that an Italian criminal law which imposed stricter sanctions on masters of vessels caught infringing water pollution rules who were Italian nationals, than on those who were not, fell outside the scope of Community law. Furthermore, the Court held that such rules, insofar as they applied without distinction to Italian ships and non-Italian ships were not prohibited by Community law.

One of the most interesting extensions of Article 59 EC during 1994 occurred in *HM Customs and Excise* v *Schindler*.[25] The Court held that the services provisions apply to lotteries, and that former UK legislation prohibiting lottery sales, although falling under Article 59, could be justified on grounds of social policy (prevention of crime, restrictions on gambling, etc.). Even such a total prohibition was not deemed disproportionate. The Court did not consider whether the objectives aimed at could not have been achieved by less restrictive means, such as supervision.

Finally, the Court also extended its case law on the free movement rights of the employees of cross-border service providers. In the earlier case of *Rush Portuguesa* v *Office National d'Immigration*[26] the Court had held that Portuguese workers employed by a Portuguese firm providing services in France were covered by the services provisions of the Treaty, rather than the provisions on workers, as temporarily posted employees. This principle was taken further in August 1994 in *Vander Elst* v *Office des Migrations Internationales*.[27] A Belgian service supplier employing Moroccan nationals, legally resident in Belgium and with Belgian work permits, may undertake work in France, using these employ-

[22] Case C-322/90 [1992] ECR I-341
[23] Case C-132/93 *Steen* v *Deutsche Bundespost (No. 2)* [1994] ECR I-2715.
[24] Case C-379/92 [1994] ECR I-3453.
[25] Case C-275/92 [1994] ECR 1039.
[26] Case C-113/89 [1990] ECR I-1417.
[27] Case C-43/93 [1994] ECR I-3803..

ees on a temporary basis without any need for work permits for the employees as 'aliens'. Although this does not extend full rights of residence or employment to third country nationals outside the country in which they are lawfully resident, it does at least not restrict them in their choice of employment within that first country by reference to the possibility that their employer might wish to provide services elsewhere in the EU.

Articles 85, 86 and 90 (competition law)

The major competition law decision of 1994 on the application of Articles 85 and 86 EC was the judgment of the Court of First Instance in the appeal by Tetra Pak against the heavy fines imposed upon it by the Commission for abuse of a dominant position, involving in particular practices of predatory pricing.[28] The application was dismissed, but a further appeal to the Court of Justice can be expected.

In the sphere of Article 90 EC, interest centres on *Commune d'Almelo* v *Energiebedrijf Ijsselmij*[29] and the Court of Justice's interpretation of the exemption from some of the rules of the Treaty for services of general economic interest contained in Article 90(2). The Court considered its application to a non-exclusive regional concession to distribute electricity where the concessionaire was given the benefit, by legislation, of an exclusive purchasing clause prohibiting local distributors from importing electricity. Essentially the Court ducked the issue by emphasizing that this is a matter for the national court, which must determine whether any restriction on competition is necessary to enable the concessionaire to perform its task of general interest.

Article 119 (equal pay)

Case law on Article 119 EC has continued to be dominated by the 'fall-out' from the *Barber* ruling[30] to the effect that occupational pension scheme payments are 'pay' within the meaning of Article 119, but limiting the retrospective effect of that decision (to the period after 17 May 1990). In an earlier group of decisions in 1993[31] the Court had already concluded that pension equality applies only to pensions awarded in respect of periods of service after the date of the *Barber* judgment (the so-called 'future service' interpretation). This is the most impor-

[28] Case T-83/91 *Tetra Pak International SA* v *Commission* (6.10.94: not yet reported).
[29] Case C-393/92 [1994] ECR 1477.
[30] Case C-262/88 *Barber* v *Guardian Royal Exchange Assurance Group* [1990] ECR I-1889.
[31] Case C-109/91 *Ten Oever* v *Stichting Bedrijfspensioenfonds voor het Glazenwassers* [1993] IRLR 601; Case C-132/92 *Birds Eye Walls Ltd* v *Roberts* [1994] IRLR 29; Case C-110/91 *Moroni* v *Firma Collo GmbH* [1994] IRLR 130; Case C-152/91 *Neath* v *Hugh Steeper Ltd* [1994] IRLR 91.

tant – and, for many, disappointing – aspect of these and the later 1994 cases.[32] The Court has in these latter cases affirmed, however, that the right to *join* a pension scheme is not limited in time, and can be backdated beyond *Barber*, although any worker wishing to take advantage must buy back years by making contributions. This is, therefore, a somewhat double-edged sword for groups such as part-time workers who were hitherto excluded. Finally, in the same group of cases, the Court took a rather blinkered approach to the question of retirement age *equalization* as the answer to problems of *equality*. Raising the retirement age of women to match that of men may have adverse consequences for them; these cannot be offset by giving them even transitional additional benefits.

IV. Enforcement and Effectiveness of Community Law

Individual Enforcement

It is, of course, one of the central features of the EU legal order that individuals may enforce rights derived under the Treaties and secondary legislation before national courts. One of the key achievements of the Court is acknowledged to be the ascription of direct effect to directives,[33] albeit only 'vertically', thereby allowing individuals to enforce the obligations contained in directives against the state and emanations of the state.[34] From the perspective of those who advocate a continuing trend towards the greater effectiveness of directives, however, 1994 was a disappointment. In *Faccini Dori* v *Recreb Srl*,[35] the Court, having dodged the issue on a number of earlier cases, was finally faced foursquare with a challenge to its earlier distinction between vertical and horizontal direct effect. However, it held, against the advice of the Advocate General in the case and a number of earlier opinions from Advocates General,[36] that an individual could not rely directly upon the protection granted in the Doorstep Selling Directive. The outcome of this case is that it continues to be very important for national courts to apply the *Marleasing* doctrine.[37] That is, they must interpret national law in the light of the wording, spirit and objectives of relevant Community rules, including directives. It may also be that the best chance for individuals of enforcing directives lies in seeking damages from the

[32] Case C-200/91 *Coloroll Pension Trustees Ltd* v *Russell* [1994] ECR I-4389; Case C-408/92 *Smith* v *Advel Systems Ltd* [1994] ECR I-4435; Case C-7/93 *Bestuur van het Algemeen Burgerlijk Pensionenfonds* v *Beune* [1994] ECR I-4474; Case C-57/93 *Vroege* v *NCIV Instituut voor Volkshuisvesting BV* [1994] ECR I-4541; Case C-128/93 *Fisscher* v *Voorhuis Hengelo BV* [1994] ECR I-4583

[33] Case 41/74 *Van Duyn* v *Home Office* [1974] ECR 1337.

[34] Case 152/94 *Marshall* v *Southampton and South West Hampshire AHA* [1986] ECR 723.

[35] Case C-91/92 [1994] ECR 3325.

[36] Case C-316/93 *Vaneetveld* [1994] ECR I-763; Case C-271/91 *Marshall* v *Southampton and South West Hampshire AHA (Marshall No. 2)* [1993] ECR I-4367.

[37] Case C-106/89 *Marleasing* [1990] ECR I4135.

state for failure to implement, under the *Francovich* doctrine.[38] The practical significance of all these cases will continue to grow as the EU adopts an ever growing body of legislation which impacts upon private commercial and economic relationships between individuals (e.g. in the fields of consumer protection and health and safety at work).

The rather conservative theme of the year was endorsed in the case of *Banks* v *British Coal Corporation*[39] in which the Court of Justice held, somewhat unexpectedly and again against the advice of the Advocate General, that the competition provisions of the ECSC Treaty are not, unlike those in the EC Treaty, capable of individual enforcement.

Enforcement by the Commission

Activity in the field of enforcement by the Commission focused not on the primary enforcement mechanisms of Articles 169–171, but on provisions such as Articles 225 and 100A(4) which set up separate enforcement mechanisms in derogation from Article 169.

Articles 224 and 225. The Court was faced with litigation arising out of the unilateral sanctions applied by Greece against the former Yugoslav Republic of Macedonia (FYROM). The Commission claimed that Greece had improperly used powers under Article 224 EC which concerns consultations between the Member States in the event of serious disturbances affecting the common market or internal stability. Greece objected that FYROM had ambitions towards creating a unified Macedonia and thus threatened Greek territorial sovereignty. In an order of 24 June 1994, the Court refused the Commission's application for interim measures against Greece.[40] The order does not determine the merits of the case, but simply establishes that the Court could not take into account the harm to FYROM as an element in determining whether interim measures should be granted, and moreover that the Commission had failed to establish that Greece had committed a manifest breach of Community law.

Article 100A(4). Article 100A(4) allows Member States to carry on applying national measures, notwithstanding the adoption of harmonization measures by the Council, on the grounds of major needs such as protection of health or the environment. It sets up an enforcement system whereby the Commission can approve the measures, and both the Commission and any Member State can bring the matter directly before the Court of Justice if it is thought that improper use of the powers is being made. *France* v *Commission (PCP)*[41] concerns the first use of its approval powers by the Commission. France challenged a Commission

[38] Case C-6/90 [1991] ECR I-5357.
[39] Case C-128/92 [1994] ECR I-1209.
[40] Case C-120/94R *Commission* v *Greece (FYROM)* [1994] ECR I-3037.
[41] Case C-41/93 [1994] ECR I-1829.

decision confirming German rules on pentachlorophenol which were more restrictive than the relevant Community harmonization measures. The French application was successful, with the Court holding, in May 1994, that the Commission had failed to state sufficient reasons for its conclusion. It did not explain the reasons of fact and law which prompted it to decide that the German rules were justified under Article 100A(4). That this is the first and so far only occasion on which Article 100A(4) has come before the Court tends to reinforce the thesis that the impact of this provision will perhaps not be as great as was feared when the Single European Act was originally concluded.

V. Protection of Individual Rights

Fundamental Rights

Rights of economic actors. Under international law, it is generally the prerogative of states to protect the interests of their citizens. The EU legal order still shares some of the characteristics of the international legal order, including a structure of procedures which makes it much easier for a Member State than an individual to bring a challenge against EU legislation which allegedly infringes the fundamental rights of citizens. The equal treatment principle, rights of property and the proportionality principle were all at issue in *Germany* v *Council (Bananas)*[42] in which Germany sought to challenge the common organization of the market in bananas instituted in 1993. This had the effect of removing a previous special arrangement for banana imports from Latin America into Germany (the 'Banana Protocol'). Bananas have always been highly political within the EU, and the German case was the culmination of a many-pronged assault on the EU's controversial policy change. While part of the challenge was based on the scope of the provisions on which the Council measures were based, much of the bulk of the decision was concerned with the protection of rights – in particular of economic operators trading in third country bananas. The Court rejected all aspects of the claim. It refused to enquire into the details of the policy, accepting the legitimacy of a distinction drawn by the EU legislators between Community and ACP banana production on the one hand, and banana production from third countries. Finally, it refused – perhaps rather contentiously – to accept arguments that the EU rules were contrary to the GATT.

Rights of EU officials. In a staff case, *X* v *Commission*,[43] the Court confirmed the right of applicants for jobs within the EU institutions to refuse to take AIDS/HIV tests on the grounds of protection of the right to respect for private life, including the right to keep his/her state of health secret, as guaranteed in Article

[42] Case C-280/93 [1994] ECR I-4873.
[43] Case C-404/92P [1994] ECR I-4737.

8 of the European Human Rights Convention (ECHR). The rights guaranteed by the ECHR were recognized by the Court as binding upon the EU as general principles of law. Indeed, in another 1994 case, the Court of First Instance referred explicitly to Article F(2) TEU, which incorporates those rights into the legal order of the Union, albeit within that part of the Treaty which is not subject to the jurisdiction of its courts.[44] However, refusal to take a test during a pre-recruitment medical examination will mean that the institution cannot be obliged to recruit the candidate. In the *X* case the Court overturned a Court of First Instance ruling that the medical officer could in certain circumstances subject candidates to tests without their consent.[45]

Competition Procedures

The procedures under which the Commission is able to enforce Articles 85 and 86 EC generate sufficient case law in themselves to merit separate attention under this heading. The most significant case of 1994 was a victory for the Commission. In *Commission* v *BASF et al.*[46] the Court overturned a Court of First Instance ruling[47] that a decision finding an infringement of Article 85 suffered from the defect of 'inexistence' just because of differences between the decision in the version which was agreed by the college of Commissioners, and the final versions notified to the alleged infringers. These were more than just changes resulting from the translation process into the various languages used by the infringers. The Court did conclude that such a decision indeed suffers from serious procedural defects and should be annulled. Thankfully for the Commission, it rejected the Court of First Instance conclusion that the decision was actually 'inexistent'. Inexistence is a category reserved for the most serious defects where it can be said that a measure is so flawed that it never really existed at all. Applying the principle in the competition context would have thrown into doubt potentially all the Commission's earlier work in this field. For example, if a decision from 1975 was inexistent for the same reason, then even though the time limit for challenging it before the Court (two months) was long past, it would still retain its defect. Consequently, logically any fine levied could be claimed back. The Commission will in any case have been forced to review its procedures in relation to translation and the adoption of decisions by the *BASF* case, but it will not now be faced with a potentially disastrous review of its earlier decisions.

A rather different case involved a complainant under the Merger Control Regulation ('MCR'). The Court of First Instance held in *Air France* v *Commis-*

[44] Case T-10/93 *A* v *Commission* ECR-SC II-387.
[45] Cases T-121/89 and 13/90 *X* v *Commission* [1992] ECR II-2195.
[46] Case C-137/92P [1994] ECR I-2555.
[47] Cases T-79/89 *BASF et al.* v *Commission* [1992] ECR II-315.

sion[48] that a statement made by the Commission spokesman that the proposed merger between Dan Air and British Airways fell outside the scope of the MCR was a measure producing legal effects for national authorities, the parties to the merger and competitors which could be reviewed by the Court. Its informal nature did not affect its legal nature. Air France had an interest in the challenge (which failed on the merits) because it had complained formally to the Commission.

Individual Rights of Redress against Community Institutions

Outside the competition law field, it is not normally so simple for an individual litigant to obtain judicial review of Community action. However, in *Codorniu* v *Council*,[49] the Court of Justice, after a period of deliberation lasting five years, widened the categories of claimants who can challenge Council legislation (as opposed to individual measures just affecting them, such as decisions). The measure in question was a Council regulation[50] which reserved the word '*crémant*' for certain quality sparkling wines produced in specified regions of France. The aim was to protect traditional descriptions. However, the applicants had produced in Spain since 1924 a wine called *Gran Cremant de Codorniu*, and marketed it under a trademark in the same name. They were precluded by the legislation from using this, and, although they were not the only producers affected (i.e. their legal situation was not unique), the Court held that they had standing to challenge the measure under Article 173 EC. It concluded that the legislation engendered unjustifiable discrimination between different categories of producers.

Having widened the categories of challenge under Article 173 EC, the Court felt justified later in the year in narrowing the circumstances in which applicants can use the Article 177 EC reference procedure to challenge measures. Where a company challenges the implementation through national measures of a Commission decision addressed to a Member State which it *could have challenged* under Article 173 (because it specifically concerned that company), the Court of Justice will refuse to review, in the context of questions put to it by the national court, the validity of the underlying Commission decision. The somewhat technical ruling in *TWD Textilwerke Deggendorf GmbH* v *Germany*[51] is nonetheless of considerable practical significance as regards the choice by potential litigants as to whether to proceed in the Court of Justice and the national courts. The former solution is likely to be shorter than the latter, as a national court

[48] Case T-3/93 [1994] ECR II-121.
[49] Case C-309/89 [1994] ECR I-1853.
[50] Regulation 2045/89 OJ 1989 L202/12.
[51] Case C-188/92 [1994] ECR I-833.

cannot invalidate the contested EU measure and must refer the matter to the Court itself.

VI. Overall Evaluation and Conclusion

1994 was a year of caution on the part of the Court, with no dramatic extensions in legal principle and a number of judgments which imply a jurisprudence of retrenchment rather than expansion. In practical terms there have been important changes in the jurisdiction of the two courts.[52] The Court of First Instance now has responsibility for all cases brought by individuals, leaving only a restricted right of appeal on matters of law to the Court of Justice itself. This perhaps explains in part the cases discussed in the previous section. It may be some years, however, before the dynamic of development which has previously dominated the Court returns in full force.

[52] Council Decision 94/149/ECSC/EC (OJ 1994 L66/29).

Journal of Common Market Studies Volume 33, Annual Review
August 1995

Developments in the Economies of the European Union

ANDREW SCOTT
University of Edinburgh

I. Overview

The dominant economic feature of 1994 was the gathering strength of the European Union's recovery from the recession of the previous three years. It is now widely accepted that economic recovery in the EU is well established, and forecasters are predicting that growth will be relatively robust, at around 3 per cent per annum, over the next few years. Following the 1991–93 recession, during which EU growth averaged less than 1 per cent per year, in 1994 EU Gross Domestic Product (GDP) increased by 2.6 per cent. This contrasts with a 0.4 per cent decline in GDP during 1993. The economic recovery in the EU during 1994 was considerably stronger than had been forecast, and this was attributable to two factors.

The first was the strength of the world economy in 1994. World economic growth excluding the EU was 3 per cent in 1994, and is forecast to increase further in both 1995 and 1996. The buoyancy of the international economy has generated a high level of demand for EU exports and, in the absence of a sustained recovery in domestic consumption or investment, it has been the performance of the export sector that has played a critical part in promoting the economic recovery. In 1994 EU exports to the rest of the world increased by over 10 per cent, assisted by high economic growth in the USA (which recorded growth in GDP of 3.9 per cent in 1994) and in the rapidly developing countries of Asia. And although economic growth in Japan during 1994 was only 0.7 per cent, there was nonetheless strong import demand with imports into Japan recording a 11 per cent increase which again benefitted the countries of the EU. At the same time EU exporters have been helped by a real depreciation of currencies. The European Commission estimates that EU currencies as a bloc have depreciated by more than 15 per cent over the period August 1992 to February 1994. It is worth noting that further currency depreciations early in 1995 are likely to enhance further the competitiveness of EU exports.

The second factor was the stronger than expected recovery of the German economy, particularly during the second half of 1994. For the year as a whole GDP in Germany grew by 2.5 per cent. In part the German recovery was based on a high demand for exports, with merchandise export volume up by almost 14 per cent on the previous year. In part too it reflected the strength of the recovery in the former East Germany, where GDP grew at over 8 per cent in 1994 and contributed positively to the overall German performance. The increasing strength of the German economy, along with the continued buoyancy of the UK economy, provided a powerful engine of economic recovery for the EU as a whole in 1994.

The EU economic performance in 1994 compared reasonably favourably with developments around the international economy. For all OECD countries the rate of growth of GDP was 2.8 per cent, slightly above the EU. However, the Japanese economy continued to emerge only slowly from recession and GDP grew at a modest 1 per cent for the year. In the USA, by contrast, GDP increased very strongly during 1994 at 3.9 per cent, although this is likely to represent the peak of the cyclical upswing with growth returning to more modest levels over the next two years. Indeed, if we consider the OECD rate of growth excluding the USA, the out-turn for 1994 is 2.2 per cent, below the EU average. The prospective weakening in economic conditions in the USA creates potential difficulties for the EU. As already noted, the USA has provided a key source of external demand for EU products with export-led growth being a central propellant in the domestic recovery. As the USA economy enters a phase of lower growth, and given the continued slow pace of recovery in Japan, the medium-term prospects of the EU economy will, consequently, come to depend on the development of domestic components of aggregate demand, i.e. consumption and investment. Further, as is discussed below, the development of domestic consumer and investor demand will hinge on the economic policy decisions of both governments and agents in the private sector. Undoubtedly policy-makers across the EU will be monitoring the movement of economic variables to guard against any resurgence of inflationary forces – this remaining the single greatest threat to future economic growth.

Despite the upturn in the economic performance of the EU in 1994, unemployment continued to rise, averaging 10.9 per cent for the year, although this is forecast to be the peak year for unemployment. The present EU situation compares unfavourably to previous years, when unemployment stood at 8.8 per cent in 1991 and 10.6 per cent in 1993. Whilst gains in employment typically lag the economic recovery, unemployment is forecast to fall only slowly over the next few years – to 10.4 per cent in 1995 and 9.8 per cent in 1996. However, this average masks considerable differences between individual Member States with the variation across the EU in 1994 ranging from 3.3 per cent in Luxembourg, to 17.7 per cent in Ireland, and 22.4 per cent in Spain. Against this background, it is to be expected that job creation will remain at the top of the EU's agenda for the foreseeable future. It is worth noting in this regard that in June 1994 the European Investment Bank launched the European Investment Fund set up as part of the economic growth initiative adopted by the EU at the Edinburgh summit in December 1992. One aspect of the Fund's activities is to provide a subsidized loan facility for small and medium-sized enterprises (SMEs) that are creating new jobs.

Unemployment in the EU remains high in comparison to other OECD countries. In the USA unemployment stood at 6 per cent in 1994, while in Japan it was slightly below 3 per cent. The OECD countries as a whole recorded an average unemployment rate of just over 8 per cent in 1994. The comparatively high and persistent level of unemployment within the EU was, of course, addressed in the 1993 White Paper on growth, competitiveness and employment. According to that document, structural reforms in the operation of EU labour markets were necessary to ensure an increase in the 'employment content' of economic growth – that is, the numbers of new jobs created as a result of each additional percentage point of economic growth. The deep-seated problem confronting the EU is the high percentage of total EU unemployment which can be described as structural unemployment – that is, unemployment which is unlikely to disappear during the recovery phase of the economic cycle. In the main, this comprises long-term unemployed – those out of work for longer than one year – which constitutes 45 per cent of total unemployment in the EU. Long-term unemployment as a percentage of total unemployment is significantly higher in the EU than in other OECD countries.

The matter of structural unemployment was addressed at the Essen European Council. The Council called for action in five areas:

1. improving employment opportunities for the labour force by promoting investment in vocational training;
2. increasing the employment intensity of growth;
3. reducing non-wage costs sufficiently to ensure that there is a noticeable

effect on decisions concerning the taking-on of employees, and in particular unqualified personnel;
4. improving the effectiveness of labour market policy;
5. improving measures to help groups which are particularly hard hit by unemployment.

If unemployment in the EU is to fall significantly, the present cyclical upswing must be transformed into sustainable medium-term economic growth. For this to occur, much depends on the fiscal and monetary policy stance adopted by EU governments over the medium term, and on the extent to which domestic sources of aggregate demand are able to compensate for a likely decline in the strength of export demand as the USA economic upswing reaches maturity. In recent reports, both the OECD and the European Commission have highlighted the critical importance of the macroeconomic stance of governments at this early stage in the economic upswing (OECD, 1994; CEC, 1994). Both authorities have pointed to three major risks which might jeopardize the recovery:

1. a resurgence of inflation as the upswing gathers momentum;
2. a failure on the part of governments to restore 'sustainable' fiscal positions;
3. failure of the labour markets reforms to promote durable job creation.

Inflation remains an ever-present danger for the EU as the recovery gathers pace. Although the average rate of inflation across the EU fell slightly from 3.1 per cent in 1993 to 2.9 per cent in 1994, forecasts suggest this will rise again to 3.1 per cent in 1995. The decline in the rate of inflation since 1991 is attributable in part to the wage-restraining effects of the recession along with gains in productivity. Both factors combined to produce a fall in nominal unit labour costs during 1994. However, movements in both short- and long-term interest rates suggest that concerns about a rekindling of inflation persist. During the second half of 1994 this fear led most EU governments to increase, modestly, short-term interest rates as monetary policy was tightened in the face of what had become a well-founded economic recovery.

Nominal long-term interest rates, on the other hand, rose sharply across the EU during 1994, resulting in relatively high real long-term borrowing rates for investors. At least part of this increase in rates at the long end of the market reflected an increase in inflationary expectations – yields on government bonds generally being a good proxy for the state of long-run inflationary expectations. An immediate potential source of inflation in the recovering economies of the EU is a speedy emergence of labour shortages which would produce upward pressure on nominal wages. Although the level of unemployment is high, it is worth recalling that approximately one half of this is long-term unemployment and can be treated as structural. Consequently, that part of total unemployment is unlikely to exercise any significant control over inflationary pressures.

Beyond this, the upward movement in long rates may be reflecting investors' fears regarding the generally over-extended situation in the public finances of most EU Member States. The prevailing state of EU public finances raises two problems. First, governments with large outstanding fiscal liabilities find it ever more costly to take recourse to further borrowing on the capital markets in order to fund expenditure programmes. Consequently, there is pressure on long-term interest rates. During the economic upswing, of course, public finances are expected to recover because revenue accruing to government increases, whilst expenditure – especially transfer payments – falls. Nonetheless, although this may restore balance to the primary deficit – that is, annual net borrowing requirement – it may not in itself ensure a reduction in the level of the structural debt. Consequently, concern about the longer-term state of health of public finances remains. Second, when a government has a large outstanding structural debt, lenders may fear a recurrence of high rates of inflation. This is likely to occur should a government take recourse to monetizing the debt in an attempt to reduce it, thereby swelling the stock of money and generating inflation. It is worth emphasizing that expectation concerning the future rate of inflation is also a key input to the wage bargaining process. If expectations adjust to anticipate a higher future rate of inflation then this will impact adversely on current wage negotiations and, in so doing, jeopardize the recovery.

The matter of returning the public finances of many EU Member States to a 'sustainable' position is, therefore, widely regarded as a necessary condition if the current upswing is to be transformed into a well-founded economic recovery. Not only will a failure to correct what is, for many Member States, an unstable public finance situation continue to put pressure on long- term interest rates, it will impede governments in their attempts to lower short-term interest rates. For the EU as a whole, interest payments on outstanding public debt represent almost 11 per cent of total public expenditure. This constitutes a significant burden on current spending plans, a burden that is added to with all further increases in interest rates.

In addition to the immediate problems they create, high levels of public sector debt conflict with attempts to progress towards the fiscal targets (convergence criteria) established in the Treaty on European Union (TEU). Although it is increasingly unlikely that monetary union will be attempted before 1999 at the earliest, the continued absence of real progress being made in some Member States towards meeting the TEU targets raises further doubts about the viability of monetary union. The lack of credibility of the timetable when set in the context of the present macroeconomic policy mix could, in itself, generate disturbances in nominal economic variables such as exchange rates and interest rates.

Another key element in the package for sustained economic recovery is labour market reform. As the OECD makes clear, unemployment is relatively higher in Europe than in other OECD countries and the emergence of high and persistent unemployment has been accompanied by rising average real wages (OECD, 1994). Undoubtedly a large part of EU unemployment is explained by low job-finding, or hiring, rates:

> The rise in unemployment [in Europe] is fully explained by rises in the average duration of unemployment resulting from falls in outflow (including job-finding/hiring) rates ... (OECD, 1994 p. 23)

Consequently, the rate of unemployment falls only slowly following a recession. Further, as the time duration of unemployment increases so the probability of finding a new job diminishes. By such a process what begins as a cyclical rise in unemployment can, over time, become structural unemployment. As the OECD report acknowledges, the policy response to this problem is usually expressed in terms of including the following elements:

> reduced payroll taxes, lower minimum wages, more liberal policies towards part-time and fixed term contracting, and reforms to the bargaining system which allow wages to better reflect local and firm conditions.*(Ibid.)*

Further, for long-term unemployment, additional measures would involve, *inter alia*,

> reforms aimed at reducing workers' reservation wages, by reducing replacement rates of unemployment assistance programmes and by tightening access to disability programmes and retirement programmes. *(Ibid.)*

Together, it is argued, these types of reforms would produce a more flexible work force and this, in turn, would result in a shortening of the time duration of unemployment spells, thereby reducing the element of structural in total unemployment. Although the Commission's 1993 White Paper was not as radical in its proposals, it did contain some elements of the package of measures proposed by the OECD.

II. Main Economic Indicators

Economic Growth

The economic recovery that began early in 1994 gathered momentum during the second half of the year resulting in an annual rate of growth of GDP of 2.6 per cent. This contrasts with the fall in GDP of 0.4 per cent during 1994. The strength of the economic upturn was as unexpected as it was welcome, and owed much in its initial phase to the strength of demand for EU exports. As can be seen from Table 1, there was a wide variation in the strength of the recovery across the EU. The strongest growth was recorded by Denmark, Ireland and the UK. In the case

Table 1: Gross Domestic Product (annual average % change, 1988–96)

	1988	*1989*	*1990*	*1991*	*1992*	*1993*	*1994*	*1995**	*1996**
Belgium	5.0	3.6	3.2	1.8	1.4	–1.7	2.2	2.7	3.1
Denmark	1.2	0.6	2.0	1.2	1.2	1.4	4.8	3.2	3.0
France	4.5	4.3	2.5	0.7	1.4	–1.0	2.2	3.2	3.2
Germany	3.7	3.6	5.7	4.5	2.1	–1.2	2.5	3.0	3.4
Greece	4.1	3.5	–0.1	1.8	1.3	–0.5	0.4	1.1	1.7
Ireland	4.2	6.2	9.0	2.6	4.8	4.0	6.0	5.6	5.3
Italy	4.1	2.9	2.1	1.3	0.9	–0.7	2.4	3.0	3.2
Luxembourg	5.7	6.7	3.2	3.1	1.9	0.3	2.3	3.0	3.2
Netherlands	2.6	4.7	4.1	2.1	1.4	0.3	2.3	3.2	3.3
Portugal	3.9	5.2	4.4	2.1	1.1	–1.2	1.1	3.0	3.2
Spain	5.2	4.7	3.6	2.2	0.8	–1.1	2.2	2.8	3.2
United Kingdom	5.0	2.2	0.4	–2.2	–0.5	2.0	3.8	2.7	2.8
EUR12	4.2	3.5	3.0	1.4	1.1	–0.4	2.6	2.9	3.2

Source: OECD.

* Forecast.

of the UK, which emerged from recession ahead of the other EU countries, 1994 is expected to record the strongest growth in the recovery phase. For the remainder of the EU, the pace of recovery is expected to quicken through 1995 before moderating somewhat during 1996. The slowest growth during 1994 was recorded by Greece and Portugal.

As previously noted, extra-EU exports initially fuelled the recovery. This is attributable to three factors: first, the strength of demand within the EU's major trading partners, especially the USA; second, the increase in the competitiveness of EU exports due to a combination of moderate wage increases and higher productivity; and third, the real depreciation of the EU currencies of more than 15 per cent over the period August 1992 to February 1994. There is now firm evidence that domestic components of aggregate demand are growing quickly. Gross investment increased by around 2.5 per cent in 1994 and is forecast to grow to around 6 per cent in both 1995 and 1996. Private consumption increased less forcefully by around 1.5 per cent in 1994 and is expected to grow by 2 per cent and 2.5 per cent in 1995 and 1996 respectively. Of course, both investment and private consumption are sensitive with respect to interest rates. Consequently, any upward pressure on either short- or long-term interest rates might well interfere with the strength of the recovery.

Table 2: Unemployment (as % of the Civilian Labour Force, 1988–96)

	1988	*1989*	*1990*	*1991*	*1992*	*1993*	*1994*	*1995**	*1996**
Belgium	10.2	8.6	7.6	7.5	8.2	9.4	10.0	9.8	9.3
Denmark	6.4	7.7	8.1	8.9	9.5	10.3	10.2	9.0	8.0
France	9.9	9.4	9.0	9.5	10.0	10.8	11.3	11.0	10.6
Germany	6.3	5.6	4.8	5.8	6.8	7.0	7.3	7.0	6.4
Greece	7.7	7.5	7.0	7.2	7.5	9.7	10.2	10.6	10.8
Ireland	17.3	15.7	14.5	16.2	17.8	18.4	17.7	16.8	15.7
Italy	10.9	10.9	10.0	10.1	10.3	11.1	11.8	11.1	10.4
Luxembourg	2.0	1.8	1.7	1.6	1.9	2.6	3.3	3.2	3.1
Netherlands	9.3	8.4	7.5	7.1	7.2	8.8	10.0	9.8	9.4
Portugal	5.7	5.0	4.6	4.0	3.9	5.1	6.1	6.0	5.6
Spain	19.3	17.1	16.2	16.4	18.2	21.8	22.4	21.9	21.2
United Kingdom	8.5	7.1	7.0	8.9	10.2	10.4	9.4	8.5	7.6
EUR12	9.8	8.9	8.3	8.9	9.7	10.6	10.9	10.4	9.8

Source: CEC.

* Forecast.

Employment and Unemployment

Despite the gathering pace of economic recovery, unemployment in the EU continued to rise throughout 1994, closing the year at just under 11 per cent. Table 2 shows a considerable variation in rates of unemployment across the EU. The poorest performing countries were Spain, Ireland and Italy, although unemployment in France also remained above the EU average. Excepting Luxembourg, the best performing EU countries were Germany, Portugal and the UK. Unemployment is expected to decline slowly over the next two years, averaging just under 10 per cent by 1996. What is clear from Table 2 is that the fall in the average rate of unemployment is spread unevenly across the EU. Unemployment is forecast to fall significantly in the UK, and to a lesser extent in Italy and Germany. Elsewhere, however, the rate of unemployment is expected to fall only slightly. Only part of this discrepancy can be attributed to demographic factors.

Inflation

The 1991–93 period of recession helped reduce the average rate of inflation in the EU from 5.4 per cent to 3.7 per cent. In 1994 inflation was further squeezed,

Table 3: Inflation (GDP Deflator, % Change on Preceding Year, 1990–96)

	1990	*1991*	*1992*	*1993*	*1994*	*1995**	*1996**
Belgium	3.1	2.7	3.4	4.4	2.1	2.3	2.4
Denmark	2.7	2.5	2.0	1.7	1.8	2.4	2.7
France	3.1	3.1	2.3	2.3	1.3	1.8	1.8
Germany	3.2	3.9	5.5	3.9	2.3	2.0	2.2
Greece	21.1	18.4	14.2	13.6	11.1	9.5	6.9
Ireland	–1.7	1.1	1.3	3.6	2.5	2.5	2.6
Italy	7.6	7.7	4.5	4.4	3.1	2.9	3.4
Luxembourg	3.0	3.0	4.5	2.5	2.8	2.7	2.9
Netherlands	2.3	2.8	2.5	1.6	1.9	1.9	2.2
Portugal	14.3	14.1	13.5	6.4	4.6	4.3	3.9
Spain	7.4	7.0	6.5	4.5	4.0	3.6	2.9
United Kingdom	6.4	6.5	4.3	3.4	2.2	2.3	2.6
EUR12	5.3	5.4	4.6	3.7	2.5	2.5	2.6

Source: OECD.
* Forecast.

with the annual rate of inflation declining to 2.5 per cent. The rate is not expected to increase over the next two years.

In addition to a fall in the rate of inflation, the period 1991–94 saw a steady convergence in rates of inflation between Member States. Although inflation remains a serious problem in Greece and, to a much lesser extent, Portugal, elsewhere there has been a steady convergence around the average for the EU as a whole. Forecasts show that inflation is likely to come down sharply in Greece over the next two years and that even greater convergence around the EU average is to be expected. This continuation in the trend towards lower inflation is all the more important occurring as it has done against a background of real exchange rate depreciation.

This positive picture with respect to price changes reflects two main factors. First, the wage-moderation legacy of the recession is still apparent and is likely to remain as long as the positive output gap between potential and actual output persists. Second, the appreciation of EU currencies against the US dollar has helped keep down the price of imported products. To the extent that expectations of future inflation can be kept low, there is no reason why the wage moderation 'learned' during the recession should not continue. However, there is always a risk that pay demands increase in line with the economic recovery as labour seeks to 'catch-up' what is perceived to be real wage erosion.

Table 4: General Government Financial Balances, Surplus (+) or Deficit (–) as % of Nominal GDP, 1990–96

	1990	*1991*	*1992*	*1993*	*1994*	*1995**	*1996**
Belgium	–5.4	–6.5	–6.7	–6.6	–5.3	–4.6	–4.1
Denmark	–1.5	–2.1	–2.6	–4.4	–4.2	–3.0	–2.2
France	–1.6	–2.2	–3.9	–5.8	–5.7	–5.0	–4.0
Germany	–2.0	–3.3	–2.9	–3.3	–2.7	–2.4	–1.8
Greece	–13.9	–13.0	–11.8	–13.5	–13.1	–11.6	–10.1
Ireland	–2.2	–2.1	–2.2	–2.4	–2.3	–2.0	–2.0
Italy	–10.9	–10.2	–9.5	–9.6	–9.7	–9.1	–7.8
Luxembourg	n/a	n/a	n/a	n/a	1.3	1.6	2.0
Netherlands	–5.1	–2.8	–3.8	–3.3	–3.8	–3.6	–2.9
Portugal	–5.4	–6.1	–3.8	–8.0	–7.1	–6.6	–5.5
Spain	–4.1	–4.9	–4.2	–7.5	–6.8	–6.1	–5.2
United Kingdom	–1.2	–2.7	–6.2	–7.7	–6.8	–4.7	–3.2
EUR12	n/a	n/a	n/a	n/a	–5.6	–4.7	–3.9

Source: OECD
* Forecast

Table 5: Gross Public Debt as % of Nominal GDP, 1990–96

	1990	*1991*	*1992*	*1993*	*1994*	*1995**	*1996**
Belgium	130.8	132.9	133.8	138.9	138.7	136.7	134.0
Denmark	59.6	64.6	68.8	79.6	81.7	82.8	83.1
France	35.4	35.8	39.6	45.8	49.5	52.4	53.8
Germany	43.8	41.5	44.1	48.1	51.1	59.1	58.3
Greece	82.6	86.1	92.3	115.3	118.8	119.3	119.4
Ireland	96.8	96.2	93.4	96.1	91.5	87.0	83.1
Italy	9.9	101.3	108.4	118.6	122.4	125.0	125.3
Luxembourg	5.4	4.9	6.1	7.8	9.2	9.8	9.9
Netherlands	78.8	78.9	79.9	81.4	80.6	81.5	81.4
Portugal	77.3	79.2	70.4	76.9	80.5	82.3	83.0
Spain	45.1	45.9	48.3	59.8	64.3	67.5	69.7
United Kingdom	n/a	35.6	41.8	48.4	53.0	55.2	55.3
EUR12	61.2	57.0	60.8	66.1	68.8	72.7	73.2

Source: OECD, CEC.
* Forecast.

Public Finance

As the economic recovery gathers pace, the state of public finances across the EU is expected to improve. Already in 1994 there was some sign of this, although no real improvement can be expected until the full effects of the upswing filter through to government revenues and expenditures. The persistence of unemployment despite economic recovery provides a limit to the degree to which both the primary and the structural deficits will improve.

The process of fiscal consolidation is proving difficult to achieve for the EU as a whole. As shown in Table 4, by 1996 the primary deficit for the EU will still be relatively high at 4 per cent of GDP, although this is lower than the 1994 level of 5.6 per cent. The problem appears to lie in the unwillingness on the part of some Member States to introduce consolidation programmes. This is evidenced by the fact that for many EU Member States the forecast improvement in the primary budget balance is expected to result from the revenue-increasing and expenditure-saving effects of the economic recovery and not, as would seem to be warranted, from a convergence programme designed to reduce long-term debt liabilities. Although Greece and Italy stand out as being the least effective in reducing the primary deficit, concerns also surround the situation in France and Spain.

Changes in the structural debt as a percentage of GDP of EU governments are shown in Table 5. Three countries stand out in terms of the extent of structural debt in terms of annual GDP – Belgium, Greece and Italy. However, many other countries have large debt to GDP ratios and there is little sign that these are set to fall in the medium term. This makes the public finances in these countries highly vulnerable to an increase in interest rates.

It is clear from Tables 4 and 5 that there is no rapid movement across the Union as a whole to fulfil the TEU convergence criteria.

III. Economic Developments in the Member States

Germany

The German economy recovered strongly during 1994, initially on the basis of increased exports but thereafter assisted by higher domestic activity, particularly in the construction industries. The five eastern Länder enjoyed buoyant growth in 1994, with GDP rising by 9 per cent and fixed investment by 17 per cent for the year as a whole (this compares with a German average of 2.5 per cent and 5.4 per cent respectively). This makes the new Länder the fastest growing area within Germany. However, unemployment in the new Länder, at 15 per cent, remains well above the national average of 7.3 per cent. Moreover, domestic demand in the new Länder exceeds GDP by two-thirds, with the difference being accounted for by fiscal transfers which amounted to more than 4 per cent of German GDP in 1994 and which mainly went to support private consumption.

In the country as a whole, unit labour costs also fell in 1994 through a combination of wage moderation and gains to labour productivity, generating higher returns to investors. Of particular significance is the deceleration in the speed at which wages in the eastern Länder are catching up with their western counterparts. Consequently, eastern unit labour costs are falling more rapidly than those in the west of the country. All of this contributes to the process of intra-German convergence.

Macroeconomic policy in Germany is cautious. The rate of growth of the money supply slowed down towards the end of the year, increasing the likelihood of the target of M3 growth of 4–6 per cent for the year as a whole being achieved. Monetary conditions eased slightly in 1994, with interest rates falling between February and May, although from then until the end of the year the discount rate and the Lombard rate remained at 4.5 per cent and 6 per cent respectively. The strength of the economic recovery argued against any further cuts in long-term interest rates, whilst the unsteady nature of developments at the long-term (bond) end of the market called for stability in short-term rates. Fiscal policy in Germany remains geared to achieving the Maastricht convergence criteria, although in this the Government is handicapped by the costs of unification. However, the primary deficit as a percentage of GDP fell from –3.3 per cent in 1993 to –2.7 per cent in 1994. The outstanding stock of debt, however, increased as a percentage of GDP, largely because of the Government taking on board all unification-related debt. That ratio is expected to continue to increase over the medium term.

France

The recession of 1992–93 was the deepest in the post-war period. However, recovery gathered momentum through 1994 and produced a 2.2 per cent rise in GDP for the year as a whole. Unemployment remains high in France at 11.3 per cent despite the increase in domestic demand and exports during the year.

Monetary conditions in France, as elsewhere, eased during the first half of the year, with the intervention rate being cut in small steps from 6.2 per cent at the beginning of the year to 5 per cent in July, after which it remained unchanged. In common with developments elsewhere, long-term interest rates in France rose quite sharply in 1994.

Fiscal policy in France is geared to the convergence criteria. The 1995 budget, adopted in September 1994, plans to cut the central government budget deficit by a combination of constraining the rise in expenditure to the rate of inflation and increases in taxation amounting to 0.2 per cent of GDP. Measures to cut the level of unemployment are a main priority of French policy. In 1994 some FF9 billion went towards reducing employers' social security contributions in respect of those on low wages. This is budgeted to rise to FF17.5 billion in 1995. Finally, it is worth recording that on 1 January 1994 the Banque de France became officially independent.

Italy

After the fall in GDP in 1993, output grew by 2.4 per cent in 1994 on the basis of high export demand and a rapidly recovering level of domestic demand. At the same time, the contractual framework governing wage increases remained in place, producing a significant lowering of unit labour costs and rising industrial profitability leading, in turn, to a recovery of investment. These trends also produced a marked reduction in the rate of inflation which, in 1994, fell to just over 3 per cent – the first time in over 20 years in which inflation has dipped below 4 per cent. Unemployment in Italy remained high in 1994, at almost 12 per cent, leading the Government to introduce a package of measures to promote employment in June.

Monetary policy was slackened somewhat during 1994. Initially the discount rate was lowered from 8 per cent in February to 7 per cent in May, only to be increased to 7.5 per cent in August. In large measure, the increase in interest rates was required to stem an outflow of capital which reflected deep-seated uncertainties concerning Italy's fiscal position. However, despite the rise in the discount rate, which was the first since the lira's exit from the Exchange Rate Mechanism in August 1992, the lira exchange rate fell to an historical low in August, fuelling fears of a revival of inflationary pressures. The fiscal situation in Italy remains highly problematic, with the primary deficit equal to 9.7 per cent of GDP and the structural deficit 122 per cent of GDP. In July 1994, the Government adopted a medium-term financial and economic plan which set out the general public finance objectives for the following three years. This envisaged a cut in the state budget deficit through a combination of higher revenues and expenditure cuts, with further measures planned for 1996 and 1997.

United Kingdom

The economic recovery in the UK began over a year earlier than elsewhere in the EU. In 1994, GDP grew by 3.8 per cent, although – unlike other EU countries – growth is forecast to fall to somewhat lower rates in 1995 and 1996. With the recovery in the EU taking hold in 1994, UK exports provided an important source of demand to complement the initially very strong growth in private consumption. However, private consumption moderated through the course of 1994 as the large tax increases announced in the 1993 budget began to have their impact. Significantly for the UK, the increase in economic activity was not accompanied by a revival of inflationary pressures. Indeed, inflation dropped to a 27-year low of 2 per cent in September, testifying to continued moderation in wage negotiations. There is now a growing sense that the labour market reforms that occurred throughout the 1980s are being reflected in a more flexible labour force and a less inflation-prone economy.

Both fiscal and monetary policies remained relatively tight during 1994. Fiscal policy was particularly restrictive as the measures designed to produce further fiscal consolidation announced in 1993 took effect. The Bank of England base rate, which was lowered to 5.25 per cent in February, was increased by 50 basis points to 5.75 per cent in September, reflecting Government concerns that the economy was overheating and that inflationary expectations were reviving. In December, the base rate was increased by a further one-half percentage point to end the year at 6.25 per cent. The concern about a revival in inflation was manifest in the behaviour of long-term interest rates which rose strongly throughout the course of 1994, moving from 6.2 per cent in January to 8.7 per cent in November. In November the Chancellor presented the budget which forecast a further reduction in the primary deficit such that the 3 per cent Maastricht criterion is expected to be met during the course of the 1995–96 financial year.

Significant Developments in Other Member States

Spain. A strong recovery in Spain ensued through 1994 on the basis of higher exports, as the benefits of three devaluations of the peseta in 1992–93 impacted on export competitiveness. Unemployment remained the single largest problem for the economy, although real wages appeared to be showing greater resistance in Spain than elsewhere. The relatively high rate of inflation in 1994 kept pressures on long-term interest rates, which rose to 11 per cent towards the end of the year. Short-term rates fell only slightly during 1994, in part explained by the continuing pressure on the peseta, and ended the year at 7.35 per cent compared to the 8 per cent at which the discount rate began 1994. In July the Government approved the revision of the convergence programme for the period 1994–97, according to which the general budget deficit is budgeted to fall from 6.7 per cent of GDP in 1994 to 5.9 per cent in 1995, 4.4 per cent in 1996, and reaching 3 per cent by 1997.

Belgium. Real GDP grew by 2.2 per cent in 1994 after the severe recession of the previous two years. As elsewhere, this upswing was built upon increased export demand, with domestic components of demand showing only a hesitant recovery during the second half of the year. Interest rates fell throughout the course of 1994 in a series of small steps. In July, the Government presented the 1995 budget which was framed in accordance with the convergence programme put in place in 1992, which aimed to reduce the budget deficit to 3 per cent of GDP by 1996. Belgium records the highest ratio of public debt to GDP anywhere in the EU (an estimated 139 per cent in 1994) although only in Belgium is this ratio forecast to decline in 1995 and 1996.

The Netherlands. Output growth of 2.3 per cent was recorded in 1994 as exports increased in response to the economic recovery in neighbouring countries. The path of interest rate policy followed closely that set in Germany, the Dutch guilder remaining the only currency within the ERM that observed the +/–2.25 per cent band of fluctuation with respect to the Deutschmark.

Ireland. This was the fastest growing economy in the EU during 1994, with GDP increasing by some 6 per cent. This expansion was the result of an easing in monetary policy and a lower income tax burden. The strong growth was also reflected in an improvement in Ireland's public finances, with the primary deficit being 2.3 per cent of GDP for the year and the ratio of public debt to GDP falling to around 87 per cent. Interest rates were reduced gradually through 1994.

Greece. Output in Greece recovered only slightly in 1994, being 0.4 per cent higher than the previous year. Unemployment continued to rise, although real wage growth remained strong – running at around 13 per cent for the year. Following the removal of restrictions on short-term capital movements in May, and in the light of the severe distortion in Greek public finances, a major speculative attack was launched on the drachma. This led to a significant reduction in foreign reserves and increases in short-term interest rates. As the crisis subsided, interest rates again were lowered, with the rediscount rate and the Lombard rate ending the year at 20.5 per cent and 24 per cent respectively.

Denmark. The Danish economy recovered strongly in 1994 with GDP rising by almost 5 per cent over the 1993 level. Indeed, the pace of recovery caused some concern that the economy may be overheating, although for the year the rate of inflation was below 2 per cent. Monetary conditions were eased only slightly during 1994, with the discount rate, which began the year at 6 per cent (the lowest rate for 25 years) reaching 5 per cent by May and not being adjusted thereafter. In November, the Government published a revised convergence programme which envisaged a step-by-step reduction in net government borrowing in order that the TEU target of 3 per cent of GDP be met by 1995.

Portugal. As elsewhere in the EU, the 1.1 per cent rise in Portuguese GDP in 1994 was mainly the result of strong export demand. Domestic demand remained low during the year, particularly consumer spending. High unemployment continued to act as a brake on nominal wage growth, facilitating a fall in inflation to 4.6 per cent, the lowest recorded for 25 years. Monetary conditions were eased as the Bank of Portugal lowered key rates, although stability of the escudo within the ERM remains a medium-term policy objective for the Government.

Luxembourg. Economic recovery continued rapidly in 1994, with GDP growing by 2.3 per cent. Once more, although the economic recovery was initially fuelled by exports, increasingly through the course of 1994 domestic components of demand gained in importance. The fiscal situation in Luxembourg remains the healthiest of all EU Member States.

References

Commission of the European Communities (1994) *1995 Annual Economic Report*, COM (94) 615 (Brussels: CEC).

OECD (1994) *OECD Economic Outlook*, No. 56, December (OECD: Paris)

Journal of Common Market Studies
Volume 33, Annual Review
August 1995

Developments in the Member States

BRIGID LAFFAN
University College Dublin

I. Introduction

This section of the *Annual Review* assesses the main developments in the Member States that had implications for the EU and the European issues that reverberated in the domestic debates on integration. Two developments had particular significance in 1994. First, this was a bumper year of elections in the Union's largest state, Germany. Second, the debate on the 1996 Intergovernmental Conference (IGC), with particular emphasis on 'differentiated integration', surfaced as different actors began to flesh out their policies and priorities.

Bilateral relations loomed large in 1994. Some strain was evident in Franco-German relations in the first half of the year when the French Ambassador to Bonn, François Scheer, complained to the media that Klaus Kinkel, the German Foreign Minister, had been too active during the EFTA accession negotiations. Apparently, the French objected to the fact that Kinkel set up a series of working parties during the Greek Presidency to try to accelerate the accession negotiations. Despite this tiff in March, both France and Germany proclaimed a joint approach to their successive Presidencies in 1994 and 1995. Anglo-French relations appeared to strengthen in the latter half of 1994 when François Mitterrand and John Major held a joint summit in Paris. Both leaders agreed to further enhance defence co-operation.

II. Elections and their Consequences

Europe endured a period of intense electioneering in 1994. Italy held a national election under its new electoral laws, the Netherlands voted in May, all Member States had European elections in June, Luxembourg voted in June, the Danes voted in August, and Germany had no fewer than 19 elections.

Germany

Germany's marathon year of elections began with the first of a series of state elections in Lower Saxony in March, included an electoral college vote for a new President in May, saw a series of local polls, and ended with national elections to the Bundestag in October. At the outset, it appeared as if Chancellor Kohl might lose office when the Social Democrats won the poll in Lower Saxony. At this stage, the Chancellor had a popularity rating of 26 per cent in contrast to 35 per cent for his SDP rival, Rudolf Scharping. The central issue in the campaign was whether or not the Germans wanted a change of government and a new Chancellor after 12 years of Kohl. By the summer Chancellor Kohl had turned the electoral tide, with Germany coming out of recession and with Kohl exploiting his role as an international statesman.

The Bundestag election on 16 October returned the centrist government of Chancellor Kohl to office for another four years, albeit with a reduced majority (See Table 1 for a summary of the election results). The ruling coalition includes his own party the Christian Democratic Union (CDU), its Bavarian sister party the Christian Social Party (CSU) and the Free Democratic Party (FDP). In total

Table 1: German General Election, October 1994

	Percentage of Vote		*Seats*	
Party	*1994*	*1990*	*1994*	*1990*
CDU	34.2	36.7	244	268
CSU	7.3	7.1	50	51
FDP (Liberals)	6.9	11.0	47	79
SPD	36.4	33.5	252	239
Greens	7.3	3.9	49	–
PDS	4.4	2.4	30	17
Republikaner	1.9	2.1	0	–
Alliance 90	–	1.2	–	8
Others	1.6	2.1	0	0
Totals	100	100	672	662

Source: Keesings, October 1994, p. 40237.

the coalition won 341 seats in the Bundestag. The opposition Social Democrats and the Greens emerged with 301 seats. The Party of Democratic Socialism (PDS), the former East German Communist Party, took 30 seats as it won three districts outright in the former East Germany. The far-right Republikaner were down to just 1.2 per cent of the vote. The election left Klaus Kinkel's FDP in a weakened position as it lost 30 seats and ceded its status as the third largest party in the Bundestag to the Greens. Chancellor Kohl's governing majority was reduced to just ten seats.

The outcome of the election appeared to offer political continuity with Chancellor Kohl, who had dominated Germany's European policy for 12 years, set to continue in office. However, the outcome of the election means that the ruling coalition will have to govern with a wafer-thin majority at a time when the Liberals are in crisis. This may make them unreliable coalition partners as they need to carve out an independent profile. Moreover, the Bundestag, the upper house, which represents the governments of the Länder, is controlled by the opposition Social Democrats. Consequently, the Government will have to work closely with the Opposition to get its programme through as the German upper house is more powerful than other second chambers in Europe. The consensual nature of German politics suggests that the Government will arrive at a *modus vivendi* with the Opposition. A possible warning for the future was seen in the success of the PDS in east Germany, whose success highlights the difficulties facing Germany as it tries to cement political unification with social unity. Many former East Germans are clearly dissatisfied with the economic and social conditions of post-unification Germany.

The guidelines agreed by the victorious coalition partners for Germany's European policy emphasize the 'consolidation of the European Union by the consistent application of the EU treaty and the further development of the EU, both internally and externally' (Coalition Agreement, 1994). Two tasks are given priority, namely stabilizing the reform in central and eastern Europe and safeguarding Europe's future as a business environment. Chancellor Kohl himself remains deeply and passionately committed to the process of European integration. In the aftermath of the election, he stated that:

> If the Germans don't realise now that German unity as a historical event will be wasted if we don't press ahead in parallel with European Unity, then there is no hope for the Germans. (*European*, 21 October 1994, p.10)

He wants to ensure that a new political generation without personal memories of the war will not dilute the achievements of European integration and Germany's commitment to Europe. Chancellor Kohl remains equally committed to a widening and a deepening of the Union. The challenge he faces is to convince both his own people and the other Member States of the benefits of his vision of the Union. The German debate on the future of integration was launched by the joint CDU/CSU paper which was published in September (see below).

Italy

The travails of the Italian political system continued in 1994. In March, Italian voters elected their 54th government since the war. At the outset, it appeared as if the Left might finally come in from the wilderness to take office with Achille Occhetto, leader of the Party of the Democratic Left (PDL, the former Communist Party), ahead in the polls and looking set to lead a progressive coalition. Then in January, Silvio Berlusconi, director of Italy's second largest company, Fininvest, decided to enter politics to provide a focus for the centre-right in the March election. Without any political infrastructure at the outset, Berlusconi managed in just three months to launch a political movement, Forza Italia, that was capable of challenging for and taking power. Berlusconi used his business empire to launch a movement based on the model of a football supporters' club backed up by the expertise of his management and his control over a number of television channels. In the lead-up to the election Berlusconi brokered an election alliance with Umberto Bossi of the Northern League and Fianfranco Fini of the MSI (a neo-fascist party rebaptized as the Alleanza Nazionale). They were opposed by the 'Progressive Alliance' led by Occhetto and the 'Pact for Italy' led by Minno Martinazzoli, leader of the remnants of the once powerful Christian Democrats. The traditional tripolar structure of Italian party politics, with a dominant centre, was transformed into a bipolar one with a strong right opposing a strong left.

The newly formed Forza Italia, buttressed by Berlusconi's control over three television channels, and its election partners secured a landslide election victory by taking 366 seats (42.9 per cent vote) in the lower house and 156 seats (42 per cent) in the upper house. The Progressive Alliance won 213 seats (34.4 per cent) and the once-powerful centre took only 46 seats (15.7 per cent) in the lower house. Berlusconi thus became Prime Minister, but internal tensions between the three successful parties became evident during the process of government formation and continued throughout the life of Berlusconi's administration. The tensions related to:

- the internal heterogeneity of the coalition: the Northern League wanted to pursue a federalist agenda and to reduce state intervention in the economy, whereas the Alleanza Nazionale, which polled strongly in the south, wanted a continuation of interventionist policies and the flow of budgetary resources to the South;

- Umberto Bossi, leader of the Northern League, was clearly unhappy about association with the neo-fascist Alleanza Nazionale whom he had labelled as 'reactionary fascists';
- there was also considerable tension between Berlusconi and Bossi, with the latter fearing that Forza Italia might try to capitalize on the fact that its supporters had been instrumental in getting most Northern League deputies elected.

The new Italian Government was thus internally divided, with a Prime Minister who had no political experience. Berlusconi's authority was further weakened when it became apparent that the judiciary was investigating possible links between his business empire and corruption scandals. From July onwards, the Government lurched from crisis to crisis and finally fell in December when Umberto Bossi decided to withdraw his support and table a vote of no confidence in the Prime Minister.

The short-lived Government had no time to develop a clear profile on European policy, beset as it was by internal division and domestic problems. Berlusconi did not display the usual rhetorical commitment to federalism characteristic of Italian politicians, and indeed was said to have admired Margaret Thatcher's approach to Europe. Moreover, the Government's failure to tackle Italy's debt and deficit problems made progress towards the Maastricht convergence criteria a tattered goal and left the lira at a historic low against the Deutschmark. The depth of Italy's economic and political problems led to Italy being the only founder Member State which was excluded from the 'hard core' defined in the German CDU/CSU paper of September.

Ministers and officials from a number of EU Member States were less than sanguine about the involvement of neo-fascist ministers in the Italian Government. There were a number of tense Council of Ministers meetings where Dutch and Belgian ministers were unwilling to show the usual welcome to new ministers by refusing to shake hands and by issuing statements about the continuing threat of fascism in Europe.

National Elections in the Netherlands, Luxembourg and Denmark

In May, the ruling Dutch centre-left coalition comprising the Christian Democratic Appeal (CDA) and the Labour Party (PvdA) had to face the electorate. Both parties experienced sizeable losses of 20 seats and 12 seats respectively. The Liberal Party, known as the People's Party for Freedom and Democracy (VVD) and the left-of-centre Democrats 66 (D66) made major gains, with the former winning an extra nine seats and D66 gaining an additional 12 seats. Pensioners' parties won a total of six seats, and the far-right Centre Democrats gained only two seats – which was less than expected. The pre-election announcement by the Prime Minister Ruud Lubbers that he was retiring from Dutch politics, in his unsuccessful bid to become President of the Commission, weakened the CDA.

Negotiations on the formation of a new coalition took until mid-August when a new Government known as the 'purple coalition', because of the inclusion of the left-wing D66 and the right-wing VVD, took office. The former Finance Minister, Wim Kok of the Labour Party, assumed leadership of the three-party coalition, with 92 seats against 58 for the opposition. Thus for the first time since the introduction of universal suffrage, the Christian Democrats are not part of the governing coalition in Holland. The change in government is not likely to lead to any major change in Dutch European policy because 'Europe' is a consensus issue in Dutch politics. That said, the need for the new coalition government to find considerable savings in the public budget has led to renewed attention to Dutch contributions to the EU budget.

In contrast to many European states, the stable nature of politics in Luxembourg was underlined by the general election in June, when the two largest parties, in coalition since 1984, – the Christian Social People's Party (CSV/PCS) and the Socialist Workers' Party (LSAP/POSL) – each lost one seat, but managed to retain a comfortable majority with 38 seats in the 60-strong Parliament. Continuity rather than change is likely to mark Luxembourg's European policy.

In August, Denmark went to the polls in an election that returned the coalition Government of Poul Nyrup Rasmussen to power, albeit with a reduced majority. Rasmussen's Social Democrats lost seven seats, whereas the opposition Liberals (V) led by Uffe Ellemann-Jensen gained an additional 13 seats. For the first time, the anti-European Union Unity list gained representation in the Folketing with six seats. As the new Government was in a minority (76 of 179 seats), it would be dependent on support from the Socialist People's Party, which opposed the Treaty on European Union (TEU) in the first Danish referendum, and the Unity List, which is opposed to any further development of the political nature of the EU. Thus the current Danish Government is likely to adopt a very restricted and minimalist approach to the 1996 IGC.

III. Political Change in Other Member States

A number of Member State Governments experienced a loss of political authority during the course of the year.

Spain

Following Felipe Gonzalez's unexpected electoral victory in 1993, his Government had a difficult year as it faced charges of financial corruption and the problems of managing the delicate relationship with the regional parties on which the Madrid Government is dependent. Allegations of corruption spread to include senior Ministers in the Socialist Party, including the Prime Minister himself. The Government was most vulnerable when faced with allegations that high-ranking security chiefs, with the knowledge of Cabinet Ministers, sanctioned a dirty war campaign against Basque terrorists in the south of France between 1986 and 1989. The succession of scandals weakened the authority of both the Government and the Prime Minister, with Gonzalez looking for a time as if he might be forced from office. The Catalan CiU (Catalan Nationalist Party), however, agreed to support the Government until after the Spanish Presidency of the Union in the latter half of 1995, thus securing the Government for one more year.

The power of the CiU was apparent during 1994. It announced in February that its continued support for the Government was dependent on a further devolution of power to the 17 Autonomous Communities. This led, in September, to the Senate unanimously approving a plan to transform the upper house into a chamber representing the Autonomous Communities. This measure is accompanied by adjustments in the system of regional spending, a greater role for the regions in formulating EU policy, and further reform of the civil service. The dependence of the Government on Jordi Pujol, President of the regional government in Catalonia, gives the regions considerable leverage over Madrid.

United Kingdom

The question of 'Europe' and British policy on the future development of the Union continued to bedevil the Conservative Government during 1994. The Prime Minister, John Major, faced repeated challenges on the issue from within the ranks of the Conservative Party, with even his Cabinet appearing deeply divided on most European issues. Moreover, the UK was in conflict with its partners in the Union on two major questions during the year:

- in March the UK Government clashed with its partners over qualified majority voting in an enlarged Union when Major resisted changes to the number of votes needed for a qualified majority despite the accession of new members;
- at the Corfu European Council, the UK objected to the appointment of Jean-Luc Dehaene, the Belgian Prime Minister, as successor to Jacques Delors as Commission President, because he was allegedly too federalist.

In the Cabinet and in Europe, the Foreign Minister, Douglas Hurd, fought to limit the impact of division on the UK's standing with its partners. He had the support of such key Cabinet figures as Trade and Industry Minister, Michael Heseltine, and Chancellor Kenneth Clarke, but met with some resistance from such as Michael Portillo, Michael Howard and Peter Lilley.

John Major tried to straddle the two wings of the Cabinet and the Party, sometimes moving to support the Eurosceptics and then back to the centre. His position was further weakened in December when he had to make the European Union Finance Bill an issue of confidence. The Prime Minister threatened a general election if the Commons failed to pass the bill which dealt with the UK's increased contributions to the EU budget arising from the financial deal brokered by Major himself at Edinburgh in 1992. In the event, nine MPs voted against the Government and were suspended from the parliamentary party, meaning that the Prime Minister did not technically have an overall majority in the House of Commons.

The prospect of an election during the latter half of 1996 or, at the latest in the spring of 1997, adds to the political complications surrounding the 1996 IGC.

Ireland

In November the Fianna Fáil/ Labour Party coalition collapsed because of a dispute concerning the appointment of the President of the High Court. Relations between the Prime Minister, Albert Reynolds, and the Foreign Minister, Dick Spring, deteriorated to the point that the Labour Party under Spring withdrew from Government. Fianna Fáil went into Opposition and was replaced by a three-party coalition consisting of Fine Gael, the Labour Party and Democratic Left. Both Labour and the Democratic Left have in the past expressed major reservations about Ireland's involvement in defence arrangements which makes the 1996 IGC highly sensitive for the newly constituted Government.

IV. Institutional Developments and Plans for 1996

National Parliaments

As part of the TEU ratification process, the French Government inserted a new Article (88.4) in the French Constitution which gave the National Assembly and the Senate the right to pass resolutions on legislative proposals from the Commission. In July 1994 there were two important, although somewhat contradictory developments concerning the French Parliament's new powers. First, the Prime Minister Edouard Balladur, in a circular to ministers and civil servants, gave a commitment that French negotiators would check whether the French Parliament intended to pass a resolution on a Commission proposal due for debate at a Council meeting, and if so, the French negotiators would enter a scrutiny reservation pending a resolution from the Assembly or the Senate. Traditionally, French Governments have been largely unfettered in their definition of French policy and interests in the Union's governance structures. Second, the *Conseil d'Etat* gave a very narrow interpretation of what was encompassed by the Article 88.4 provision. It ruled that the new article included legislative acts of the Community but excluded items under pillars two and three of the TEU and all major policy documents that would not lead to specific legislative proposals. This judgment severely limits the new found power of the French Parliament.

Transparency and Openness

In February, the Dutch government began proceedings against the Council of Ministers in the European Court of Justice in an attempt to get the Council's internal regulations on secrecy overturned. This followed a decision by the Council in December 1993 that it had a right to refuse information if it considered the request 'manifestly unreasonable, which is to say a request that could be contrary to the efficiency and good order of the institution'. This blanket refusal clause was inserted at the behest of the UK, Belgium, Germany and Portugal, but opposed by the Netherlands, Denmark and Greece. The Dutch Government action is the first time that a Member State has taken an institution to the Court without having a direct national interest in the issue.

Proposals for 1996

The process of constitution-building and Treaty change in the Union has started to build towards the opening of the 1996 IGC. A number of major proposals or projects for constitutional change appeared in the latter half of 1994. These were:

- CDU/CSU paper (published on 1 September) entitled 'Reflections on European Policy', produced by a group including Wolfgang Schäuble and Karl Lamers (Chancellor Kohl's Foreign Policy adviser);
- articles by the French European Minister, Alain Lamassoure in May, followed by two articles by the Prime Minister, Edouard Balladur in *Le Figaro* (30 August) and *Le Monde* (30 November) on 'A Europe of Concentric Circles';
- a speech by the British Prime Minister, John Major, in Leiden (7 September) in Holland entitled 'Europe: A Future that Works'.

All three contributions suggested that the battle of ideas about the future of integration was opening once again. All papers attempt to deal with the twin issues of constitutional design and institutional change, because of the pressures for a Continental enlargement of the Union. All address the issue of diversity and the prospect for differentiated integration in contemporary Europe either in terms of variable speed (time), variable space (geographic) or variable policy reach of Union activities . The contents of the three contributions are discussed in the Editorial by Neill Nugent.

V. Presidencies

Greece and Germany held the Presidency during 1994. Hopes were not high for the Greek Presidency: a new Government was constituted in Athens at the beginning of the Greek Presidency which led to concerns about the smooth workings of the Council; Andreas Papandreou, the new Greek Prime Minister, was 76, very feeble and not able to take on the full burden of executive government which meant that he could not be as active a President of the European Council as might be required; and the Greek Permanent Representative was changed just weeks before the Presidency began. In addition, the Greek Minister for European Affairs, Theodoros Pangalos, did not endear himself to Bonn when he described Germany as 'a bestial giant with a child's brain' just weeks before the Presidency began. Relations between Greece and its partners further deteriorated in February when Greece banned the Former Yugoslav Republic of Macedonia from using the Greek port of Thesaloniki because of its opposition to the new Republic's use of the name Macedonia. Convention usually required the Member State holding the Presidency to show restraint on national issues during the six months in the chair. The Commission claimed that the Greek ban was illegal under the terms of the common commercial policy and proceeded to take Greece to Court. The case has not yet been completed.

The priorities of the Greek Presidency were outlined to the European Parliament in January as:

- completion of the accession negotiations with the EFTA applicants;
- implementation of the provisions of the TEU;
- progress with an action plan for combatting unemployment;
- bringing the Union closer to its citizens.

The most significant achievement of the Presidency was the completion in March of a number of very difficult dossiers in the enlargement negotiations (see the keynote article by Fraser Cameron). In the view of many, the Presidency was greatly helped on enlargement by the Germans, who set up a number of informal working parties to push the contentious dossiers along. That said, the negotiations were concluded despite the difficulty of many of the outstanding issues. Another area of progress concerned the Commission's White Paper on growth, competitiveness and employment, on which discussions proceeded in a number of different Council formations.

Presidencies are increasingly judged by the outcome of the summit meeting held at the end of each term of office. The main achievements of the European Council held during the Greek Presidency in Corfu were:

1. agreement on a priority list for 11 trans-European network projects;
2. the establishment of a Reflection Group to prepare for the 1996 IGC;
3. a partnership and co-operation agreement was signed with Russia at the meeting;
4. explicit reference was made to the future accession of Cyprus and Malta to the EU.

The Corfu meeting failed, however, to agree on the appointment of a replacement for Jacques Delors as Commission President, which lent some support to the view that the European Council had failed in its most important task. Views about responsibility for the failure to choose a replacement differ – on the one hand, the UK felt that the French and Germans were trying to impose their candidate without sufficient consultation. On the other hand, the Greek Prime Minister was too ill to engage in the usual pre-summit tour of the other capitals which might have alerted him to the looming problem, and his replacement, Theodoros Pangalos, was not seen by all of the Member State Prime Ministers.

Germany assumed the Presidency in the latter half of the year. In the lead-up to the Presidency much was made of the notion of a 'joint Presidency' between France and Germany for their two successive periods in the chair. The objective was to give renewed momentum to the process of integration. President Mitterrand spoke of a 'continuous, if not common, Franco-German Presidency' after a bilateral summit meeting with Chancellor Kohl in May. In the event, there appeared to be little evidence of any intensification of co-operation between the Germans and the French, partly because bilateral contact is already highly developed.

One of the first tasks of the German Presidency was to call a special European Council to deal with the unfinished business of Corfu. At the July summit, Jacques Santer, Prime Minister of Luxembourg, was unanimously approved as the next Commission President. In July, the German Foreign Minister, Klaus Kinkel, outlined the priorities of the German Presidency:

- to make progress in environmental policy;
- a strengthening of the social dimension of integration;
- the development of a practical strategy for bringing the countries of central and eastern Europe nearer to accession;
- further development of Mediterranean policy.

Partly, perhaps, because it was distracted by domestic elections, the German Presidency gave the impression that consolidation, rather than any attempt to develop grandiose initiatives, was its priority. Once the Bundestag elections were out of the way in October, however, Chancellor Kohl concentrated his energies on achieving a successful conclusion to the Presidency at the Essen European Council in December. The main objective was to have a discussion and conclusions on a German paper dealing with the integration of six former communist countries, the leaders of which had been invited to the Council. The main thrust of the paper was accepted by the other Member States with the proviso that it be accompanied by a new strategy towards the southern Mediterranean. Other issues dealt with at Essen were:

1. continuing work on the Delors White Paper, particularly the trans-European networks;
2. strengthening the Union's action in the area of internal security;
3. a further commitment, largely symbolic, to enhancing the Union's democratic legitimacy.

The conclusions at Essen were essentially what Chancellor Kohl was looking for. Nevertheless, the German Presidency came in for considerable criticism from the European Parliament in December. MEPs were critical of the fact that, despite 28 meetings on Europol, little progress had been made on the necessary convention. Doubts were also expressed on the Union's policies towards Bosnia and on refugees from the former Yugoslavia. The Essen summit marked the end of an era in Union politics in many respects as it was the last Council attended by both President Mitterrand and Jacques Delors. Chancellor Kohl is the only remaining part of the triad that did so much to shape European integration since the early 1980s. Essen was also the beginning of a Continental-wide Union; the customary photograph of the Heads of Government included the 12 EU leaders, the three acceding states and the six leaders from central and eastern Europe.

VI. Policy Developments

EMU

Despite the currency crisis in 1993 which effectively transformed the ERM, stage II of EMU began on schedule in January 1994. This further stimulated debate in the Member States on the desirability and feasibility of implementing the TEU commitments on EMU. The progression towards EMU means that in most Member States, national budgets are now being framed in the context of the Maastricht convergence criteria. Furthermore, national Finance Ministers are being questioned in the Council by their partners about their strategy for achieving the TEU targets. During the course of 1994, ten of the 12 Member States (Ireland and Luxembourg excluded) were found to be in breach of the strict budget deficit standards set out in the TEU. The fact that Ireland was not subjected to a stiff grilling despite its high debt–GDP ratio, offers a glimmer of future discussions on the strictness of the convergence criteria. The Italian Government began to discuss the prospect of bringing the lira back into the ERM but did not do so.

Scepticism about the feasibility of the 1997 deadline was continually expressed during 1994 because of the problem of excessive public debt in many of the Member States. However, the end of the recession made the prospect of a limited EMU involving a select number of currencies by 1999 more realistic. EMU which looked a bleak prospect during the 1992–93 currency crisis was back on the agenda. Hence the Member States began to pay more attention to their likely place in the single currency line-up. In February, Spain began to voice its fears about the impact of the EFTA enlargement on its prospects for inclusion in EMU. It wanted to ensure that it could, together with the other three Mediterranean states, form a blocking minority in 1996, the first target date on EMU. A declaration was therefore annexed to the Treaties of Accession to take account of Spain's difficulties. In November, Hans Tietmeyer, President of the Bundesbank, argued that the maximum permissible budget deficits in the TEU were too high, which suggests that the Bundesbank is not in any way reconciled to the prospect of a single currency. Chancellor Kohl's foreign policy adviser, Karl Lamers, on the other hand, spoke of the compelling case for monetary union. The prospect of a referendum on EMU was mooted in the UK and in France during the course of 1994.

Structural Policy and Regional Issues

Regional policy proved not to be too contentious during 1994, as the big decisions on the implementation of Delors II were taken in 1993. That said, the Commission approved a series of programmes under the Community initiative part of the Structural Funds, assessed the development plans submitted by the Objective 1 regions and decided on the distribution of monies allocated to the Objective 2 and 3 priorities. France and the UK received the lion's share of the funds under these two Objectives.

The first meeting of the Committee of the Regions, due to take place in January, was delayed because Portugal failed to submit its list of nominees to the Council. The problem in Portugal appeared to be a conflict about whether elected office holders or officials should represent Portugal on the Committee. The growing mobilization of Europe's regions and cities was again evident during 1994 with meetings of the Council of European Municipalities and Regions, the Atlantic Rim, the Association of Euro-cities and Europe's Maritime regions.

Agriculture

The 1993 agreement on the terms of the GATT round and the MacSharry proposals provided the framework for agricultural policy during 1994. That said, the Commission's price proposals for 1994–95 were hugely resisted by the Agricultural Ministers. The majority of Ministers argued that the price proposals went beyond what was required by the MacSharry reforms and the GATT. Opposition was voiced by the German, French, Dutch, Portuguese and Irish Ministers. In contrast, the British Minister argued that the proposals did not go far enough and that measures to contain CAP expenditure were vital. Apart from prices, the operation of the milk quota system in Italy was the subject of considerable criticism, with a Commission report of March 1994 concluding that Italy had failed to operate its milk quota system properly since 1989 and thus owed the Community a considerable amount of money. The Italians lobbied successfully to have the amount of the fine reduced by linking the issue to its agreement to the new 'own resources' provisions. German restrictions on the importation of British beef because of BSE ('mad cow disease') continued to cause controversy during the year.

Fisheries

The Common Fisheries Policy (CFP) experienced considerable strain in 1994. French fishermen resorted to violent demonstrations at ports, retail outlets and fish markets in protest against low import prices. This led the French Government to request minimum import prices for nine fish species in February, a request which was endorsed by the Commission. In March the Commission was forced to continue the minimum price regime when France threatened to hold up the accession negotiations on Norwegian fishing. In the summer a 'tuna war' in the Bay of Biscay broke out between Spanish fishermen who continue to fish for tuna using baited lines, and boats from the UK, France and Ireland with large driftnets. There were repeated violent clashes between the Spaniards and the other fishermen. The Spaniards maintain that there is systematic flaunting of EU rules on driftnet size.

In December the accession of the EFTA states was threatened when Spain vowed to prevent their membership by 1 January unless they were given full participation in the CFP. Spain and Portugal were promised in March that they would be fully integrated into the CFP from 1996 , six years ahead of the date agreed in their 1985 accession treaties. The UK and Irish Governments accepted that the Iberian states should have greater access to their waters but were concerned by the threat of over-fishing in what is known as the Irish Box because of depleting fish stocks. In December, after a series of marathon Council meetings, the UK and Ireland agreed to give Spanish vessels greater access to their waters provided there was tighter monitoring of their activities.

Immigration, Free Movement of People and Border Controls

Free movement and immigration loomed large in domestic debates about European integration. Growing strife in Algeria where 10,000 people have been killed since 1992, has done much to fuel fears of instability and Islam in the southern Member States. An ongoing tightening of asylum procedures is apparent in the Member States, with stricter measures in Germany leading to a rise in asylum-seekers in Belgium and Holland, which in turn led these states to review their laws and procedures. A proposal put to the Commission by the Social Affairs Commissioner to grant citizenship to immigrants legally resident in the EU was rejected by the German Commissioners in February.

The elimination of border controls was one of the most sensitive issues on the post-1992 agenda. The planned full implementation of the Schengen Accord in February was further delayed (the fourth delay in two years) because of France's continued hesitation. Although most border controls have been eliminated between the five original Schengen states, passport controls continue at airports. The official French line is that the Schengen Information System, based in Strasbourg, is not yet technically sound. France's partners are unconvinced by this argument and cite the hard-line approach of Charles Pasqua, the Interior Minister, as the real explanation. In December the Schengen states reached agreement on another deadline (March 1995) for the full elimination of border controls.

Social Policy

The Social Policy protocol, attached to the TEU, was used for the first time as Britain's long-standing opposition to an extensive EU role in social policy continued to make itself felt. The Commission resorts to the Social Protocol only if the UK cannot be brought on board in the Council. Implacable UK opposition to the Works' Council Directive, originally tabled 24 years ago, meant that it was dealt with under the procedures of the Social Protocol. The Eleven adopted a Common Position on the directive in June and formally adopted it in September. At the same Council meeting, Michael Portillo, the UK Employment Secretary, vetoed a directive on parental leave which will now be tabled under the protocol.

State Aid and Subsidies

State aid to industries in difficulty are usually one of the most contentious issues in relations between Brussels and the Member States. During 1994, the fate of airline national flag carriers and the continuing crisis in the steel industry were among the most intractable issues faced by the Commission. In 1986 when the Commission launched its deregulation of air transport, it was agreed that there would be a complete opening of European skies in 1997. However, liberalization in air transport poses a considerable challenge to many of Europe's national carriers that had traditionally been heavily subsidized by their national exchequers. In response to pressure from the national governments concerned, the Commission agreed that flag carriers should be allowed one last injection of public funds if it was accompanied by meaningful restructuring. During 1994, however, there was considerable acrimony when the French Government proposed to inject sizeable amounts into Air France. Europe's privatized carriers – British Airways, KLM and Lufthansa – objected strongly to the cash injection. When the subsidy was approved by the Commission in July, together with smaller amounts to TAP (Air Portugal) and the Greek Olympia Airline, the privatized carriers proceeded to take the case to the European Court of Justice. In December Iberia was looking for further handouts as it faces bankruptcy. The difficulty for the Commission is that, having already approved a cash injection for the Spanish flag carrier just two years ago, this further request runs counter to its 'one last time' policy. The decision on Iberia will be made in 1995.

The steel industry also bedevils the Commission's state aid policy. The December 1993 agreement on a rescue plan for Europe's beleaguered steel industry quickly ran into trouble in 1994. The extent and nature of aid to the Italian industry was the central bone of contention. There were clashes in the Commission between the Competition Commissioner, Karel van Miert, and the External Affairs Commissioner, Sir Leon Brittan, with the latter arguing for a very strict interpretation of EU laws which would have limited the level of subsidy allowed to the steel industry. There was also pressure on the Commission from the unsubsidized steel producers, notably British Steel, who threatened to take the Commission to the European Court of Justice. The steel rescue plan itself was abandoned in the latter part of the year when the industry failed to deliver the required cuts. Both these industries highlight the difficulties facing the Commission when faced by national governments that are prey to powerful domestic interests.

Environment

Although the Environmental Council agreed a number of important environmental provisions during 1994, it failed to make progress on the question of an energy tax. By the end of the German Presidency, it appeared as if British opposition to the proposed CO_2 tax 'in principle', and French opposition to the inclusion of nuclear energy, had killed of the tax proposal for an energy tax for the time being. Moreover, the high standards environmental states – Germany, the Netherlands and Denmark – were defeated on a packaging waste directive.

VII. Public Opinion

One of the main legacies of the TEU ratification crisis is the heightened interest in the 'people' dimension of European integration and in the attitude of Europe's public to developments in the European Union. All political leaders and EU officials are aware that they will not only have to win a negotiating battle in the 1996 IGC, but will also have to convince Europe's electorates. The most significant indicator of public opinion during 1994 was the further decline in turnout (56.5 per cent) for EP elections. Just before the Euro-elections, only half of all EU citizens had heard of them.

As is usual, two *Eurobarometer* surveys – numbers 41 and 42 – were taken in 1994, one in the spring and one in the autumn (see Tables 2 and 3). *Eurobarometers* 41 and 42 suggest that the standard indicators of support for the European Union continue to fall in some Member States but are consolidating in others. A downward trend in support for EU membership is now evident for three years since an all-time high (72 per cent believing that 'EC membership a good thing') was registered in spring 1991. In *Eurobarometer* 41 those believing that EU membership was a good thing for their country fell by three percentage points, to 54 per cent, from the figure recorded at the end of 1993. However the proportion rose to 58.5 per cent in the autumn poll. Support was over 70 per cent in Ireland, Luxembourg and the Netherlands, and 60 per cent or over in Italy, Belgium, Germany and Greece. The lowest recorded figures were Denmark (53 per cent), Spain (47.3 per cent), and the UK (42.8 per cent).

During 1994, the proportion of people believing that their country benefits from EU membership consolidated with, in the autumn, 49 per cent perceiving 'benefits' against 52 per cent who disagreed or were uncertain. Majorities perceiving benefits were recorded in all Member States with the exception of Germany (49.7 per cent), Spain (33.5 per cent), France (42 per cent) and the UK (38.4 per cent). These figures suggest that possible referendums on the 1996 IGC would be hard fought in France and the UK, where it is quite possible they will be held.

VIII. Implementation[1]

The implementation and enforcement of EC law has received increased attention from the Commission, the Council and the Member States in recent years. The Commission as 'guardian of the Treaties' is responsible for managing the process set out in Article 169 of the Treaty of Rome which deals with infringement proceedings. The process operates on the basis on three phases: a 'letter of

[1]The Commission's *Annual Report to the EP on the Implementation of EU Law* appears too late for inclusion in this volume. The 1993 report was published in June 1994. The reference is COM(94) 500 in *OJ* C154, 6.6.1994.

Table 2: National Attitudes Towards EU Membership

	B	*DK*	*F*	*G*	*GR*	*IRL*	*I*	*L*	*NL*	*P*	*S*	*UK*	*EU*
Good thing	61+5	53 0	58+8	61+11	65+1	82+10	70+2	80+9	77 0	56+2	47–3	43 0	58+4
Bad thing	7–3	2–4	12–1	10–2	8–1	5–2	5–0	5–4	4–1	11–2	18+4	22 0	13+1
Neither	28–2	23+5	27–6	25–8	22+2	10–6	17–3	13–4	15–1	28–4	28–3	28–1	23–4
Don't know	3–1	2–1	2–2	4–1	5–2	3–2	8+1	2–1	4+2	5+2	5 0	6–1	5–3
Total	99	100	100	100	100	100	100	100	100	100	99	99	99

Source: Eurobarometer 42. Column 1 shows data from No. 42 and column 2 shows the change from No. 41. All figures are percentages.

Table 3: Perceived Benefits of EU Membership

	B	*DK*	*F*	*G*	*GR*	*IRL*	*I*	*L*	*NL*	*P*	*S*	*UK*	*EU 12*
Benefited	51+1	61–5	42+3	50+7	72+4	89+6	54+1	72+4	69–3	70+1	34–8	38–6	49+1
Not benefited	25–1	27+1	36–4	31–7	17 0	5–5	17–6	18–0	17+5	21–3	46+1	45–1	32–3
Don't know	23–1	12+4	22+1	20+1	11–4	5–2	28+4	11–3	14–3	10+3	20+7	16+6	20+3
Total	99	100	100	101	100	99	99	101	100	101	100	99	101

Source: Eurobarometer 42. Column 1 shows data from No. 42 and column 2 shows the change from No. 41. All figures are percentages.

notice' to the Member State asking for information; a 'reasoned opinion' which outlines the Commission's views; and finally, the institution of proceedings at the Court. In 1994, the Commission commenced 974 infringement proceedings, issued 546 reasoned opinions, and referred 89 cases to the Court of Justice. The breakdown by country of cases was as follows: Belgium 10, Denmark 0, Germany 5, Greece 17, Spain 9, France 8, Ireland 12, Italy 12, Luxembourg 6, the Netherlands 4, Portugal 5 and the United Kingdom 1.

During 1994 the Commission turned its attention from implementation to the operation of legislation on the ground. In so doing, it began to scrutinize the quality of national implementing legislation to determine if it conforms to EU law.

By the end of 1994, 89 per cent of internal market legislation was implemented (see Table 4). However, this high percentage masks considerable variation from one sector to another and from one Member State to another. The sectors causing most difficulty are industrial property (62.5 per cent), public procurement (63.5 per cent), and insurance (72.2 per cent). Greece, with a total of 43 measures not notified at the end of 1994 had the worst record of implementing internal market legislation, followed by Germany (26), Ireland (24), Spain (22) and Italy (21). Denmark and the UK maintained their good record on implementation with failure to notify just 8 and 14 measures respectively. The French and Dutch records are also very good. The general improvement in the level of implementation suggests that in most Member States the increasing attention paid to internal market legislation has borne fruit.

Table 4: Implementation of Internal Market Measures (November 1994)

Country	*Measures Notified*	*Not Notified*	*Not Applicable/Derogation*
Belgium	190	17	–
Denmark	217	8	1
France	204	9	–
Germany	180	26	1
Greece	165	43	4
Ireland	190	24	1
Italy	189	21	3
Luxembourg	196	19	2
Netherlands	206	11	1
Portugal	187	19	5
Spain	185	22	4
UK	197	14	–

Source: Background Briefing for Internal Market Council, 8 December 1994.

Journal of Common Market Studies
Volume 33, Annual Review
August 1995

A Guide to the Documentation of the European Union

IAN THOMSON AND DUNCAN MITCHELL
University of Cardiff

Abbreviations

Bull.EU: *Bulletin of the European Union*

COM: Commission document

EC: European Community (when noted as the publisher, 'EC' means the Office for Official Publications of the European Communities (EUR-OP), L-2985, Luxembourg. EC publications may be obtained from the sales agents of EUR-OP in the Member States and elsewhere. In the UK the sales agent is HMSO.)

EP: European Parliament

EU: European Union

OJ: *Official Journal of the European Communities*
– Annex: Debates of the European Parliament
– C: Information
– L: Legislation

PE DOC: Committee Report of the European Parliament

SEC: Internal Commission General Secretariat Document

Most publications cited in this *Guide* are available for reference in European Documentation Centres (EDCs, mainly based in academic libraries) and EC Depository Libraries throughout the world. Access to electronic sources is also available to EDCs and Depository Libraries.

Introduction

In this *Guide* a selection of the key EU documents and publications of 1994 is listed, highlighting important policy activities and initiatives of the European Union. (It should, however, be noted that although the EU has formally existed since November 1993, there is still something of a dilemma as to how to refer to documentation, much of which emanates from the EC 'pillar' of the Union. 'EC' remains the standard term for material published by the Office for Official Publications of the European Communities (EUR-OP).) Some titles issued in the closing weeks of 1993, or published in 1993 but which only became available in 1994, are included, as are some titles from 1994 which became available early in 1995. The *Guide* is divided into five sections:

General
Governance and Institutional Developments
Financing the Union
Internal Policy Developments
External Policies and Relations

For reasons of space, specific legislative proposals and legislation adopted during the year are not included. Such documents are listed in the 'Recent references' section of the current awareness bulletin *European Access* (edited by Ian Thomson) under the appropriate heading and are also brought together at the beginning of 'Recent publications of interest' in each issue of *European Access*.

The Commission continued in 1994 to respond to calls for transparency and openness in EU decision-making by issuing more Green and White Papers (specific examples are listed below) and by releasing as *COM* documents material which might previously have remained categorized as internal documents. A Users' Advisory Council on Information met for the first time in October 1994. An initiative was launched to produce consolidated texts of EU legislation which has been heavily amended. The Commission issued a guide explaining new procedures for access to Commission documents.

General

For an overview of the activities of the EU in 1994 see the European Commission's *XXVIIIth General Report on the Activities of the European Union 1994* (published in February 1995) and issues of the monthly *Bulletin of the European Union*. Specialist annual reports compiled by the Commission covering agriculture and competition policy in 1994 will also be published during the course of 1995. Overview reports from other Union institutions, where available, are listed below under the appropriate heading in the section on Governance and Institutional Developments.

The 'Chronology' in each issue of *European Access* during 1994 lists important events and initiatives of the previous two months and directs readers to the section of 'Recent references' where appropriate information sources are listed.

The Treaty on European Union

The Treaty on European Union (TEU) came into force on 1 November 1993 and it was expected, from previous experience, that the authoritative version of the Treaty would be published in the 'L' series of the *OJ*. However, this did not happen, and the authoritative version is now said to be the text published in *OJ* C191, 29.7.92, pp. 1–112.

In the previous *Annual Review* an announced four-volume compilation of all EU primary legislation was cited. Although the first volume appeared in 1993, the subsequent three volumes did not make their anticipated appearance. A revised four-volume set is reportedly to be published in 1995, taking into account the accession of Austria, Finland and Sweden to the EU on 1 January 1995.

Governance and Institutional Developments

Enlargement

The institutional impact of enlargement to 15 Member States is presented in:

> 95/1/EC, Euratom, ECSC: *Decision of the Council of the European Union of 1.1.95 adjusting the instruments concerning the accession of new Member States to the European Union. OJ* L1, 1.1.95, pp. 1–13

Commission

The Commission's legislative programme for 1994 was first announced in November 1993 (*COM* (93)588 final). It was republished in 1994 along with the Institutions' *Joint Declaration on the Legislative Programme*, and the relevant Council Declaration and Parliament Resolution:

> Parliament/Commission: *Legislative programme of the Commission for 1994. OJ* C60, 28.2.94, pp. 1–30/*Bull.EU: Supplement* No. 1, 1994

The Commission was not due to issue its legislative programme for 1995 until following the inauguration of the new Commission under Jacques Santer in January 1995.

After the meeting of the (then) 21 nominated Members of the new Commission in Senningen (Luxembourg) on 29 October 1994, Jacques Santer announced the final division of portfolios for the new Commission as from 1995:

Commission, Spokesman's Service: *Division of portfolios in the new Commission. Press Release*, IP/94/1002 (29.10.94) (available on *Rapid*). (Note that this assumed the accession of Norway to the EU.)

The Presidency, the European Council and the Council of the European Union

The programmes of the six-monthly Presidencies of the EU are presented to the European Parliament (EP) in January and July each year. For the Greek Presidency (January–June 1994) see *OJ*: Annex, No. 3-441 (1994), pp. 109–30; for the German Presidency (July–December 1994) see *OJ*: Annex, No. 4-449 (1994), pp. 37–55.

Similarly, a review and debate of each Presidency takes place in the EP usually during the last months of each Presidency and following the European Council. The review of the Greek Presidency and the Corfu European Council (June 1994) took place in July 1994 (*OJ*: Annex, No. 4-449 (1994), pp. 20–37 and 55–57); the review of the German Presidency and the Essen European Council (December 1994) took place in December 1994 and will appear in *OJ*: Annex, No. 4-455 (1994).

The conclusions adopted at the end of European Council meetings are published in the *Bull.EU* and issued on the *Rapid* database. For the European Council in Corfu, 24–25 June 1994, see *Bull.EU*, No. 6, 1994, pp. 7–20 or DOC/94/1 on *Rapid*. For the European Council in Essen, 9–10 December 1994, see *Bull.EU*, No. 12, 1994 (not published at the time of compilation) or DOC/94/4 on *Rapid*.

The full text of common positions adopted by the Council under the co-operation procedure were published for the first time in 1994 in the 'C' series of the *OJ*, beginning with *OJ* C101, 9.4.94, p. 1. Agendas and reports of all regular Council meetings are now routinely available on the *Rapid* database with the prefix *PRES*.

The Council has continued its attempts to publish its *Annual Report* more quickly, issuing the reports for 1992 and 1993 in 1994:

Council, General Secretariat: *Fortieth Review of the Council's Work (The Secretary-General's Report) 1 January –1 December 1992*. EC, 1994; ISBN: 92-824-1052-8; EC No. BX-79-93-922-EN-C

Council, General Secretariat: *Forty-First Review of the Council's Work (The Secretary-General's Report) 1 January–December 1993)*. EC, 1994; ISBN: 92-824-1134-6; EC No. BX-24-94-002-EN-C

A further manifestation of the Council's initiative is the publication of a summary of the principal decisions and facts of a year as soon as possible after the year: this is to be called *Part One of the Review*, and will be reprinted at a later date alongside a more detailed analysis (*Part Two*). Part One, covering 1993, was published in April 1994:

Council, General Secretariat: *Forty-first Review of the Council's Work (The Secretary-General's Report) 1 January–31 December 1993*. Part 1 – Summary. EC, 1994; ISBN: 92-824-1141-9; EC No. BX-24-94-001-EN-C

Finally, at the beginning of 1994 the row erupted over the adjustment of weighted votes in Qualified Majority Voting (QMV) following enlargement. A settlement of sorts (the 'Ioannina compromise') was reached in April:

Council: *Council Decision of 29 March 1994 concerning the taking of Decision by qualified majority by the Council. OJ* C105, 13.4.94, p. 1 (*OJ* C1, 1.1.95, p.1 gives effect to the adjustment required following Norway's decision not to join the EU)

The European Parliament

Periodically the EP issues a volume of *Fact Sheets*, providing a substantial synopsis of the development of Community/Union policies and highlighting the EP's role. The latest edition was published in 1994 to coincide with the campaign for the June elections:

Parliament, DG IV: *Fact Sheets on the European Parliament and the activities of the European Union.* (6th ed.) EC, 1994; ISBN: 92-823-0551-1; EC No. AX-80-93-533-EN-C

The Treaty on European Union (TEU) created the office of Ombudsman, whose function will be to safeguard European citizens' political, civil and social rights. Attempts were made during 1994 to establish the office although, by the end of 1994, procedural difficulties within the EP had prevented a choice of person:

Parliament: *94/262/ECSC, EC, Euratom: Decision of the European Parliament of 9.3.94 on the regulations and general conditions governing the Ombudsman's duties. OJ* L113, 4.5.94, pp. 15–18

Parliament: *Call for nominations for the office of Ombudsman. OJ* C210, 30.7.94, p. 21

The fourth direct elections to the EP were held in June 1994. The Parliament does not seem formally to publish the results. Its Information and Publications Directorate-General did, however, issue the following:

Parliament, DG III: *European elections 1994. Results and elected Members.* (Provisional edition, 15.6.94.) EC, 1994

Parliament, DG III: *European elections 1994. Biographical notes on the 567 Members.* (Provisional edition, 5.7.94) EC, 1994

Parliament's zeal for institutional reform is undimmed. In Februrary 1994, looking towards the 1996 Intergovernmental Conference (IGC), the EP criticized the perceived failings of the TEU and called on the new EP to continue campaigning on the basis of the Committee on Institutional Affairs' draft Constitution for the EU (annexed to the Resolution):

Parliament: *Resolution on the Constitution of the European Union* (10.2.94). *OJ* C61, 28.2.94, pp. 155–70

The Economic and Social Committee

The annual report of the Economic and Social Committee for 1993 was published, and new rules of procedure adopted at the June plenary:

> Economic and Social Committee: *Annual report 1993*. EC, 1994; ISBN: 92-830-0256-3; EC No. EX-82-94-189-EN-C
>
> Economic and Social Committee: *Rules of procedure (Adopted at the plenary session held on 2.6.94)*. *OJ* L257, 5.10.94, pp. 32–53

The European Court of Justice

The European Court of Justice (ECJ) has investigated ways of reducing delays in publishing the full number of language versions of its judgments. While the French-language text of the judgments (French being the Court's official working language) has appeared reasonably rapidly, the English version has been published around two years after the judgment was made.

In 1994 two major decisions were implemented to improve the situation. Firstly, the Translation Directorate now aims to translate judgments into all official languages on the day of the judgment. Individual judgments are then available directly from the Court in Luxembourg. Secondly, the full text of the hearing of each case (as opposed to the judgment) will no longer be translated into all official languages and will be available only in the language of the case. As a result of these changes, the first judgments of 1994 of the ECJ (and Court of First Instance (CFI)) were published in mid-1994 in the series *Reports of Cases before the Court of Justice and the Court of First Instance*. This series is now published in two parts: one for the ECJ, the other for the CFI. (Note that from 1994 those CFI cases involving disputes between the EU institutions and their staff have been separated from the main set of law reports and published separately in *Reports of European Community Staff Cases*.)

The European Court of Auditors

The European Court of Auditors continues to receive most prominence in December each year when it publishes its annual report on the legality and the soundness of the management of revenue and expenditure of the Community and its institutions for the previous financial year:

> European Court of Auditors: *Annual report concerning the financial year 1993 together with the institutions' replies*. *OJ* C327, 24.11.94, pp. 1–484

The Court became a full Community institution under the TEU's provisions in November 1993, and has recently sought to publicize its work. In addition to *Information Notes* issued to coincide with its annual and special reports, the Court issued in 1994 a new edition of a brochure describing its function and working methods:

> European Court of Auditors, External Relations Department: *The European Court of Auditors. Auditing the Community's finances*. EC, 1994; ISBN: 92-826-8128-9; EC No. MX-81-93-898-EN-C

Other EU Institutions and Organizations

The Committee of the Regions was established by the TEU as a representative voice for local and regional interests in the EU, and is consulted on issues and legislative proposals of relevance to those interests. Following its inaugural session on 9–10 March 1994, the texts of its opinions have begun to be published in the 'C' series of the *OJ*, beginning with *OJ* C217, 6.8.94, p. 1. The Committee adopted its rules of procedure in May:

> Committee of the Regions: *Rules of procedure adopted by the Committee of the Regions at its third Plenary Session on 17–18 May 1994: approved by the Council of the European Union at its 1759th meeting on 25 May 1994. OJ* L132, 27.5.94, pp. 49–54

The location of other new organizations and institutions was finally agreed at the European Council in November 1993 (*OJ* C323, 30.11.93, p. 1/*Bull.EC*, No. 10, 1993, p. 110). During 1994 a number of these organizations and institutions were established and began to recruit staff. Few, however, started issuing information in a formal sense apart from the European Environment Agency in Copenhagen (Kongens Nytorv 6, DK-1050, Copenhagen, Denmark), which launched a newsletter in October 1994.

Application of Community Law

After the virtual completion of the single market programme, attention in 1994 shifted increasingly to questions of implementation. The Commission's annual report on the application of law has grown since its inception in 1984, both in size and political significance:

> Commission: *Eleventh annual report on monitoring the application of Community law (1993). COM* (94)500 final (29.3.94)/*OJ* C154, 6.6.94, pp. 1–177

Transparency and Subsidiarity

The trauma of ratifying the TEU has turned a spotlight onto the openness of decision-making and its closeness to EU citizens. The Commission now reports annually on progress in applying subsidiarity:

> Commission: *Report to the European Council on the application of the subsidiarity principle 1994. COM* (94)533 final (25.11.94)

The Commission also produced two glossy publications which further signalled its collaboration with the new spirit. The first was a collection of documents approved by the Commission in 1993 and 1994 on information policy and transparency in decision-making; the second was a joint Commission-Council initiative following the TEU, setting out practical details on access to documents:

> Commission, DG X: *Information, communication, openness*. EC 1994; ISBN: 92-826-7653-6; EC No. CC-82-94-852-EN-C

> Commission, DG X: *Access to Commission documents. Users' guide*. EC, 1994; ISBN: 92-826-8446-6; EC No. CM-84-94-791-EN-C

Financing the Community

1994 Budget

The full text of the EU budget for 1994 was published in:

> Parliament: *94/56/ECSC, EC, Euratom: Final adoption of the general budget for the European Union for the financial year 1994. OJ* L34, 7.2.94, pp. 1–1757

Amending and supplementary budgets are sometimes adopted during the year to accommodate unexpected circumstances. Two such were adopted in 1994 (*OJ* L169, 4.7.94, pp. 1–127; *OJ* L362, 21.12.94, pp. 1–195).

1995 Budget

The full texts of the draft budget as it passes through the various legislative stages are not published. Summaries are available in various secondary sources such as the *Bull.EU* for the appropriate months. To trace the progress of the 1995 budget see 'Finance from Europe News' in each issue of *European Access* during 1994 and No. 1, February 1995.

The Commission adopted the preliminary draft budget for 1995 on 17 April 1994 (*Bull.EU*, No. 4, 1994, p. 86). The Council adopted a first reading draft 1995 budget on 25 July 1994 (*Bull.EU*, No. 7–8, 1994, p. 97). The EP voted on the first reading of the draft 1995 budget on 27 October 1994 (*Bull.EU*, No. 10, 1994, p. 76). The Council approved a draft 1995 budget at a second reading on 16 November 1994 (*Bull.EU*, No. 11, 1994, p. 102). The European Parliament adopted the 1995 budget on 13 December 1994 and following the vote the EP President Klaus Hänsch signed the budget. The 1995 budget has been published in *OJ* L369, 31.12.94, pp. 1–1913.

Financial Management

(For the annual report of the Court of Auditors see above.) The Commission's annual report on the execution of the budget for 1992 was published in 1994:

> Commission: *Financial report 1992*. EC, 1994; ISBN: 92-826-6584-4; EC No. C6-79-93-627-EN-C

Budget fraud is becoming an increasingly salient and politically sensitive issue. The EP held public hearings on the subject in 1993, and the Copenhagen European Council (21–22 June 1993) requested the Commission to present proposals to strengthen anti-fraud action. In 1994 the Commission published its report for 1993:

> Commission: *Protecting the financial interests of the Community. The fight against fraud. 1993 annual report.* EC, 1994; ISBN: 92-826-7804-0; EC No. CM-22-94-001-EN-C/*COM* (94)94 final (23.4.94)

The action programme arising from this report, setting out the Commission's new anti-fraud strategy and developing a partnership with the Member States, was published separately from the report:

Commission: *Protecting the financial interests of the Community. The fight against fraud. The Commission's anti-fraud strategy work programme for 1994.* EC, 1994; ISBN: 92-826-7815-6; EC No. CM-22-94-002-EN-C/*COM* (94)92 final (23.3.94)

Much responsibility for action against fraud remains at the national level. In December 1994 the Council tackled the variety of legal provisions to counter fraud in different Member States, looking for voluntary measures to make national provisions more compatible:

Council: *Council Resolution of 6.12.94 on the legal protection of the financial interests of the Communities. OJ* C355, 14.12.94, pp. 2–3

Miscellaneous

The Commission reports twice annually on borrowing and lending operations, guarantees to third parties, and corresponding risks:

Commission: *Commission Report ... on guarantees covered by the General Budget – Situation at 30 June 1993. COM* (93)687 final (26.1.94)

Commission: *Commission Report ... on guarantees covered by the General Budget – Situation at 31 December 1993. COM* (94)364 final (8.9.94)

As EC relationships with third countries, and especially central and eastern European countries, have developed, EU financial activities have expanded and diversified. The Commission's annual report on these activities is becoming increasingly important:

Commission, DG II: *Reports on the borrowing and lending activities of the Community in 1993. European Economy: Supplement A*, No. 10, October 1994/*COM* (94)317 final (18.7.94)

The Edinburgh European Council of December 1992 agreed on the financial perspective for the EC for 1993–99, and envisaged the gradual replacement of the VAT element as the main source of revenue by the GNP-based 'fourth resource' between 1995 and 1999.

There are still many problems to be ironed out, however, particularly in questions of the comparability of Member States' GNP:

Commission: *Communication ... on progress in harmonisation of GNP and the evaluation of financial support. COM* (94)16 final (4.2.94)

Finally, in anticipation of enlargement in 1995, and in accordance with the Interinstitutional Agreement of 1993, the Commission reported to the Budgetary Authority on adjustments which would be required to the financial perspective:

Commission: *Communication ... Adjustment of the financial perspective with a view to enlargement of the European Union* (+ legislative proposal). *COM* (94)398 final (4.10.94)/*OJ* C395, 31.12.94, pp. 1–3

Internal Policy Developments

In this section, attention is focused primarily on substantive consultative reports from the Commission (increasingly called Green or White Papers) which suggest future Commission action or which report on existing policies. Also included is a selection of further publications which present significant information.

Space limitations make it impossible to deal with the mass of legislative proposals and adoptions which is published every year. In 1994 the Commission adopted 7,034 instruments (regulations, decisions, directives, recommendations and opinions), compared to 7,335 in 1993, and sent the Council 558 proposals, recommendations or draft instruments plus 272 communications, memoranda and reports (in 1993 the figures were 619 and 343 respectively). The Council adopted 46 directives, 274 regulations and 148 decisions (63, 319 and 164 respectively in 1993).

The entries for the specific policies are presented in alphabetical order.

Agriculture

The Commission's annual report on EU agriculture, published in conjunction with the *General Report*, appeared later than usual in 1994, to allow for the inclusion of a summary of the agricultural chapter of the GATT Uruguay Round, concluded on 15 December 1993:

> Commission: *The agricultural situation in the Community. 1993 report*. EC, 1994; ISBN: 92-826-6991-2; EC No. CM-81-93-422-EN-C

The annual report on the EAGGF (Guarantee Section) was published in October:

> Commission: *Twenty-third financial report on the European Agricultural Guidance and Guarantee Fund (EAGGF) Guarantee Section 1993. COM* (94)464 final (31.10.94)

A new agrimonetary system was introduced at the same time as the entry into force of the single market in 1993 and the removal of border controls. The first report on the new system was published in 1994, accompanied by a proposal for improvements to deal with the monetary turbulence experienced in the EC in 1993:

> Commission: *Report ... on the agrimonetary system for the Single Market. Period from 1 January 1993 to 30 June 1994 ... (+ legislative proposal). COM* (94)498 final (16.11.94)

In these circumstances, the annual report on the relationship between expenditure and exchange rate fluctuations had an added significance:

> Commission: *Report on the impact on EAGGF Guarantee Section expenditure of movements of the dollar/ECU exchange rate; increases in the correcting factor resulting from monetary realignments within the European Monetary System. COM* (94)463 final (28.10.94)

CAP reform continues to be an issue. The Commission published the findings and recommendations of an independent, international group of experts, with a view to stimulating debate:

> Commission, DG II: *EC agricultural policy for the 21st century. European Economy; Reports and Studies*, No. 4, 1994

In addition to these major publications, a series of reports, discussion papers and communications on individual areas of the CAP appeared throughout the year. Some of the more significant are listed below:

> Commission: *Report ... on the development of vineyards in the European Community and the relationship between production and consumption in the wine sector. COM* (94)28 final (21.3.94)

> Commission: *Communication concerning the programme of measures for promoting consumption in the Community and expanding the markets for milk and milk products in 1994/95. OJ* C121, 3.5.94, pp. 8–10

> Commission: *Communication ... Discussion paper on European apiculture. COM* (94)256 final (24.6.94)

> Commission: *Communication ... Development and future of Community policy in the fruit and vegetables sector. COM* (94)360 final (27.7.94). (Related publication: *COM* (94)271 final (6.7.94))

> Commission: *Report ... concerning application of Council Regulation (EEC) No. 2990/82 on the sale of butter at reduced prices to persons receiving social assistance. COM* (94)472 final (3.11.94)

> Commission: *First report ... on the statistics on the number of animals used for experimental and other scientific purposes. COM* (94)195 final (27.5.94)

Competition

As with agriculture, the Commission publishes a specialized annual report on competition policy as a supplement to the *General Report*:

> Commission: *XXIIIrd Competition Report From the Commission – 1993*. EC, 1994; ISBN: 92-826-8374-5; EC No. CM-82-94-650-EN-C/*COM* (94)161 final (5.5.94)

The Commission also published a booklet summarizing the principles of EC competition policy and the ways it was applied in 1993:

> Commission, DG IV: *Community competition policy in 1993*. EC, 1994; ISBN: 92-826-7996-9; EC No. CM-83-94-127-EN-C

DG IV embarked on a process of publicizing competition rules in order to ensure their observance:

Commission, DG IV: *Competition law in the European Communities. Vol. IA: Rules applicable to undertakings. Situation at 30.6.94*. EC, 1994; ISBN: 92-826-6759-6; EC No. CM-29-93-A01-EN-C

Two further volumes will complete the set but were not published in 1994.

The 1990 Merger Regulation is to be reviewed in 1996. The Commission launched the process in 1994 by documenting the working of the new Regulation:

Commission, DG II: *Competition and integration. Community merger control policy. European Economy*, No.57 (1994)

Other publications in 1994 commented on various aspects of state aids:

Commission, DG II: *State aid control in the context of other Community policies. European Economy: Supplement A*, No.4, April 1994, pp. 1–12

Commission: *Community guidelines on state aid for environmental protection. OJ* C72, 10.3.94, pp. 3–9

Commission: *Community guidelines on state aid for rescuing and restructuring firms in difficulty. OJ* C368, 23.12.94, pp. 12–20

In the ongoing campaign to achieve transparency, the Commission is seeking to publicize its approach and decision-making practice by launching a newsletter:

Commission, DG IV: *Competition Policy Newsletter, 1994–* (Quarterly).

Consumer Policy

The 1985 directive on liability for defective products made no provision for services. In 1990 the Commission proposed another directive to plug the gap, but the Council failed to agree. The Commission finally withdrew its proposal in 1994, but issued a communication restating its commitment to making services safe:

Commission: *Communication ... on new directions on the liability of suppliers of services. COM* (94)260 final (23.6.94)

There was one other report of note on consumer policy in 1994:

Commission: *Report ... on the application of Article 14 of Council Directive 89/397/EEC of 14.6.89 on the official control of foodstuffs. COM* (94)567 final (6.12.94)

Culture

A compilation of texts relating to culture was published, mainly for the use of people involved in work for relevant ministries or in the implementation of decisions:

Council, General Secretariat: *Texts concerning culture at European Community level*. EC, 1994; ISBN: 92-824-1036-6; EC No. BX-78-93-718-EN-C

The EC has had – since 1991 – the legal authority to co-ordinate the Member States' activities with regard to broadcasting activities in the EU. The Commission reported on EC activities in the period from 3 October 1991 to 31 December 1993:

Commission: *Communication ... on the application of Articles 4 and 5 of Directive 89/552/EEC. Television without frontiers. COM* (94)57 final (3.3.94)

In 1992 the Commission indicated that it would act in support of culture more vigorously once the TEU, with its specific cultural provisions, was in force. In 1994 the Commission laid out the framework for EC support measures in the cultural field, on the new basis:

Commission: *Communication ... European Community action in support of culture (+ legislative proposals to establish Kaleidoscope 2000 and Ariane Programmes). COM* (94)356 final (27.7.94)/*OJ* C324, 22.11.94, p. 5

Economic and Monetary Situation

Annual reports analysing the state of the European economy on both a Community-wide and individual Member State basis appeared in March and December:

Commission: *Annual Economic Report for 1994. COM* (94)90 final (23.3.94)/ *European Economy*, No.56 (1994)

Commission: *Annual Economic Report for 1995. COM* (94)615 final (13.12.94)

Updated economic forecasts are issued periodically throughout the year:

Commission, DG II: *Economic forecasts for 1994–1995. European Economy: Supplement A*, No. 5, May 1994

Commission, DG II: *Economic forecasts for 1994–1996. European Economy: Supplement A*, No.11–12, November–December 1994

Article 103(2) of the TEU provides the framework for the co-ordination of the Community's and Member States' economic policies from the start of Stage II of EMU. The Commission now publishes annual guidelines, which are designed to act as a key point of reference for the conduct of national policies in attaining the convergence criteria:

Commission: *Commission Recommendation for the Broad Guidelines of the Economic Policies of the Member States and the Community drawn up in conformity with Article 103(2) of the Treaty on European Union. COM* (94) 217 final (1.6.94)/*European Economy*, No.58 (1994), pp. 1–29 (includes the Council Recommendation of 11 July and an annex of the main economic indicators)

Education, Training and Research and Technological Development (RTD)

A new magazine in 1994 brought together policy-related articles and operational information on the activities of the Commission's Task Force, to reflect the integration of the various EC education and training programmes into SOCRATES, LEONARDO and Youth for Europe III from 1995:

Commission, Task Force: Human Resources, Education, Training and Youth: *Le Magazine*, No. 1, 1994–. ISSN: 1023-3725

The 1993 White Paper on growth, competitiveness and employment (*COM* (93)700 final) has had a considerable impact on education and training policy, as has the reformed framework for policy-making as a result of the TEU. In November 1994 the Commission set out its thoughts on education and training policy, and in particular on areas where it felt large-scale measures were necessary:

Commission: *Communication ... Education and training in the face of technological, industrial and social challenges: First thoughts. COM* (94)528 final (23.11.94)

In December, the Council called for greater efforts to provide high quality and attractive vocational education and training, as the number of non-skilled jobs in the economy shrinks and rapid structural and technological changes take place:

Council: *Resolution ... on the quality and attractiveness of vocational education and training. OJ* C374, 30.12.94, pp. 1–4

The Council reinforced its message by establishing the 'Leonardo da Vinci' action programme to support and supplement national programmes. This programme will run from 1 January 1995 to 31 December 1999, superseding the five existing programmes in this area:

Council: *Decision ... establishing an action programme for the implementation of EC vocational training policy. OJ* L340, 29.12.94, pp. 8–24

Free movement of people is still restricted by differences in educational systems and lack of recognition of professional and educational qualifications. The Commission launched a debate on this issue, with the aim of strengthening existing initiatives and establishing new ones:

Commission: *Communication ... on recognition of qualifications for academic and professional purposes. COM* (94)596 final (13.12.94)

The new SOCRATES educational programme includes specific action in favour of the children of legally-established migrants and gypsies. The Commission published a document in March explaining the background to this decision:

Commission: *Report on the education of migrants' children in the European Union. COM* (94)80 final (25.3.94)

A long series of reports was published in 1994, reflecting the conclusion of a number of education and training-related programmes, including Petra (*COM* (93)704 final (14.1.94)), Comett (*COM* (94)368 final (9.9.94)), Force (*COM* (94)418 final (13.10.94)), Lingua (*COM* (94)280 final (6.7.94)), Value II (*COM* (94)548 final (5.12.94)), Eurotra (*COM* (94)69 final (20.9.94)), Tempus (*COM* (94)142 final (20.4.94)) and Erasmus (*COM* (94)281 final (6.7.94)).

Discussions in 1993 on the successor programme to the Third Research and Technological Development (RTD) programme came to fruition, and the Fourth Programme was adopted via the co-decision procedure in April 1994:

> Council/Parliament: *Decision No.1110/94/EC of the European Parliament and of the Council ... concerning the fourth framework programme of the EC activities in the field of research and technological development and demonstration (1994-98). OJ* L126, 18.5.94, pp. 1–33

The Commission also published a colourful report on the development of EC RTD policy and the detail of the Fourth Programme:

> Commission, DG XIII: *Community research and technological development policy. The main issues at stake in the EU's fourth framework programme for research and technological development (1994-98).* EUR 15637; EC, 1994; ISBN: 92-826-7849-0; EC No: CG-NA-15637-EN-C

The task of co-ordinating national and European policies has not been tackled effectively. The Commission set out its thoughts on the subject in October:

> Commission: *Communication ... Research and technological development. Achieving coordination through cooperation. COM* (94)438 final (19.10.94)

The Commission also published a huge first information report, with the aim of providing a common information base. This is to be the first in a series of regularly updated studies:

> Commission: *The European Report on Science and Technology Indicators 1994.* Report EUR 15897 EN, October 1994

The Commission's second annual report on the Community's Joint Research Centre (JRC) was followed by Council conclusions that the JRC should take a new approach and progressively enter the competitive arena:

> Commission: *Joint Research Centre: 1993 annual report. COM* (94)87 final (23.3.94)

> Council: *Council Conclusions ... on the role of the Joint Research Centre (JRC). OJ* C126, 7.5.94, pp. 1–4

The White Paper on growth, competitiveness and employment placed a great deal of emphasis on RTD. This was reflected in the series of reports on Community programmes published in 1994:

> Commission: *Communication ... a review of the implementation and performance of the RTD Programme 'Telematic Systems in Areas of General Interest' (1991–1994). COM* (94)185 final (26.5.94)

> Commission: *Communication ... Telematics applications for transport in Europe. COM* (94)469 final (4.11.94)

Commission: *Communication ... Biotechnology and the White Paper on growth, competitiveness and employment. Preparing the next stage. COM* (94)219 final (1.6.94)

Commission: *Report ... R&D in advanced communications technologies for Europe (RACE) – Mid-term report on Phase II of RACE (1990–94). COM* (94)306 final (14.7.94)

Energy

As the pace of debate over energy policy in the EU accelerated, the Commission's glossy, expanded report on recent developments appeared as a special issue of *Energy in Europe*:

Commission, DG XVII: *1993 – Annual Energy Review. Energy in Europe,* Special Issue, June 1994

Energy is increasingly being identified as requiring special attention, both indirectly by the TEU's emphasis on the role of horizontal measures in promoting cohesion, and directly by the Fifth Environmental Action Programme, which stresses the importance of energy in promoting sustainability. In February 1994, the Commission proposed that an overall approach to the problems of energy and cohesion should be adopted:

Commission: *Communication ... Energy and economic and social cohesion. COM* (93)645 final (14.2.94)

Since the TEU the Commission has been discussing the need for trans-European energy networks, but the European dimension is still lacking. Proposals for a more proactive approach were published in January 1994:

Commission: *Communication ... on Community guidelines on trans-European energy networks (+ related legislative proposals). COM* (93)685 final (19.1.94)

The European Energy Charter was signed in December 1991, with the aim of stabilizing relations between the countries of central and eastern Europe (CCEE) and potential OECD investors. In September 1994 the Chair of the Conference for negotiations on the Charter issued a draft Treaty, which the Commission believed the Community should sign, as an important step forward in co-operation with the CCEE:

Commission: *Communication ... on the signing and provisional application by the EC of the European Energy Charter Treaty (+ legislative proposals). COM* (94)405 final (21.9.94)

The Treaty was signed in Lisbon on 17 December 1994.

Finally, the Commission sought to launch a debate on energy policy, to maintain the EU's competitiveness, security of supply and environmental protection:

Commission: *Green Paper: For a European Union energy policy. COM* (94)659 final (11.1.95)

Environment

The Fifth Environmental Action Programe requires the Commission to review the implementation of the Programme at regular intervals. The first of these reports appeared at the end of June 1994, half-way to the mid-term review of the Action Programme at the end of 1995:

> Commission: *Interim review of implementation of the European Community Programme of Policy and Action in Relation to the Environment and Sustainable Development 'Towards Sustainability'. COM* (94)453 final (30.11.94)

Member States were requested by the Council between 1990 and 1993 to prepare national programmes for the control of CO_2 and other greenhouse gas emissions. Following the signature by the EC and Member States of the Rio Convention on Climate Change in June 1992, the Council decided in June 1993 to require the Member States to publish their programmes. The first evaluation of these programmes was published in March 1994:

> Commission: *Report ... under Council Decision 93/389/EEC. First evaluation of existing national programmes under the monitoring mechanism of Community CO_2 and other greenhouse gas emissions. COM* (94)67 final (10.3.94)

Sustainability is now a formal goal of the Union, and environmental policy is to be integrated into other policies. The definition of 'prosperity' is to be widened to include environmental goals. The Fifth Action Programme and the White Paper on growth, competitiveness and employment are thus linked; but putting this into practical terms is no easy task. The Commission published its first, tentative analysis of the situation and the implications for economic and fiscal policy-making in November 1994:

> Commission: *Communication ... economic growth and the environment. Some implications for economic policy making. COM* (94)465 final (3.11.94)

As a first step, the Commission went on to suggest a European system to allow for comparisons between Member States and the 'greening' of national accounts:

> Commission: *Communication ... Directions for the EU on environmental indicators and green national accounting. The integration of environmental and economic information systems. COM* (94)670 final (21.12.94)

One other report of note was published in 1994:

> Commission: *Convention on International Trade in Endangered Species of Wild Fauna and Flora. 7th EC Annual Report. COM* (94)104 final (7.4.94)

Fisheries

French vessels were given a derogation to the Common Fisheries Policy (CFP) in 1991 which allowed them to continue to use large driftnets until the end of 1993, despite the environmental damage caused by such equipment. The Commission reported in 1994 that, far from extending the derogation, an eventual ban on all driftnets should be aimed for:

> Commission: *Communication ... The use of large driftnets under the Common Fisheries Policy. COM* (94)50 final (8.4.94)

The current multi-annual guidance programme for fisheries runs from 1993 to 1996 and aims to manage the reduction in national fishing fleets' capacities. The Commission's annual report indicates the extent of attainment of objectives:

> Commission: *Annual report ... on the progress of the multiannual programmes for the fishing fleet at the end of 1993. COM* (94)208 final (1.6.94)

There are, however, gaps in the CFP. EC regulations do not refer to the use of passive gear, although the trend towards the use of such equipment poses a threat to stock management. The Commission pressed for urgent action in 1994:

> Commission: *Communication ... Fishing with passive gear in the Community. The need for management, its desirability and feasibility. COM* (94)235 final (10.6.94)

Despite all these actions, the worst recession in the EC industry's history hit fishing in 1993. Emergency measures had been introduced by the Commission to safeguard producer incomes, but the need for fundamental structural reforms was clear. The Commission put forward some tentative suggestions:

> Commission: *Communication: The crisis in the Community's fishing industry. COM* (94)335 final (19.7.94)

The crisis led the Commission to propose catch restrictions for types of fish the stocks of which were in a particularly desperate state. These proposals took into account Sweden and Finland's accession:

> Commission: *Proposal for a Council Regulation(EC) fixing, for certain fish stocks and groups of fish stocks, the total allowable catches for 1995. COM* (94)566 final (7.12.94)

Health

Prior to the TEU's entry into force, the Commission had already proposed a framework for action, but the TEU's provisions on public health allow the Commission to develop policy in a more coherent fashion. In June 1994, the Council invited the Commission to bring forward proposals for action in the priority areas it identified in its framework proposal:

> Council: *Council Resolution ... on the framework for Community action in the field of public health. OJ* C165, 17.6.94, pp. 1–2

Specific proposals for multi-annual action programmes on health promotion and action against cancer had either already been submitted or followed rapidly:

Commission: *Communication ... adopting a programme of Community action on health promotion, information, education and training within the framework for action in the field of public health. COM* (94)202 final (1.6.94). (The proposal for a Council and EP Decision was published in *OJ* C252, 9.9.94, pp. 3–6)

Commission: *Communication concerning the fight against cancer in the field of public health (+ related legislative proposal). COM* (94)83 final (29.3.94)

Commission: *Communication ... concerning a Community action programme on the prevention of AIDS and certain other communicable diseases in the context of the framework for action in the field of public health (+ legislative proposal). COM* (94)413 final (9.11.94)/*OJ* C333, 29.11.94, p. 34

However, in some ways the TEU only constitutionalized the *status quo*, as is shown by the existing programmes:

Commission: *'Europe against Cancer' programme. Report from the Commission ... on the execution of the programme in 1993. COM* (94)550 final (5.12.94)

Commission: *'Europe against AIDS' Programme 1991–1993. Commission report on the implementation of the Action Plan 1993. COM* (94)515 final (23.11.94)

Commission: *Communication ... Blood safety and self-sufficiency in the European Community. COM* (94)652 final (21.12.94)

Industry

The Commission's annual review of the situation of, and outlook for, manufacturing and service industries in the EU is a massive and important reference work:

Commission, DG III/Eurostat: *Panorama of EU industry 1994*. EC, 1994; ISBN: 92-826-7670-6; EC No. CO-80-93-468-EN-C

Industrial policy remains a politically sensitive subject for the EU. However, the TEU calls on the EU and its Member States to act to lay the basis of a European policy, and the White Paper on growth, competitiveness and employment was endorsed by the European Council as the benchmark for EU and Member State action. On the basis of the 1990 communication, *Industrial Policy in an Open and Competitive Environment*, the Commission outlined priorities for action and identified the steps which could be taken:

Commission: *Communication ... An industrial competitiveness policy for the European Union. COM* (94)319 final (14.9.94)/*Bull.EU: Supplement*, No.3, 1994

The Commission and Eurostat have worked together over several years, making progress in harmonizing and expanding statistics, to produce information on the structure and behaviour of enterprises, which is essential for the development of any enterprise policy:

Commission, DG XXIII/Eurostat: *Enterprises in Europe*. Third report. 2 vols. EC, 1994; ISBN: 92-826-7692-7; EC No. CT-02-93-001-EN-C

The Commission also published a report detailing current actions falling under enterprise policy and other Community policies, with the aim of improving their visibility and coherence:

Commission: *Fourth Commission activity report on enterprise policy. COM* (94)221 final (7.9.94)

The role of small and medium-sized enterprises (SMEs) was emphasized in the White Paper on growth, competitiveness and employment. The Commission set out its approach to assist SMEs in the fields of taxation and the transfer of businesses. It also published its own conclusions arising out of an examination of the results of a Round Table of bankers which reported in 1994 on relationships between banks and SMEs:

Commission: *Communication ... The improvement of the fiscal environment of small and medium-sized enterprises. COM* (94)206 final (25.5.94)

Commission: *Communication from the Commission on the transfer of businesses. Actions in favour of SMEs. OJ* C204, 23.7.94, pp. 1–23

Commission: *Communication ... Round Table of leading representatives from the banking sector. COM* (94)435 final (28.10.94)

The European Observatory for SMEs was established in December 1992 as an independent network to produce reports on the situation of and prospects for SMEs in Europe, which were designed to provide the basis for EC policy:

Commission: *Communication ... The European Observatory for SMEs. Comments by the Commission on the Second Annual Report. COM* (94)352 final (7.9.94)

On a rather different scale, the crisis in the European steel industry brought about by overcapacity and recession has been an ongoing problem. Unanimous agreement in the Council on restructuring was not reached until the end of 1993, although the Commission had been organizing a number of flanking measures to ease the pain since February 1993. Throughout 1994 the Commission grew increasingly frustrated, as the industry failed to agree a package of cuts in capacity, and finally withdrew the flanking measures altogether. The process can be traced through the published documentation:

Commission: *Forward programme for steel for the first half of 1994 and for 1994 as a whole. OJ* C10, 14.1.94, pp. 2–12

Commission: *Communication ... Intermediate report on the restructuring of the steel industry. COM* (94)125 final (13.4.94)

Commission: *Communication ... Fresh impetus for restructuring the steel industry in the Community. COM* (94)265 final (21.6.94)

Commission: *Communication ... Restructuring the Community steel industry: Final assessment and conclusions. COM* (94)466 final (25.10.94)

In the space available here, it is impossible to include, let alone comment on, all of the documents which appeared during 1994 covering industrial sectors. The following is an indicative list of the most important:

Commission: *Communication ... concerning an 'Agreement respecting normal competitive conditions in the commercial shipbuilding and repair industry' within the framework of the OECD (+ legislative proposal). COM* (94)460 final (3.11.94)/*OJ* C375, 30.12.94, p. 1

Commission: *Communication ... on the European Union automobile industry. COM* (94)49 final (23.2.94)

Commission: *Communication ... on the outlines of an industrial policy for the pharmaceutical sector in the European Community. COM* (93)718 final (2.3.94)

Commission: *Communication ... Strengthening the competitiveness of the European machinery construction industry. COM* (94)380 final/2 (22.11.94)

A group of prominent persons was established by the December 1993 Brussels European Council, to report on specific measures on information infrastructures to the Corfu summit in June 1994. Chaired by Martin Bangemann, the Group's report, which called for a regulatory approach to create a Europe-wide market for information services, was published in July, and also appeared as a supplement to the *Bull.EU*:

Commission: *Europe and the global information society. Recommendations of the high-level group on the information society (Bangemann Group Report). Bull.EU: Supplement,* No.2, 1994, pp. 5–39

The Bangemann Report came on top of an existing programme to establish a European information services market, the mid-term review of which appeared in 1994:

Commission: *Communication ... on the mid-term review of the implementation of the Community programme 'Establishment of an internal information services market, 1991–1995'. COM* (94)183 final (21.6.94)

One of the most sensitive areas of Commission action is the liberalization of telecommunications and cable television. In 1994 the Commission brought forward initial guidelines for discussion:

Commission: *Communication ... Green Paper on the liberalisation of telecommunications infrastructure and cable television. COM* (94)440 final (25.10.94)

Commission: *Green Paper on the liberalisation of telecommunications infrastructure and cable television networks. Part II: A common approach to the provision of infrastructure for telecommunications in the EU. COM* (94)682 final (25.1.95)

The White Paper on growth, competitiveness and employment placed a great deal of emphasis on the information society and the audiovisual sector's potential for growth and job creation. The Bangemann Report added to the momentum. The Commission published a series of communications in 1994 dealing with various aspects of communications and media:

Commission: *Strategy options to strengthen the European Programme Industry in the context of the audiovisual policy of the European Union. Green Paper. COM* (94)96 final (6.4.94)

Commission: *Communication ... Follow-up to the consultation process relating to the Green Paper on 'Pluralism and media concentration in the Internal Market – an assessment of the need for Community action'. COM* (94)353 final (5.10.94)

Commission: *Towards the personal communications environment: Green Paper on a common approach in the field of mobile and personal communications in the European Union. COM* (94)145 final (27.4.94)

Commission: *Communication ... on the consultation on the Green Paper on mobile and personal communications (+ legislative proposal). COM* (94)492 final (23.11.94)

Commission: *Communication ... on satellite communications. The provision of – and access to – space segment capacity. COM* (94)210 final (10.6.94)

Commission: *Communication ... Present status and future approach for open access to telecommunications networks and services (Open Network Provision). COM* (94)513 final (29.11.94)

Justice and Home Affairs

Progress in this area is dependent upon the existence of a consensus among Member States that a collective approach is necessary. The Commission's initiation of a debate on immigration and asylum policy was therefore couched in terms of the common interest and the need to address issues in the context of a single institutional framework:

Commission: *Communication ... on immigration and asylum policies. COM* (94)23 final (23.2.94)

Single Market

The first annual report on the operation of the single market was published in March 1994:

Commission: *The Community internal market. 1993 report. COM* (94)55 final (14.3.94)/EC, 1994; ISBN: 92-826-7633-1; EC No. C1-01-93-001-EN-C. (A summary of the report is also available: ISBN: 92-826-7644-7)

The high-level Sutherland Group examined the operation of the single market in 1992.

In response to the Group's suggestions, the Commission presented its work on administrative co-operation between Member States, and between Member States and the Commission:

> Commission: *Communication ... on the development of administrative cooperation in the implementation and enforcement of Community legislation in the Internal Market. COM* (94)29 final (16.2.94)

The number of cross-border transfers of funds is growing, and in order to ensure that payment systems operate properly and efficiently (and to assist progress towards EMU) the Commission presented its position at the end of the year:

> Commission: *Communication ... EU funds transfers: Transparency, performance and stability (+ legislative proposals and draft Notice). COM* (94)436 final (18.11.94)

The abolition of border controls has required measures to adapt VAT in relation to intra-EC trade:

> Commission: *Communication and report ... Common system of value added tax: arrangements for taxing transactions carried out by non-established taxable persons. COM* (94)471 final (3.11.94)

> Commission: *Report ... on the operation of the transitional arrangements for charging VAT in intra-Community trade. COM* (94)515 final (23.11.94)

At the end of the year, the Commission provided an overview of VAT arrangements, to enable the Council to decide whether amendments needed to be made:

> Commission: *Report ... on the harmonisation of the laws of the Member States relating to turn-over taxes – Common system of value-added tax: uniform basis of asessment. COM* (94)584 final (13.12.94)

Management and investment funds are a major source of investment capital for EU industry. The Commission proposed a directive to regulate the system in the EC in 1991, but withdrew the proposal when Member States demanded amendments. The Commission then sought urgently to clarify its intentions:

> Commission: *Communication on the freedom of management and investment of funds held by institutions for retirement provision. Communication on an internal market for pension funds. OJ* C360, 17.12.94, pp. 7–11

Finally, the Commission published a practical manual for all working on the harmonization of technical regulations:

> Commission: *Guide to the implementation of Community harmonisation directives based on the new approach and the global approach.* EC, 1994; ISBN: 92-826-8584-5; EC No. CO-81-93-551-EN-C

Social Policy and the Labour Market

Since 1992 the Commission, rather than seeking to harmonize social systems, has instead set common objectives in social policy, leaving Member States free to decide how to operate and finance their own systems. This new approach makes the circulation of information crucial, and in 1994 a first report was published (supplementing the *Employment in Europe* report), with the aim of giving Member States and social protection organizations the information they need to define their options and possible actions:

Commission, DG V: *Social protection in Europe 1993*. EC, 1994; ISBN: 92-826-6973-4; EC No. CE-79-93-978-EN-C

The December 1993 Brussels European Council endorsed the Commission's White Paper on growth, competitiveness and employment. DG V had had considerable input into the White Paper, and provided further analysis of the situation in 1994:

Commission, DG V: *Employment in Europe 1994*. EC, 1994; ISBN: 92-826-8965-4; EC No. CE-85-94-042-EN-C

Commissioner Padraig Flynn undertook a tour of national capitals, to hold discussions with governments and social partners at the national level:

Commission: *Progress report on employment. Results of Mr Flynn's tour of capitals. Bull.EU: Supplement*, No.2, 1994, pp. 103–24

The outcome of this activity, following the 1993 White Paper, and the Green Paper on Social Policy of 1993 (*COM* (93)551 final (17.11.93)) was a major White Paper in July, which sought to preserve the 'European social model' whilst facing the challenges of the 1990s:

Commission: *European social policy – a way forward for the Union. COM* (94)333 final (27.7.94). 2 vols

The Council noted the White Paper on Social Policy and looked forward to a detailed Work Programme from the Commission in 1995, listing some of the central objectives towards which Social Policy could be directed:

Council: *Council Resolution ... on certain aspects for a European Union social policy: a contribution to economic and social convergence in the Union. OJ* C368, 23.12.94, pp. 6–10

There were a number of publications relating to equal treatment of the sexes in 1994:

Commission: *Memorandum on equal pay. COM* (94)6 final (23.6.94)

Commission: *Report ... on the implementation of Council Directive 86/613/ EEC of 11.12.86 on the application of the principle of equal treatment between men and women engaged in an activity, including agriculture, in a self-employed capacity, and on the protection of self-employed women during pregnancy and motherhood. COM* (94)163 final (15.9.94)

Council: *Resolution of the Council ... of 6.12.94 on equal participation by women in an employment-intensive economic growth strategy within the EU. OJ* C368, 23.12.94, pp. 3–6

The TEU's Social Protocol was used for the first time in September 1994, with the British Secretary of State for Employment not participating in the final Council vote on legislation, which consequently will not apply to the UK:

Council: *Council Directive 94/45/EC of 22.9.94 on the establishment of a European Works Council or a procedure in Community-scale undertakings and Community-scale groups of undertakings for the purposes of informing and consulting employees. OJ* L254, 30.9.94, pp. 64–72

The Commission published a review of Community action on health and safety at work since the SEA, with the full texts of EC legislation:

Commission, DG V: *Europe for safety and health at work. Social Europe*, No.3, 1993 (published 1994)

The TEU identified drug dependence as a priority area for Community action. The Commission reviewed the situation in 1994 and then put forward proposals for a new action programme:

Commission: *Communication ... Community action in the field of drug dependence (1995–1999) (+ legislative proposal). COM* (94)223 final (21.6.94). (Legislative proposal also published as *OJ* C257, 14.9.94, pp. 4–6)

The Commission also called for reinforced efforts against drugs, a complex issue affecting all three pillars of the EU. The TEU's entry into force made it necessary to look again at the European Plan against Drugs, approved by the December 1992 Edinburgh European Council:

Commission: *Communication ... on a European Union action plan to combat drugs (1995–1999). COM* (94)234 final (23.6.94)

The HELIOS II programme for disabled people was established in 1993. Among the measures introduced was the Handynet computerized information and documentation system. The Commission's 1994 report included a legislative proposal for the development of Handynet:

Commission: *Report ... Implementation of the Handynet computerised information and documentation system. COM* (94)303 final (12.7.94)/*OJ* C222, 10.8.94, p. 19

1994 saw the launch of a new, thrice-yearly journal, with features on the activities of DG V in the areas of social protection, social exclusion, family and older people:

Commission, DG V: *Solidarity*, No.1, 1994–

The TEU's Social Protocol instructs the Commission to make an annual report on the demographic situation in the Community. As the 1994 report was the first, the

Commission published it separately to other reports requested by the Protocol:

Commission: *The demographic situation of the European Union. 1994 report. COM* (94)595 final (13.12.94)

Finally, the Commission laid out the EU's platform in advance of the UN summit on Social Development in Copenhagen:

Commission: *Communication ... The European Union's priorities for the World Summit for Social Development (Copenhagen, March 1995). COM* (94)669 final (21.12.94)

Structural Policy

Against the background of the TEU's commitment to increasing solidarity and the Edinburgh budget settlement, the Commission sees a regular update of knowledge of regional trends and related developments as vital. This is the principal aim of the Commission's periodic reports:

Commission, DG XVI: *Competitiveness and cohesion: trends in the regions. Fifth periodic report on the social and economic situation and development of the regions in the Community. COM* (94)322 final (19.7.94). (Also published, with foreword, as EC, 1994; ISBN: 92-826-8631-0; EC No. CX-85-94-147-EN-C)

The Commission is required to report each year on the operation of the Structural Funds, in the light of their reform in 1989. The fourth such report was published in 1994:

Commission, DG XVI: *The implementation of the reform of the Structural Funds 1992. Fourth annual report.* EC, 1994; ISBN: 92-826-7082-1; EC No. C2-81-93-866-EN-C

Looking ahead to the 1994–99 period, the Commission published a booklet on current regional problems:

Commission, DG XVI: *Europe at the service of regional development.* EC, 1994; ISBN: 92-826-8864-X; EC No. CX-85-94-640-EN-C

The European Social Fund (ESF) is now required to take on the new task of facilitating adaptation to industrial change and changes in production systems, in particular through vocational training and retraining. The Commission approved most of the programming documents relating to Objective 4 in 1994, and reported on the first stage of implementation:

Commission: *Communication ... European Social Fund – the new Objective 4. COM* (94)510 final (16.11.94)

The Commission also informed Member States of the commitment appropriations from the Structural Funds for agricultural Objective 5(a) areas for the period 1994–99:

Commission: *Communication ... Objective 5(a). Indicative breakdown by Member State of commitment appropriations from the Structural Funds. COM* (94)268 final (27.6.94)

A framework for the future of Community Initiatives (CIs) was set out in a Green Paper in 1993, and the responses were set out in a communication which also contained draft proposals for the revision of the CIs:

Commission: *The future of Community Initiatives under the Structural Funds. COM* (94)46 final (16.3.94)

Having adopted guidelines on CIs for the period 1994–99, in June, the Commission published a practical guide for potential beneficiaries:

Commission: *Guide to the Community Initiatives 1994–99*. 1st ed. EC, 1994; ISBN: 92-826-8437-7; EC No. CM-84-94-056-EN-C

Cities are becoming an increasing focus of CIs, and the Commission is looking for a more ambitious and better co-ordinated approach in the coming period:

Commission: *Community Initiative concerning Urban Areas (URBAN). COM* (94)61 final (2.3.94)

The Christophersen Group, established by the December 1993 Brussels European Council to assist the Commission in leading and co-ordinating the speedy and efficient implementation of trans-European networks (TENs) in transport and energy, reported to the June 1994 Corfu European Council:

Commission: *Trans-European networks. Interim report of the group of personal representatives of the Heads of State or Government (Christophersen Group). Bull.EU: Supplement*, No. 2, 1994, pp. 41–102

As a complement to its mammoth *Europe of the Regions* review, the Commission brought out a similar survey of the EU's 440 inhabited islands:

Commission, DG XVI/Eurostat: *Portrait of the Islands*. EC, 1994; ISBN: 92-826-6259-4; EC No. CA-75-92-300-EN-C

The Commission also reported on a programme of options specifically relating to the remoteness and insularity of Madeira and the Azores:

Commission: *1992–93 report on the progress achieved in implementing Poseima. COM* (94)476 final (9.12.94)

Transport

A committee was appointed in June 1993 to investigate the economic and social situation in the vital road freight transport sector, and to make recommendations on its future development. The committee reported in July 1994:

Committee of Enquiry on Road Freight Transport: *Road freight transport in the Single European Market. Report of the Committee of Enquiry, July 1994*. EC, 1994 (available direct from DG VII)

A committee established to report on the future of the European air transport industry suggested practical solutions in January, and formed the basis of a Commission communication in June:

Comité des Sages for Air Transport to the European Commission: *Expanding horizons. Civil aviation in Europe, an action programme for the future. A report by the Comité des Sages for Air Transport to the European Commission*. EC, 1994 (available direct from DG VII)

Commission: *Communication ... The way forward for Civil Aviation in Europe. COM* (94)218 final (1.6.94)

For the full effects of liberalization in the air transport industry to be felt, the Commission argued that ancillary services must be included:

Commission: *Ground-handling services. Consultation paper. OJ* C41, 11.2.94, pp. 2–8

The Commission began in 1971 to report annually on rail, road and inland waterway infrastructure. 1994 saw only the fifteenth report, which the Commission blamed partly on non-co-operation from the Member States:

Commission: *15th report ... on expenditure on and utilisation of rail, road and inland waterway infrastructure: 1987–1988–1989. COM* (94)47 final (28.2.94)

The Council decided in 1992 that EC-level action on tourism was appropriate and requested an annual report from the Commission, the first of which covered the period to December 1993:

Commission: *Report ... on Community measures affecting tourism (Council Decision 92/421/EEC). COM* (94)74 final (6.4.94)

Miscellaneous

The outbreak of peace in Northern Ireland in 1994 led to the creation of a special Commission Task Force for the province, and the establishment of priorities for a new package of aid to assist the peace process:

Commission: *Communication ... A special support programme for peace and reconciliation in Northern Ireland. COM* (94)607 final (7.12.94)

External Policies and Relations

General

The Commission updates the summary of agreements with third countries annually:

> Commission, DG IA: *Annotated summary of Agreements linking the Communities with Non-Member Countries (as at 31 December 1993 – with a list of recent developments updated to June 1994)*. EC, 1994 (available directly from DG IA)

Asia

The Commission sought to spark a policy debate about the EU's response to the growing political and economic power of Asian countries:

> Commission: *Communication ... Towards a new Asia strategy. COM* (94)314 final (13.7.94)

Common Foreign and Security Policy (CFSP)

Statements adopted by EU Foreign Ministers within the framework of the CFSP are published as *Press Releases from the Council of the European Union* and are available on the *Rapid* database with the prefix *PESC*. (Press Releases reporting General Affairs Councils relevant to CFSP activities are available with the prefix *PRES*.)

Eastern and Central Europe

Member States agreed in June 1993 at the Copenhagen European Council that any of the CCEE which wanted to join the EU could do so, as soon as they were able to assume the responsibilities of membership. The June 1994 Corfu European Council requested a paper from the Commission on the development of the Europe Agreements with the CCEE, and a strategy to prepare them for accession to the EU. The first response was published in July, followed quickly by specific proposals:

> Commission: *Communication ... The Europe Agreements and beyond: a strategy to prepare the countries of Central and Eastern Europe for accession. COM* (94)320 final (13.7.94)

> Commission: *Communication ... Follow-up to Commission Communication on 'The Europe Agreements and beyond'. COM* (94)361 final (5.8.94)

The Commission complied with a request for a proposal for the structure and role of a Task Force to help the CCEE to bring their laws into line with those of the EU, but suggested that subcommittees of the Europe Agreements would be more suitable bodies:

> Commission: *Communication ... Relations with the associated countries of Central and Eastern Europe. Task Force on Approximation of Laws (Follow-up of the European Council of Copenhagen). COM* (94)391 final (16.9.94)

The Commission's surveys of the CCEE demonstrated an urgent need to help their economies:

> Commission, DG II: *Economic situation and economic reform in central and eastern Europe. European Economy: Supplement A,* No. 8–9, August–September 1994, pp. 1–19

Macro-financial assistance was originally designed to support intra-EC balance of payments, but has been extended since 1990 to support third countries, in particular the CCEE:

> Commission, DG II: *Report on the implementation of macro-financial assistance to third countries – Communication from the Commission. European Economy,* No.58 (1994), pp. 31–104

On a different note, concern grew through the summer of 1994 about the illicit export of dangerous materials from the former USSR. The Commission proposed measures to tackle the problem:

> Commission: *Communication ... The illicit traffic in radioactive substances and nuclear materials. COM* (94)383 final (7.9.94)

The EC has provided scientific and technological support for the CCEE and the former USSR since 1990, with the aim of smoothing the transition to a market economy. This co-operation is now to be extended to the whole of the Fourth Framework Programme (see above), paving the way to the integration of research and technology throughout Europe:

> Commission: *Communication ... Cooperation in science and technology between the European Union and the countries of Central and Eastern Europe on the one hand and the new independent States of the former Soviet Union on the other. COM* (94)420 final (24.11.94)

Enlargement

The Commission approved the accession applications from the four candidates in April 1994:

> Commission: *Commission Opinion on the application for accession to the European Union by the Republic of Austria, the Kingdom of Sweden, the Republic of Finland and the Kingdom of Norway. COM* (94)148 final (19.4.94)

Various documents relating to these accessions, including the text of the Accession Treaty, the Final Act and the minutes of the Treaty signing, can be found in:

> *Documents concerning the accession of the Republic of Austria, the Kingdom of Sweden, the Republic of Finland and the Kingdom of Norway to the European Union. OJ* C241, 29.8.94, pp. 1–404

European Economic Area

The European Economic Area (EEA) came into operation on 1 January 1994. The agreement was published, with the Protocols following the Swiss referendum:

Council/Commission: *Agreement on the European Economic Area. OJ* L1, 3.1.94, pp. 1–605

There followed a series of implementing decisions:

EEA Joint Committee: *Decision of the EEA Joint Committee No. 1/94 of 8 February 1994 adopting the rules of procedure of the EEA Joint Committee. OJ* L85, 30.3.94, pp. 60–63

EFTA Surveillance Authority: *Rules of procedure of the EFTA Surveillance Authority. OJ* L113, 4.5.94, pp. 19–21

EEA Council: *Decision of the EEA Council No. 1/94 of 17.5.94 adopting the rules of procedure of the EEA Council. OJ* L138, 2.6.94, pp. 39–40

European Economic Area: *Rules of procedure of the EFTA Court, adopted on 4 January and 1 February 1994. OJ* L278, 27.10.94, pp. 1–26

European Economic Area: *Agreement between the EFTA States on the establishment of a surveillance authority and a Court of Justice. OJ* L344, 31.12.94, pp. 1–83

European Economic Area: *Rules of procedure adopted by the EEA Consultative Committee at its Constituent Meeting held on 8 February 1994 in Brussels. OJ* L301, 24.11.94, p. 10

External Trade

The conclusion of the GATT Uruguay Round in December 1993 was the first major external relations decision taken by the EU after the entry into force of the TEU. The Commission outlined the challenges and potential benefits of the agreement:

Commission, DG I: *The Uruguay Round. Global agreement. Global benefits.* EC, 1994; ISBN: 92-826-7794-X; EC No. CC-83-94-143-EN-C

Following the signature of the Final Act in April 1994, the Commission urged the Council to adopt the results in formal terms:

Commission: *Proposal for a Council Decision Concerning the conclusion of the Uruguay Round of Multilateral Trade Negotiations. COM* (94)143 final (15.4.94)

However, by October the Council had still not acted. The new World Trade Organization was due to begin operations in January 1995, and the Commission was convinced that further delay would be damaging. Again, the Council was urged to make the necessary amendments and additions to EC law:

Commission: *Uruguay Round. Implementing legislation. COM* (94)414 final (5.10.94)

Latin America

The Commission responded to various requests for a report on the strengthening of ties with Latin America and regional groupings, proposing short-term measures to facilitate a long-term strategy:

Commission: *Communication ... The European Community and Mercosur: an enhanced policy. COM* (94)428 final (19.10.94)

The Essen European Council endorsed the Commission's strategy, which was also received positively at a Mercosur Presidential meeting. The EU and Mercosur then reached an understanding on co-operation:

Council: *Solemn joint declaration between the Council of the European Union and the European Commission, on the one hand, and the Mercosur Member States on the other. OJ* C377, 31.12.94, pp. 1–2

Mediterranean

Concerns about the economic and social stability of the EU's southern flank are growing. The Corfu European Council invited the Commission to submit proposals for the creation of a zone of stability:

Commission: *Communication ... Strengthening the Mediterranean policy of the European Union: establishing a Euro-Mediterranean partnership. COM* (94)427 final (19.10.94)

The Commission also reported on existing financing projects in the region:

Commission: *Report ... on the implementation of financial and technical cooperation with Mediterranean non-member countries and on financial cooperation with those countries as a group. COM* (94)384 final (18.11.94)

North America

EC and USA competition rules affect each other's trade increasingly. In order to avoid conflict, the Commission concluded a Co-operation Agreement with the US in 1991, but this was overturned by the European Court on the grounds that only the Council had the authority to conclude such an agreement. The Commission urged the Council to validate the agreement as quickly as possible:

Commission: *Communication ... concerning cooperation with the United States of America regarding the application of their competition rules (+ legislative proposal). COM* (94)430 final (12.10.94)

Relations with Developing Countries

Commission co-operation with non-governmental development organizations gives practical expression to the EC contribution to the Third World. This mostly takes the form of co-financing of development programmes, but has become increasingly diverse in recent years:

Commission: *Report from the Commission on cooperation with European non-governmental development organisations (NGDOs) in spheres concerning developing countries (1992 financial year). COM* (94)7 final (27.1.94)

Commission: *Report from the Commission on cooperation with European non-governmental development organisations (NGDOs) in respect of developing countries (1993 financial year). COM* (94)468 final (3.11.94)

The EC's Humanitarian Office (ECHO) was established in April 1992 to improve the efficiency of humanitarian aid delivery and to raise the programme's profile. 1993 was ECHO's first full year of operation and the first of what will be annual reports was issued in 1994:

Commission: *Humanitarian aid. Annual report 1993. COM* (94)40 final (16.2.94)/EC, 1994; ISBN: 92-826-7928-4; EC No. CM-83-94-604-EN-C

The Commission reported on positive actions to help developing countries improve their human rights records, and on measures taken against serious infringements:

Commission: *Report ... on the implementation in 1993 of the Resolution of the Council and of the Member States ... on human rights, democracy and development on 28.11.91. COM* (94)42 final (23.2.94)

The EC Investment Partners programme, designed to encourage private investment in the Third World, is becoming more important than official development assistance and helps such countries become part of the world economy. The programme expired at the end of 1994, prompting the Commission to propose its extension:

Commission: *Communication ... for the continuation and consolidation of the EC Investment Partners (ECIP) financial instrument for the countries of Latin America, Asia, the Mediterranean region and South Africa. COM* (94)358 final (27.7.94).

The Member States and Commission agreed in December 1993 to co-ordinate their approach to population growth at the 1994 Cairo World Conference on Population and Development:

Commission: *Communication ... The European Community and the challenge of population growth: proposed position of the Community at the World Conference on Population and Development, Cairo, 5–13 September 1994. COM* (94)100 final (4.5.94)

Finally, there was a series of reports and other communications in 1994 on various aspects of policy towards developing countries. The most important of these were:

Commission: *Fifteenth annual report ... on the implementation of financial and technical assistance to Asian and Latin American developing countries at 31.12.91. COM* (94)541 final (2.12.94)

Commission: *Communication ... Integration of developing countries in the international trading system. Role of the GSP 1995–2004. COM* (94)212 final (1.6.94)

Commission: *Communication ... Balance sheets and accounts of the fifth, sixth and seventh European Development Funds for the financial year 1993. COM* (94)365 final (5.8.94)

Commission: *Communication ... Community support for structural adjustment in the ACP countries towards the consolidation and strengthening of a realistic and concerted approach. COM* (94)447 final (27.10.94)

Commission: *Communication ... on the mid-term review of the Association of the overseas countries and territories with the European Community. COM* (94)538 final (21.12.94)

Eurostat: *ACP basic statistics 1994*. EC, 1994; ISBN: 92-826-7447-9; EC No. CA-81-93-042-EN-C

Commission, DG VIII: *EU–ACP cooperation (1993). The Courier*, Special edition, May 1994

South Africa

As a strong signal of support for the new, democratically elected South African Government, the Commission proposed a package of initial support measures with a quick interim agreement, whilst a comprehensive long-term settlement was negotiated:

Commission: *Communication: Proposal for measures to be presented to the new Government of South Africa (initial measures and interim agreement). COM* (94)123 final (6.4.94)

A Co-operation Agreement was reached at the end of the year:

Council: *Decision ... concerning the conclusion of a Cooperation Agreement between the EC and the Republic of South Africa. OJ* L341, 30.12.94, pp. 61–65

Journal of Common Market Studies Volume 33, Annual Review
August 1995

Chronology of Key Events

NEILL NUGENT
Manchester Metropolitan University

January 1 Greece assumes the Council Presidency.

1 Second stage of Economic and Monetary Union begins.

1 European Economic Area comes into being.

19 Theodoras Pangalos, Greece's Deputy Foreign Minister, outlines the priorities of the Greek Presidency to the EP. The priorities include: taking action to combat unemployment, including following up on the Commission's White Paper on growth, competitiveness and employment; developing the social dimension; completing the enlargement negotiations with the EFTAns and paving the way for the future accession of Cyprus and Malta; and developing the common foreign policy, not least by furthering relations with the Mediterranean region and the Baltic States, by increasing co-operation with central and eastern Europe, and by finalizing a partnership agreement with Russia.

26 Commission adopts its proposals for 1994–95 farm prices.

February 1 Europe Agreements with Poland and Hungary enter into force.

7 For the first time, MEPs use their powers under the co-decision

procedure to announce their intention to reject a common position. The proposed legislation concerns a ban on powerful motor cycles.

9 Commission and EP adopt a joint declaration on the 1994 legislative programme.

16 Formal launch of Europol.

March 1 Negotiations for the accession of Austria, Finland, and Sweden to the EU are completed.

7 and 8 The General Council agrees on measures which will give effect to the June 1993 Copenhagen Council declaration that there should be a more structured relationship between the EU and the associated countries of central and eastern Europe.

9 The Committee of the Regions meets for the first time.

15 With the resolution of differences over fisheries, negotiations for the accession of Norway to the EU are completed.

27–28 General election in Italy marks the end of the party political system which became established after World War II. The dominant Christian Democrats are largely replaced by the right-wing Freedom Alliance led by the media tycoon Silvio Berlusconi. The overall results are: the right: 42 per cent of the vote and 366 seats in the 630 Chamber of Deputies; the centre (including the former Christian Democrats: 15.7 per cent and 46 seats; the left: 34.4 per cent and 213 seats; others: 8.0 per cent and 5 seats.

29 In what becomes known as the 'Ioannina compromise', the way is cleared for enlargement of the EU after the UK Government accepts arrangements on future voting procedures in the Council of Ministers. It is agreed that after Austria, Finland, Sweden and Norway join the EU, 64 votes out of the total 90 Council votes will constitute a qualified majority and 27 votes will constitute a blocking minority; however, it also agreed 'if members of the Council representing a total of 23 to 26 votes indicate their intention to oppose the adoption by the Council of a decision by a qualified majority, the Council will do all within its power to reach, within a reasonable time … a satisfactory solution that can be adopted by at least 68 votes'. (In December, following the Norwegian referendum, the Council amends these voting figures: with the total number of Council votes numbering 87, 62 votes becomes a qualified majority and 26 votes becomes a blocking majority; 23 to 26 becomes 23 to 25; and 68 becomes 65.)

31 Hungary applies for membership of the EU.

April	5	Poland applies for membership of the EU.
	15	The GATT Uruguay Round agreement is formally signed in Marrakesh.
	19	Commission announces preliminary draft budget for 1995.
	20	Following a conciliation meeting with the Council under the co-decision procedure, the EP gives approval to the size (12.3bn ECU) and shape of the Fourth Framework Research Programme for the 1994–98 period. This is the first time the TEU co-decision powers have been used in this way.
	20	For the first time, the EP uses its TEU granted power to request the Commission to submit a legislative proposal. A resolution is adopted calling on the Commission to bring forward a directive on civil liability in respect of future damage to the environment.
May	3	General election in the Netherlands. The two main government coalition parties – the Christian Democrats and Labour – both lose votes. The principal gainers are the left-of-centre and strongly pro-European Democrats 66 (a breakaway from the Liberal VVD) and the VVD.
	4	EP votes overwhelmingly in favour of the accession of the four EFTAn states. The votes are: Austria: 374 for, 24 against, 61 abstentions; Finland: 377 for, 21 against, 61 abstentions; Norway: 374 for, 24 against, 58 abstentions; Sweden: 380 for, 21 against, 60 abstentions.
	9	A meeting of WEU Foreign and Defence Ministers admits nine eastern European and Baltic States as 'associate partners': Poland, Hungary, the Czech Republic, Slovakia, Romania, Bulgaria, Lithuania, Latvia, and Estonia.
June	9–12	EP elections. The overall size of the major groupings and the political balance between them is only marginally affected, but the right becomes internally more heterogeneous. There is an increase in the representation of smaller parties, with the largest single new addition to the Parliament being that of Forza Europa (the name under which Berlusconi's Forza Italia contest the elections). When the new EP convenes in July, nine political groups are constituted, with the PES (Socialists) being the largest group with 198 MEPs and the EPP (Christian Democrats) being the second largest with 157. Twenty-seven MEPs are non-attached.

12 Austrian referendum on EU membership. The people vote in favour of accession by 66.4 per cent to 33.6 per cent on an 81 per cent turnout.

14 Partnership and Co-operation Agreement between the EC, its Member States, and the Ukraine is signed. This replaces the Agreement with the former Soviet Union which was signed in 1989.

22 Russia signs NATO's Partnership for Peace Agreement. As well as including the 'standard' partnership agreement on co-operation between armed forces (which countries such as Poland hope will lead to NATO membership), Russia is given the promise of dialogue and co-operation which matches its status as a 'major European, world and nuclear power'. (Later in 1994, negotiations with Russia on the application of the Agreement run into considerable difficulties.)

24 On the occasion of the European Council meeting in Corfu, President Yeltsin meets with the EU leaders and signs the Partnership and Co-operation Agreement which has been negotiated between the EU, its Member States, and Russia. This replaces the Agreement signed with the former Soviet Union in 1989.

24–25 Corfu European Council. The main business is the nomination of a new Commission President. On the first round of voting there are 8 votes for the Belgian Prime Minister Jean-Luc Dehaene, 3 for the Dutch Prime Minister Ruud Lubbers (Spain, Italy, and the Netherlands), and 1 for the External Trade Commissioner Sir Leon Brittan (UK). Lubbers and Brittan then withdraw their candidacies but the UK vetoes Dehaene, claiming that he is too federalist by nature.

Other business covered at the summit includes: the formal signing of a Treaty on Accession by the Heads of Government of Austria, Sweden, Finland and Norway; the adoption of a number of recommendations and decisions to give effect to the Commission's White Paper on growth, competitiveness and employment; the welcoming of work being undertaken within the JHA pillar of the TEU and an invitation to the JHA Council to make progress on the establishment and extension of the remit of Europol; and agreement to establish a Reflection Group to prepare for the 1996 IGC – the Group to be made up of representatives of Ministers of Foreign Affairs, of the President of the Commission, and of the EP, and to begin its work in June 1995.

At the conclusion of the summit, Chancellor Kohl announces he will call a special summit in July to settle the unresolved matter of the Commission Presidency.

27 Following the signing of the Treaty on Accession at the Corfu summit, Ministers from Austria, Finland, Sweden, and Norway attend a Council meeting (the Research Council) for the first time. They are 'active observers' – with the right to speak but not to vote.

July 1 Germany assumes the Council Presidency.

8–10 Western Economic Summit meeting in Naples followed by a meeting of the G 7 leaders with Russia. At the latter meeting, it is agreed that 'the political arm' of the Group of Seven will become the Group of Eight.

12 In a landmark judgment, Germany's Constitutional Court removes the constitutional restraint that German politicians have imposed on themselves regarding military involvement overseas by ruling that German troops can be deployed beyond the NATO area.

15 Jacques Santer, the Luxembourg Prime Minister, is nominated as the new Commission President at a special half-day European Council meeting in Brussels.

18 Jurgen Trumpf, the German State Secretary for Foreign Affairs, is appointed as the successor of Niels Ersball as Secretary-General of the Council of the European Union. He will take up his post on 1 September.

18 Free trade agreements are signed between the European Communities and the three Baltic States of Estonia, Latvia and Lithuania. They replace the chapters on trade in the Trade and Co-operation Agreements with the Baltic States which have been in force since 1993 and also include some accompanying measures. The Agreements are scheduled to enter into force on 1 January 1995.

18 New Co-operation Agreement (replacing the 1975 Agreement) between the EC and Sri Lanka is signed.

18–19 Following protracted negotiations, the Agriculture Ministers reach a political agreement, by a qualified majority, on the 1994–95 prices package. The agreement is quickly put into the form of regulations which are adopted at the Ecofin Council on 27 July.

19 Klaus Hänsch of the PES (Socialist) Group is elected President of the EP. In a straight contest with ELDR (Liberal) candidate Yves

Galland he polls 365 votes, with Galland polling 87 votes, and 82 votes being spoiled.

19 For the first time, the EP rejects a Council common position under the co-decision procedure. The directive in question concerns voice telephony.

20 Klaus Kinkel, German Foreign Minister, outlines the priorities of the German Presidency to the EP. Priorities include: combatting unemployment via continued implementation of measures identified in the Commission's White Paper, notably, deregulation, modernizing industry, restructuring, innovation, promoting research, and developing trans-European networks; further development of EU foreign and security policy, with joint approaches increasingly being the norm and agreements being reached on implementing decisions; clarification and consolidation of a common approach to eastern European states following enlargement to the EFTAns; progress on arrangements for dealing with cross-border drug trafficking, terrorism, and the status and nature of Europol.

21 Jacques Santer's nomination for the Commission Presidency is endorsed by the EP by 260 votes to 238 with 23 abstentions.

25 Budget Council. First reading of the 1995 budget.

27 Commission adopts its long-awaited White Paper on social policy.

September 1 Chancellor Kohl's CDU party issues a policy paper, 'Reflections on European Policy', which is highly integrationist in tone and which supports the idea of a strengthened inner core of five to seven countries. The paper attracts considerable attention throughout the EU. Chancellor Kohl emphasizes that it is a party and not a government document, but he does little to distance himself from its central thrust.

7 UK Prime Minister, John Major, delivers a much publicized speech at Leiden in which he calls for the European integration process to be flexible, with some Member States integrating more closely, or more quickly in certain areas, than others. He rejects, however, the notion of an inner core or of a two-speed Europe.

14 The Commission adopts a communication on the competitiveness of European industry.

18 General election in Sweden. There is a marked move to the left, with the Social Democrats attracting 45 per cent of the vote, the former Communists 6 per cent and the Greens 5 per cent. The parties of the centre-right coalition government lose ground, with the Conservatives

attracting 22 per cent, the Centre 8 per cent, the Liberals 7 per cent, and the Christian Democrats 4 per cent. The Conservative Prime Minister, Carl Bildt, is replaced by the Social Democrat leader Ingvar Carlsson.

21 General election in Denmark. The four party centre-left coalition led by Prime Minister Poul Nyrup Rasmussen wins 42 per cent of the vote and the three party opposition wins 44.7 per cent. With Rasmussen able to rely on the support in Parliament of two other left-wing parties which win 10.4 per cent between them, he continues in office.

22 The first directive is adopted on the basis of the TEU's Agreement on Social Policy. The Council as eleven unanimously adopt, with Portugal abstaining, the directive on the establishment of a European works council or a procedure in Community-scale undertakings and Community-scale groups of undertakings for the purposes of informing and consulting employees.

October 9 General election in Austria. The far right and fringe parties make big gains and the two large centre parties which have ruled in coalition for eight years lose support. The main results are: Social Democrats: 35 per cent of the vote and 66 seats; Austria People's Party (conservatives): 28 per cent and 52 seats; Freedom party (far right): 23 per cent and 42 seats. The Social Democrat/People's Party continues in power (there are 183 seats in the Austrian Parliament), but loses the two-thirds majority in Parliament which is necessary for constitutional reforms.

10 Co-operation Agreement is signed between the EC and South Africa.

16 General election in Germany. The coalition led by Chancellor Kohl is returned to power, though with its majority reduced from 134 to 10. The overall results are: CDU/CSU: 41.5 per cent of the vote and 294 seats in the 672 member Bundestag; FDP (Kohl's partners in government): 6.9 per cent and 47 seats; SPD: 36.4 per cent and 252 seats; Greens: 7.3 per cent and 49 seats; PDS (former Communists) 4.4 per cent and 30 seats.

16 Referendum in Finland on EU membership. The people vote in favour of accession by 57 per cent to 43 per cent on a 74 per cent turnout.

25 EP first reading of 1995 budget.

Jacques Santer meets with the other members-designate of the incoming Commission to settle the distribution of portfolios.

31 At a meeting in Luxembourg between the Foreign Ministers of the 12, of the four would-be accession states, and of six eastern European

countries (Poland, Hungary, the Czech Republic, Romania, Bulgaria, and Slovakia), a range of measures are agreed designed to bring the EU and the countries of eastern Europe more closely together.

November 13 Referendum in Sweden on EU membership. The people vote in favour of accession by 52.2 per cent to 46.9 per cent on an 82 per cent turnout.

15 Court of Justice delivers a key ruling in a case between the Commission and the Member States concerning negotiating rights in international trade negotiations.

16 Budget Council. Second reading of the 1995 budget.

27–28 Referendum in Norway on EU membership. The people reject accession by 52.2 per cent to 47.8 per cent on an 88.6 per cent turnout.

29 At a trialogue meeting, the Commission, Council, and EP agree on adjustments to the financial perspective to allow for the enlargement of the EU to 15 Member States. Maximum expenditure for 1995 is set at 80.9bn ECU, rising to 92.4bn ECU in 1999. The Council agrees the adjustments on 5 December and the EP does so on 13 December.

December 5–6 Summit meeting in Budapest of the 53 member country Conference on Security and Co-operation in Europe. Little progress, except for an agreement to a change in name to the Organization for Security and Co-operation in Europe. The change of name is intended to reflect the body's now permanent status.

9–10 Essen European Council. A relatively low-key meeting, with much of the agenda devoted to confirming and/or clarifying existing commitments and policies. The main areas of progress are: measures are urged on the Member States in the context of the growth initiative; on trans-European networks, a list of priority projects is confirmed; the importance of strengthening the Union's internal security is stressed, especially the need to conclude the Europol Convention; a Council report on strengthening the EU's Mediterranean policy is welcomed; and a Council/Commission strategy for preparing central and eastern European countries which have Europe Agreements for EU membership is accepted and is discussed with the leaders of these countries at the conclusion of the summit meeting.

11 Jacques Delors announces that he will not be a candidate in the 1996 French presidential election.

13 The EP approves the 1995 budget and it is then signed by President Klaus Hänsch. It amounts to 80.89bn ECU in commitments and

76.53bn ECU in payments. This represents a 12 per cent increase over the 1994 budget, but it is for 15 countries rather than 12.

17 The European Energy Charter Treaty is signed in Lisbon by 45 of the 51 negotiating partners.

20 Second meeting of the EEA Council. It is decided that existing structural arrangements will continue, in an appropriately modified form, when Austria, Finland and Sweden leave EFTA and join the EU on 1 January 1995. It is also decided that Liechtenstein will become part of the EEA on 1 May 1995 subject to certain conditions being met.

The Italian Prime Minister, Silvio Berlusconi, resigns so as to avoid a vote of no confidence in the Chamber of Deputies after a component part of his coalition (the Northern League) withdraws support from him.

22 Member States within the Schengen Group agree that they will remove remaining frontier controls on 26 March 1995.

Journal of Common Market Studies
Volume 33, Annual Review
August 1995

Books on European Integration

CLIVE H. CHURCH
University of Kent

The following list includes all those books submitted to the *Journal of Common Market Studies* during 1994, whether these were reviewed or not. Each book is entered only once even though, inevitably, some titles are of relevance to more than one section.

General Studies

Blacksell, M and Williams, A M: *The European Challenge: Geography and Development in the European Community* (Oxford, Oxford University Press, 1994, ISBN hb 0198741766, pb 0198741774) xiv + 430 pp., hb £45.00. pb £15.95.

Caesar, R and Scharrer, H-E (eds): *Maastricht: Königsweg oder Irrweg zur Wirtschafts- und Währungsunion?* (Bonn, Europa Union Verlag, 1994, ISBN 3771304865) 520 pp., DM 58.00.

Church, C and Phinnemore, D: *European Union and European Community: A Handbook and Commentary on the Post-Maastricht Treaties* (Hemel Hempstead, Harvester Wheatsheaf, 1994, ISBN 0745014712) xxv + 575 pp., £15.95.

Dehousse, R (ed): *Europe After Maastricht: An Ever Closer Union ?* (Munich, Beck, 1994, ISBN 3406383424) xi + 318 pp., DM 78.00.

Dinan, D: *Ever Closer Union ? An Introduction to the European Community* (Basingstoke, Macmillan, 1994, ISBN hb 0333616863, pb 033361871) 533 pp., hb £40.00, pb £12.99.

Duff A, Pinder, J and Pryce, R for the Federal Trust: *Maastricht and Beyond: Building the European Union* (London, Routledge, 1994, ISBN hb 0415108179, pb 0415108187) xiv + 311 pp., hb £40.00, pb £12.99.

Esterbauer, F: *Europäische Integration von den Anfängen zum Vertrag von Maastricht* (Vienna, Wilhelm Braumüller, 1994, ISBN 3700310498) 110 pp., öS195.

Goodman, S: *The European Community* (Basingstoke, Macmillan, 1993, 2nd edn, ISBN 0333583566) 255 pp., £35.00.

Guigou, E: *Pour les Européens* (Paris, Flammarion, 1994, ISBN 2080669699) 245 pp., FF110.

Henning, C R, Hochreiter, E and Hufbauer, G C (eds): *Reviving the European Union* (Washington D.C. / London, Institute for International Economics / Longman, 1994, ISBN 0881322083) 184 pp., £15.99.

Lewis, D: *The Road to Europe* (Bern, Peter Lang, 1994, ISBN hb 0820416401, pb 0820421138) 260 pp., np.

Lodge, J (ed): *The European Community and the Challenge of the Future* (London, Pinter, 1993, 2nd edn, ISBN hb 1855670569, pb 1855671417) 450 pp., hb £39.50, pb £14.99.

Lützeler, P M: *Europe after Maastricht: American and European Perspectives* (Oxford /Providence, Berghahn Books, 1994, ISBN 157181020X) viii + 224 pp., £23.00 / $29.95.

Maris, B: *Jacques Delors: artiste et martyre* (Paris, Albin Michel, 1993, ISBN 2226061630) 326 pp., £35.00.

Miall, H (ed): *Redefining Europe: New Patterns of Conflict and Cooperation* (London, Pinter, 1994, ISBN hb 185567257X, pb 1855672588) xiii + 293 pp., hb £45.00, pb £14.99.

Rees, G W: *International Politics in Europe* (London, Routledge, 1993, ISBN hb 041508282X, pb 0415082838) 191 pp., hb £37.50, pb £10.99.

Rollat, A: *Delors* (Paris, Flammarion, 1993, ISBN 2080667262) 301 pp., FF120.

Schönberger, P: *Hauptsache Europa* (Berlin, Duncker & Humblot, 1994, ISBN 3428080548) 128 pp., DM 88.00.

Stirk, P (ed): *Mitteleuropa* (Edinburgh, Edinburgh University Press, 1994, ISBN 0748604499) xiii + 175 pp., £25.00.

Weidenfeld, W and Wessels, W: *Jahrbuch der Europäischen Integration* (Bonn, Europa Union, 1993, ISBN 3771304458) 560 pp., np.

Williams, A M: *The European Community* (Oxford, Blackwell, 1994, 2nd edn, ISBN hb 063119172, pb 0631191720) xviii + 263 pp., hb £35.00, pb £11.99 / $ 19.95.

Government and Institutions

Brouwer, F, Lintner, V and Newman, M (eds): *Economic Policy Making & the European Union* (London, Federal Trust, 1994, ISBN 0901573450) 133 pp., £9.95.

Bueno de Mesquita, B and Stokman, F (eds): *European Community Decision Making* (London and New Haven, Yale University Press, 1994, ISBN 0300057598) 259 pp., £20.00.

CEPR Annual Report: *Making Sense of Subsidiarity: How Much Centralization for Europe?* (London, CEPR, 1994, ISBN 1898128030) xvii + 165 pp., £10.00.

Delwit, P and De Waele, J M: *La Gauche face aux mututions en Europe* (Brussels, Editions de l'Université, 1993, ISBN 2800410701) 218 pp., 595 BF.

Duff, A (ed): *Subsidiarity within the European Community* (London, Federal Trust, 1994, ISBN 0901573426) 134 pp., £17.95.

Edwards, G and Spence, D: *The European Commission* (Harlow, Longman, 1994, ISBN 0582210194) xiii + 311 pp., £36.25.

Harris, G: *The Dark Side of Europe: The Extreme Right Today* (Edinburgh, Edinburgh University Press, 1994, 2nd edn, ISBN 0748604669) xi + 265 pp., £12.99.

Hrbek, R and Weyand, S: *Betrifft: das Europa der Regionen* (Munich, Beck, 1994, ISBN 3406374751) 208 pp., np.

Lasok, K P E: *The European Court of Justice: Practice and Procedure* (Sevenoaks, Kent, Butterworth Law Publishers, 1994, 2nd edn, ISBN 0406006210) xc + 739 pp., £125.00.

Macqueen, H L (ed): *In Search of New Constitutions* (Edinburgh, Edinburgh University Press, 1994, ISBN 0748605150) ix + 99 pp., £9.95.

Merten, D (ed): *Die Subsidiarität Europas* (Berlin, Duncker & Humblot, 1994, 2nd edn, ISBN 3428081072) 146 pp., DM 48.00.

Monar, J and Morgan, R: *The Third Pillar of the European Union. Cooperation in the Fields of Justice and Home Affairs* (Brussels, Presses Interuniversitaires Européennes, 1994, ISBN 9052014019) 245 pp., BF 950.

Morass, M: *Regionale Interessen auf dem Weg in die Europäische Union* (Vienna, Braumüller, 1994, ISBN 3700310641) 565 pp., np.

Nugent, N: *The Government and Politics of the European Union* (Basingstoke, Macmillan, 1994, 3rd edn, ISBN hb 0333614445, pb 0333614453) xxi + 473 pp., hb £40.00, pb £12.99.

O'Keeffe, D and Twomey, P (eds): *Legal Issues of the Maastricht Treaty* (London, Chancery/Wiley, 1994, ISBN 0471941999) 374 pp., £45.

Rausch, R: *Die Kontrolle von Tatsachenfeststellungen und -würdigungen durch den Gerichtshof der Europäischen Gemeinschaften* (Berlin, Duncker & Humblot, 1994, ISBN 3428080882) 329 pp., DM 92.00.

Robles Carillo, M A: *El control de la Política Exterior por el Parlamento Europeo* (Madrid, Editorial Civitas, 1994, ISBN 8447003337) 563 pp., np.

Smith, J: *Citizens' Europe? The European Elections and the Role of the European Parliament* (London, RIIA, 1994, ISBN 0905031849) vii + 75 pp., £9.00.

Spierenburg, D and Poidevin, R: *The History of the High Authority of the European Coal and Steel Community: Supranationality in Operation* (London, Weidenfeld and Nicholson, 1994, ISBN 0297821725) xxvi + 686 pp., £70.00.

Westlake, M: *A Modern Guide to the European Parliament* (London, Pinter, 1994, ISBN 1855672014) xv + 302 pp., £12.95.

Westlake, M: *Britain's Emerging Euro-Elite? The British in the Directly-Elected European Parliament, 1979–1992* (Aldershot, Dartmouth, 1994, ISBN 1855215292) xv + 319 pp., £35.00.

Internal Policies and the Law

Ackrill, R: *Information Sources on the Common Agricultural Policy* (Manchester, European Information Association, 1994, ISBN 0948272252) vi + 98 pp., £25.00 (£21.50 EIA members).

Anderson, M and Den Boer, M (eds): *Policing Across National Boundaries* (London, Pinter, 1994, ISBN 1855671956) 203 pp., £35.00.

Benoît-Guilbot, O and Gallie, D: *Long Term Unemployment* (London, Pinter, 1994, ISBN hb 1855672480, pb 185567212X) 182 pp., hb £28.50, pb £9.99.

Benyon, J *et al.*: *Police Cooperation in Europe: An Investigation* (Leicester, CSPO, Leicester University, 1994, ISBN 1874493308) 351 pp., £47.50.

Brewster, C and Hegewisch, A (eds): *Policy & Practice in European Human Resource Management* (London, Avebury, 1994, ISBN hb 0415065291, pb 0415065305) xiii + 398 pp., hb £50.00, pb £18.99.

Brown, P and Crompton, R: *Economic Restructuring and Social Exclusion* (London, UCL Press, 1994, ISBN hb 1857281497, pb 1857281500) vii + 248 pp., hb £35.00, pb £12.95.

Burnett, J and Oddy, D (eds): *The Origins and Development of Food Policies in Europe* (London, Pinter, 1994, ISBN hb 0718514742, pb 071851694X) 265 pp., hb £45.00, pb £18.99.

Button, K: *Transport Policy: Ways into Europe's Future* (Gütersloh, Bertelsmann Foundation, 1994, ISBN 3892040656) 227 pp., np.

Clasen, J: *Paying the Jobless* (Aldershot, Avebury, 1994, ISBN 1856285197) 243 pp., £35.00.

Clout, H: *Europe's Cities in the Late Twentieth Century* (Utrecht/Amsterdam, Royal Dutch Geographical, 1994, ISBN 9068091905) 218 pp., Dfl 35.00.

Collinson, S: *Europe and International Migration* (London, Pinter/RIIA, 1994, ISBN hb 1855672960, pb 1855672979) xiv + 210 pp., hb £37.95, pb £12.99.

Crouch, C: *The Future of Employment in Western Europe: Reconciling Demands for Flexibility, Quality and Security* (Brighton, Sussex European Institute, 1994, No ISBN) 14 pp., £5.00.

Dai, X, Cawson, A and Holmes, P: *Competition, Collaboration and Public Policy: A Case Study of the European HDTV Strategy* (Brighton, Sussex European Institute, 1994, No ISBN), 33 pp., £5.00.

Dassetto, F and Dumoulin, M: *Naissance et Développement de l'Information Européenne* (Bern, Peter Lang, 1994, ISBN 326104599X) 146 pp., SF 17.00.

Gibb, R (ed): *The Channel Tunnel: A Geographical Perspective* (Chichester, Wiley, 1994, ISBN 0471949086) xvi + 244 pp., £29.95 / $47.95.

Heffernan, L: *Human Rights: A European Perspective* (Dublin, Round Hall Press, 1994, ISBN hb 1858000335, pb 1858000238) 436 pp., hb £47.00, pb np.

Hugman, R: *Aging and the Care of Older People in Europe* (Basingstoke, Macmillan, 1994, ISBN hb 0333587480, pb 0333587499) x + 199 pp., hb £30.00, pb £10.99.

Hyman, R and Ferner, A: *New Frontiers in European Industrial Relations* (Oxford, Blackwell, 1994, ISBN 0631186069) xv + 414 pp., £19.99 / $29.95.

Jamieson, A (ed): *Terrorism and Drug Trafficking in the 1990s* (Aldershot, Dartmouth, 1994, ISBN 1855215322) xv + 285 pp., np.
Kiriazidis, T: *European Transport: Problems and Policies* (Aldershot, Hants, Avebury, 1994, ISBN 1856286142) 127 pp., £32.50.
Lawrence, E: *Gender and Trade Unions* (Basingstoke, Taylor & Francis, 1994, ISBN hb 0748401466, pb 0748401474), 180 pp. 208, hb £34.00, pb £11.95.
Leonardi, R and Nanetti, R: *Regional Development in a Modern European Economy* (London, Pinter, 1994, ISBN 1855671557) 260 pp., £35.00.
Miall, H (ed): *Minority Rights in Europe: The scope for a transnational regime* (London, Pinter, 1994, ISBN hb 1855672308, pb 1855672316) 120 pp., hb £22.50, pb £9.95.
Nielsen, R and Szyszczak, E: *The Social Dimension of the European Community* (Copenhagen, Handelshojskolens Forlag, 1993, 2nd edn, ISBN 8716132165) 298 pp., DKK 236.
Portwood, T: *Mergers Under EEC Competition Law* (London, Athlone Press, 1994, ISBN 0485700093) xiv + 210 pp., £45.00.
Rasmussen, H: *European Community Case Law: Summaries of Leading EC Court Cases* (Copenhagen, Handelshojskolens Forlag, 1993, ISBN 8716132211) 560 pp., np.
Rootes, C and Davis, H (eds): *Social Change & Political Transformation* (London, UCL Press, 1994, ISBN hb 1857281470, pb 1857281489) 224 pp., hb £35.00, pb £12.95.
Schäffer, H (ed): *Wirtschaftsrecht und Europäishce Regionen* (Berlin, Duncker & Humblot, 1994, ISBN 3428080343) 212 pp., DM 98.00.
Scott, J: *Development Dilemmas in the European Community* (Buckingham, Open University Press, 1995, ISBN hb 0335191223, pb 0335191215) xvi +192 pp., hb £40.99, pb £16.99.
Six, P and Vidal, I (eds): *Delivering Welfare: Repositioning Non-Profit and Cooperrative Action in Western European Welfare States* (Barcelona, CIES, 1994, ISBN 8460495140) 409 pp., np.
Slot, P J and McDonnell, A (eds): *Procedure and Enforcement in EC and US Competition Law: Proceedings of the Leiden Europa Institute Seminar on User-Friendly Law* (London, Sweet & Maxwell, 1993, ISBN 042149400X) 274 pp., £75.00.
Vogel, L: *Prevention at the Workplace* (Brussels, European Trade Union Tech Bureau for Health/Safety, 1994, ISBN 2930003103) xvi + 402 pp., BF 1,600 + BF 100 p&p.
Wintle, M J (ed): *Rhetoric and Reality in Environmental Policy* (Aldershot, Avebury, ISBN 1856289273) ix + 144 pp., £32.50.

External Relations and Developments

Babarinde, O A: *The Lomé Conventions and Development: An Empirical Assessment* (Aldershot, Avebury, 1994, ISBN 1856286789) xiv + 250 pp., £37.50.
Baylis, T A: *The West and Eastern Europe* (Connecticut, Praeger, 1994, ISBN hb 0275946762, pb 0275947343) 240 pp., hb £48.50, pb £17.95.
Bojicic, V and Dyker, D: *Sanctions on Serbia: Sledgehammer or Scalpel?* (Brighton, Sussex European Institute, 1993, No ISBN) 23 pp., £5.00.

Burghardt, G: *The Future for a European Foreign and Security Policy* (Brighton, Sussex European Institute, 1993, No ISBN) 15 pp., £5.00.

Carlsnaes, W and Smith, S (eds): *European Foreign Policy: The EC and Changing Perspectives in Europe* (London, Sage, 1994, ISBN hb 0803988168, pb 0803988176) vi + 312 pp., hb £40.00, pb £14.95.

Frellesen, T and Ginsberg, R: *EU–US Foreign Policy Cooperation in the 1990s: Elements of Partnership* (Brussels, CEPS, 1994, ISBN 9290791764) 67 pp., BF 675 & p+p.

Ludlow, P: *Europe and the Mediterranean* (London, Brasseys for CEPS, 1994, ISBN 1857530594) v + 262 pp., £35.00.

Ludlow, P: *The Fourth Enlargement – Public Opinion on Membership in the Nordic Candidate Countries* (Brussels, CEPS, 1994, ISBN 9290791705) 96 pp., BF600.

Miall, H (ed): *Shaping a New European Order* (New York, Council on Foreign Relations for RIIA, 1994, ISBN 0876091575) vii + 118 pp., $14.95.

Norberg, S, Hökborg, K, Johansson, M, Ediasson, D and Dedichen, J: *The European Economic Area: EEA Law* (Stockholm, Fritzes, 1994, ISBN 9138922002) 893 pp., SEK 1,530.

Papisca, A and Vela, D: *I Rapporti verso l'esterno della Communità dopo il 1992* (Bari, Cacucci Editore, 1993, No ISBN) 311 pp., Lit 38,000.

Pedersen, T: *European Union and the EFTA Countries* (London, Pinter, 1994, ISBN 1855671484) vii + 200 pp., £35.00.

Regelsberger, E (ed): *Gemeinsame Aussen und Sicherheitspolitik der Europäische Union* (Bonn, Europa Union, 1993, ISBN 3771304652) 211 pp., np.

Schmidt, K: *Collective Western European Resort to Armed Force* (Copenhagen, DJOF Publishing, 1994, ISBN 8757430233) 82 pp., DK KR 95.00.

Stubbs, R and Underhill, G: *Political Economy and the Changing Global Order* (Basingstoke, Macmillan, 1994, ISBN 033361688X) 553 pp., £14.99.

Winand, P: *Eisenhower, Kennedy and the United States of Europe* (Basingstoke, Macmillan, 1993, ISBN 0333613570) xvi + 432 pp., £40.00.

Economic Developments in Europe and Beyond

Baldwin, R: *Towards an Integrated Europe* (London, CEPR, 1994, ISBN 1898128138) xxvi + 234 pp., £12.95.

Burda, M and Wyplosz, C: *Macroeconomics: A European Text* (Oxford, Oxford University Press, 1994, ISBN hb 0198773056, pb 0198773064) 486 pp., hb £45.00, pb £18.95.

Cobham, D: *European Monetary Upheavals* (Manchester, Manchester University Press, 1994, ISBN hb 071904443X, pb 0719044448) 247 pp., hb £35.00, pb £12.99.

Collignon, S with Bofinger, P, Johnson, C and de Maigret, B: *Europe's Monetary Future* (Pinter, London, 1994, ISBN 1855672537) xxx + 238 pp., £25.00.

Edmonds, J: *Industrial Relations: Will the European Community Change Everything?* (Brighton, Sussex European Institute, 1994, No ISBN) ii + 10 pp., £5.00.

Eeckhout, P: *The European Internal Market and International Trade: A Legal Analysis* (Oxford, Oxford University Press, 1994, ISBN 0198259034) xxxi + 399 pp., £50.00.

El-Agraa, A M: *The Economics of the European Community* (Hemel Hempstead, Harvester Wheatsheaf, 1994, 4th edn, ISBN 0745015794) xxxvii + 565 pp., £17.95.

Georgakopoulos, T, Paraskevopoulos, A and Smithin, J: *Economic Integration between Unequal Partners* (Aldershot, Edward Elgar, 1994, ISBN 185278878X) 336 pp., £49.95.

Gibb, R and Michalak, W (eds): *Continental Trading Blocs: The Growth of Regionalism in the World Economy* (Chichester, Wiley, 1994, ISBN 0471949094) 224 pp., £29.95.

Greenaway, D and Winters, L A: *Surveys in International Trade* (Oxford, Blackwell, 1994, ISBN hb 0631178929, pb 0631185895) 336 pp., hb £55.00, pb £19.99.

Johnson, C and Collignon, S: *The Monetary Economics of Europe* (Pinter, London, 1994, ISBN 1855672545) vi + 312 pp., £45.00.

Kenen, P J: *Exchange Rates and the Monetary System: Selected Essays of Peter B Kenen* (Aldershot, Edward Elgar, 1994, ISBN 1852789433) xix + 557 pp., £59.95.

Moran, M and Prosser, T (eds): *Privatization and Regulatory Change in Europe* (Buckingham, Open University Press, 1994, ISBN hb 0335190731, pb 0335190723) viii + 168 pp., hb £40.00, pb £16.99.

Mourik, A van: *Wages and European Integration* (Maastricht, BIV Publications, 1994, ISBN 9090074759) xiii + 187 pp., np.

Nugent, N and O'Donnell, R: *The European Business Environment* (Basingstoke, Macmillan, 1994, ISBN hb 0333566424, pb 0333566432) x + 260 pp., hb £42.50, pb £13.99.

Oxelheim, L (ed): *The Global Race for Foreign Direct Investment* (Heidleberg, Springer, 1994, ISBN 3540568468), 273 pp., DM 140.00.

Pelkmans, J: *Opening up the Euro-Market for Textiles* (Brussels, CEPS, 1993, ISBN 9290791594) 178 pp., BF600.

Perry, K: *Business and the European Community* (Oxford, Butterworth-Heinemann, 1994, ISBN 0750615699) x + 308 pp., £9.95.

Revell, J (ed): *The Changing Face of European Banks and Securities Markets* (Basingstoke, Macmillan, 1994, ISBN 0333604784) xxviii + 296 pp., £47.50.

Round, J I (ed): *The European Economy in Perspective: Essays in Honour of Edward Nevin* (Cardiff, University of Wales Press, 1994, ISBN 0708312403) xii + 350 pp., £35.00.

Somers, F *et al.*: *European Community Economies* (London, Pitman, 1994, 2nd edn, ISBN 0273603477) 338 pp., £19.99.

Soros, G: *The Alchemy of Finance* (Chichester, Wiley, 1994, 2nd edn, ISBN hb 0471043133, pb 0471042064) x + 368 pp., hb £29.95, pb £14.95 / $19.95.

Torres, F and Giavazzi, F (eds): *Adjustment and Growth in the European Monetary Union* (Cambridge, Cambridge University Press, 1993, ISBN 052144019X) xxiv + 388 pp., £37.50 / $59.95.

Welfens, P J J: *European Monetary Integration: EMS Developments and International Post-Maastricht Perspectives* (New York / Heidelberg, Springer, 1994, 2nd edn, ISBN 0387574115) x+361 pp., DM 148.

Wilks, S: *The Revival of Japanese Competition Policy and its Importance for EU–Japan Relations* (London, RIIA, 1994, ISBN 0905031830) xiii + 53 pp., £8.00.

Member States

Benoît-Rohmer, F and Hardeman, H: *The Minority Question in Europe: Towards the Creation of a Coherent European Regime* (Brussels, CEPS, 1994, ISBN 9290791691) v + 57 pp., BF 600.

Da Silva Lopes, J (ed): *Portugal and EC Membership Evaluated* (London, Pinter, 1994, ISBN 0861871049) 256 pp., £35.00.

Ehrhart, G, Kreikemeyer, A and Zagorski, A (eds): *The Former Soviet Union and European Security: Between Integration and Re-Nationalization* (Baden-Baden, Nomos, 1993, No ISBN) 276 pp., DM 42.00.

Gates-Coon, R: *Eastern Europe Bibliography* (Metuchen, New Jersey, Scarecrow Press Inc, 1994, ISBN 0810827751) iv + 175 pp., £25.00.

Jones, A: *The New Germany: A Human Geography* (Chichester, Wiley, 1994, ISBN hb 0471949299, pb 0471949329) xiii + 228 pp., hb £35.00, pb £11.95 / $56.00.

Komorowski, J and Stawarska, R (eds): *Poland and the European Communities: Proceedings of April 21–23 Conference 1993* (Poznán, Poznán University of Economics, 1994, ISBN 8385530304) 143 pp., np.

Lane, J E and Ersson, S: *Politics and Society in Western Europe* 2nd edn (London, Sage, 1994, ISBN 0803977956), 418 pp., £11.95.

Lippert, B: *Deutschland und Ungarn: Partner im neuen Europa* (Bonn, Europa Union, 1993, ISBN 3771304520) 96 pp., DM21.80.

Maxwell, K and Spiegel, S: *The New Spain: From Isolation to Influence* (New York, Council on Foreign Relations Press, 1994, ISBN 087609163X) xi + 126 pp., $14.95.

Pantelouris, E M: *Greece: Perspective 2000* (Moffat, Scotland, Blueacre Books, 1994, ISBN hb 0950681458, pb 095068144X) 162 pp., hb £22.50, pb £9.50.

Pridham, G, Herring, E and Sanford, G: *Building Democracy? The International Dimension of Democratisation in Eastern Europe* (London, Leicester University Press, 1994, ISBN 0718514599) vii + 224 pp., £37.50.

Redmond, R: *Prospective Europeans: New Members for the European Union* (Hemel Hempstead, Harvester Wheatsheaf, 1994, ISBN 0745015948) xiv + 204 pp., £14.95.

Scott, D: *Ireland's Contribution to the European Union* (Dublin, Institute of European Affairs, 1994, ISBN 1874109087) 41 pp., IR£7.50.

Wolff, L: *Inventing Eastern Europe* (Cambridge, Cambridge University Press, 1994, ISBN 0804723141), xiv + 420 pp., £35.00.

Zetterholm, S (ed): *National Cultures and European Integration* (Oxford, Berg, 1994, ISBN 1859730515) vii + 175 pp., £12.95.

Index